Please turn the page for more

D1352152

SCREENPLAY

"Quite simply, the only manual to be taken seriously by aspiring screenwriters."
—TONY BILL, coproducer of *The Sting*, director of *My Bodyguard*

"The complete primer, a step-by-step guide from the first glimmer of an idea to marketing the finished script."
—*New West*

"A much-needed book . . . straightforward and informed . . . facts and figures on markets, production details, layout of script, the nuts and bolts, are accurate and clear, and should be enormously helpful to novices."
—*Fade-In*

"Experienced advice on story development, creation and definition of characters, structure of action, and a direction of participants. Easy-to-follow guidelines and a commonsense approach mark this highly useful manual."
—*Video*

"This basics of the craft in terms simple enough to enable any beginner to develop an idea into a submittable script."
—*American Cinematographer*

"Full of common sense, an uncommon commodity."
—*Esquire*

"Impressive . . . His easy-to-follow step-by-step approaches are comforting and his emphasis on right attitude and motivation is uplifting."
—*Los Angeles Times Book Review*

SELLING A SCREENPLAY

"Syd Field is the preeminent analyzer in the study of American screenplays. Incredibly, he manages to remain idealistic while tendering practical 'how to' books."

—JAMES L. BROOKS, scriptwriter, *The Mary Tyler Moore Show, Terms of Endearment, Broadcast News*

"An informative, engaging look at the inside of the dream factory. This is a terrific aid for screenwriters who are trying to gain insight into the Hollywood system."

—DAVID KIRKPATRICK, producer, former head of Production, Paramount Pictures

"A wonderful book that should be in every filmmaker's library."

—HOWARD KAZANJIAN, producer, *Raiders of the Lost Ark, Return of the Jedi, More American Graffiti*

Also by Syd Field:

The Screenwriter's Workbook

Screenplay

Selling a Screenplay: The Screenwriter's Guide to Hollywood

Four Screenplays

THE SCREENWRITER'S PROBLEM SOLVER

How to recognize, identify, and define screenwriting problems

SYD FIELD

A Dell Trade Paperback

A DELL TRADE PAPERBACK

Published by
Dell Publishing
a division of
Bantam Doubleday Dell Publishing Group, Inc.
1540 Broadway
New York, New York 10036

Grateful acknowledgment is made to the following for permission
to use selected materials from the following films:

The Shawshank Redemption .Copyright 1994 Castle Rock
Entertainment. All Rights Reserved. Reprinted by permission of
Castle Rock Entertainment.

Thelma & Louise .Copyright 1991 Metro-Goldwyn Mayer Inc. All
Rights Reserved.

The Silence of the Lambs Copyright 1991 Orion Pictures
Corporation. All Rights Reserved.

For additional credits, see the Acknowledgments page, which
constitutes an extension of the copyright page.

Library of Congress Cataloging in Publication Data
Field, Syd.
   The screenwriter's problem solver : how to recognize,
identify, and define screenwriting problems / Syd Field.
      p.   cm.
   ISBN 0-440-50491-0
   1. Motion picture authorship. 2. Motion picture plays—
Technique. I. Title.
PN1996.F439 1998
808.2'3—dc21   97-30241
                                                      CIP

Printed in the United States of America

Published simultaneously in Canada

March 1998

10 9 8 7 6 5 4 3

BVG

*Once again, to all my students,
who showed me how to put
the pieces together. . . .*

Acknowledgments

A Special Thanks to:

Doug, Steve, Jim, Adam, Michael,
and all the others in my
Thursday-night class for their
continual help, encouragement, and
extraordinary insight;

To Trish Todd, who took what I had,
turned it inside out, and pointed
me in the right direction;

And to Jessie, Hugh, Steve, Gabriele, Mark,
and the rest of the staff at
the Writer's Computer Store;

And, of course, to Aviva,
and the path we've
chosen to
follow together. . . .

Grateful acknowledgment to the following: To Frank Darabont for *The Shawshank Redemption*; to David Koepp for letting me quote from *Jurassic Park*; to Quentin Tarantino for letting me quote from *Pulp Fiction*; to Lisa Chambers and Patricia Troy for letting me quote from the article "Lethal Weapon" from *Written By*, the Journal of the Writers Guild of America; to MDP Worldwide for granting me permission to discuss *Loved*.

And, a very special thanks to Jim Cameron and Will Wisher for their keen insight in *Terminator 2: Judgment Day*; to Jerry Bruckheimer for supporting my efforts to analyze *Crimson Tide*, to Alvin Sargent for his great insights, and to Doug, Cherry, and Joan for letting me pick apart and analyze their screenplays.

Contents

Part IV   **PROBLEMS OF STRUCTURE**

The World is as you see it. . . .

from YOGA VĀSISTHA

"What you try that doesn't work always shows you what does work."

THE
SCREENWRITER'S
PROBLEM
SOLVER

Introduction

When I first started thinking about writing this book, I wanted to find some kind of tool that the screenwriter could use in order to recognize and define various problems of screenwriting. But as I began writing, I became aware that I was really writing about the *solutions* to various problems, and not really identifying them. It just didn't work. So I began to rethink my approach. To solve any kind of a problem means you have to be able to recognize it, identify it, and then define it; only in that way can any problem really be solved.

The more I began thinking about the "problem," the more it became clear that most screenwriters don't know exactly what the problem really is. There's a vague and somewhat tenuous feeling somewhere that something is not working; either the plot is too thin or too thick; or the character is too strong or too weak; or there's not enough action, or the character disappears off the page, or the story is told all in dialogue.

So I began analyzing the Problem-Solving process. The only way I could make this book work, I realized, was to recognize and define the various *symptoms* of the problem, very much the way a medical doctor isolates the various symptoms of his patients before he can treat the disease.

When I approached the *Problem-Solving* process from this point of view (and it *is* a process), I began to see that there's usually not just *one* symptom, but *many* symptoms. It soon became clear that many of the problems in screenwriting share the same symptoms, but the problems themselves are different in kind; only when you analyze the *context of the problem* can a distinction be made, and it is those distinctions that lead us on the path of recognizing, defining, and solving. For the truth is that you can't solve a problem until you know what it is.

With that in mind I began to understand that there are only three distinct categories of *The Problem*; when you're writing a screenplay, all problems spring either from *Plot*, *Character*, or *Structure*.

The art of Problem Solving is really the art of recognition.

You can look at any problem in two ways: the first is to accept the fact that a problem is *something that doesn't work*. If that's the case, you can avoid it, deny it, and pretend it doesn't exist. That's the easy way.

But there's another way of approaching the problem, and that's to look at any creative problem as a challenge, an *opportunity* for you to expand your screenwriting skills.

They are really both sides of the same coin. How you look at it is up to you.

"The World is as you see it."

1

The Art of Problem Solving

A few weeks ago, during one of my screenwriting workshops, a student turned in some pages from her screenplay with a somewhat worried and concerned expression on her face. I didn't say anything, I simply took the pages and read them.

The scene she had written took place at the beginning of the Second Act, as the main character, a lawyer, is investigating the mysterious and unexpected death of her mother, who had died while recovering from a simple surgical procedure in the hospital.

Stunned and grieving, she is trying to find out why her mother had suddenly died, but no one has any answers, and no one is talking. The doctors placate her, the nurses know nothing, and the hospital administrator is concerned and suggests she join a grieving group. Her grief turns to anger, and she's determined to find out what happened. Pursuing lead after lead, she manages to locate one of the nurses who had taken care of her mother right before she died. The nurse had mysteriously quit the hospital a few days after the mother's death, had changed her address and literally disappeared. But through her own persistence, and some lawyer friends, she manages to track the nurse down. And now, she's going to talk to her.

This was the scene my student had just written. As I read her pages, I began to get some insight into why she appeared to be concerned about it. She had written the scene like an interrogation; the main character questions the nurse, who is reluctant to say anything about her mother's death.

This was an important scene, and it had to be handled in such a way that it both moved the story forward and revealed information about the main character. She's tough, feisty, and smart, and she's not just going to accept what happened, but she's determined to find out why it happened. And this scene is the first real clue the main character has which confirms her suspicion that some kind of cover-up is going on. Somebody made a mistake here, and because of it, her mother is dead.

I waited until the people in the class had finished reading the pages, then I turned to the young woman who had written the scene, and asked, "What do you think?"

She was very quick to answer. "I think something's wrong," she said, "it just doesn't feel right."

She was right. She had a *problem.*

Problems are common in screenwriting. The old expression "Writing is rewriting" is very true. But in my experience there are two ways you can look at a problem:

The first is to say that a problem is something that doesn't work. Very simple.

The second way is to say that a problem is an opportunity, a challenge that will allow you to ultimately improve your craft of screenwriting.

Two different points of view. But any way you look at it is the same: a *problem becomes the fuel of creativity.* You either view it as an obstacle or an opportunity; either a problem is something that doesn't work, or an opportunity for you to move up to another level.

It's up to you.

For some people the simple knowledge that they have a problem in their script can create a panic attack; it's a horrible, much-to-be-dreaded experience.

I have traveled all over the world conducting screenwriting seminars and workshops, and I hear the same thing in country after country; screenwriters describe their scripts in terms of the problems they are encountering. "Well," they say, "my problem is that my structure's not working," or "my character's weak," or "the dialogue's flat."

And I tell them there are no problems, there are only solutions. They laugh at that, because they think I'm kidding. But I'm not.

I think what scares most screenwriters, or anyone for that matter, is that most of the time they know there's a problem, they just don't know what it is. *They can't define or describe it.* It exists only as a vague sense of discomfort, an imprecise dissatisfaction, a knot in the gut or a lump in the throat.

My student knew, *or felt*, she had a problem with these pages, she just didn't know what it was. The art of Problem Solving means being aware of those hazy and undefined feelings, and using them as some kind of a guide to lead you into an examination of the cause or source of the problem. The art of Problem Solving is really *the art of recognition.*

In my student's case the main character, the lawyer, has knocked and entered, and she and the nurse have a dialogue scene. The scene was smooth and well written, but the overall effect was really somewhat dull and boring. Basically, talking heads. That's not screenwriting. That's playwriting. There was no sense of threat, no tension. And when I read pages that are slow and boring, the first thing I do is look for the source of conflict. And in these pages there was hardly any conflict at all.

I wanted to find out what her feelings were about the scene, so I looked at her for a long moment, and then asked, "What do you think?"

"I think something's wrong," she replied, "something's just not working."

"Like what?" I said, wanting to get specific.

"Oh, I don't know. It just feels like there's something wrong."

"So what do you think it is?" I persisted.

She thought about it for a moment, then said, "I think it's soft; it feels fuzzy."

Soft and fuzzy.

That's a pretty accurate description. It lets you know that something's not working as well as you think it should. And if you don't pay attention to that little "itch," that little "soft and fuzzy" feeling, the chances are it could evolve into a much larger *problem* later on.

Writing a screenplay is such a specific and demanding craft that when something doesn't work, whether a scene, or sequence, or character, it casts a long shadow across the page. It becomes the seed that will erupt into a full-blown problem later on. So it's important to catch and take note of these *symptoms* as they occur.

If you feel you have a *problem*, and can't articulate or define it, there's not much you can do to fix it. That's just a natural law. *You can't fix something if you don't know what's wrong with it.*

When you get down to it, the art of Problem Solving is

the *art of recognition*. And it is a definite skill that relies on the writer's sense of recognition and self-awareness. If you feel there's a problem—maybe the script is too long, too talky, or the characters are too weak or too thin—what can you do to fix it?

Nothing. At least not until you can accurately describe it. Until you know what the problem is, all you can do is piddle around with it; you can't fix something until you know what's wrong with it. There are many screenwriters who piddle around with a problem without fixing it, and it will probably remain as one of those scenes that never seem to work, no matter what you do. And you just let it go and hope no one notices it.

It happens all the time. The ostrich syndrome.

But if you know how to define and articulate the problem—maybe the main character is too passive and seemingly disappears from the action, or is too unsympathetic, or maybe the dialogue's too direct—you've got a handle on it and you can solve it to the best of your ability.

So, in this process of what we call Problem Solving, how do we go about fixing "soft and fuzzy"?

First, define the problem. That means generally rethinking the material. Go back into the material; analyze your *intentions*. What is the purpose of the scene? Why is it there? What is the character's *dramatic need*—what does your main character want to win, gain, get, or achieve during the course of the screenplay?

It's usually something that can be described fairly simply; in *Thelma & Louise* (Callie Khouri) it is their need to escape safely to Mexico. In *Dances With Wolves* it is John Dunbar's dramatic need to go to the farthermost edge of the frontier and adapt to the ways of the land and the people.

So, what is your character's dramatic need? Define it within the context of the scene. If you can illuminate this dramatic need—either through action or dialogue—you gain more subtext and texture, and thus add more dimension to the scene.

The first step in Problem Solving means to rethink the needs of a scene; you must take it apart in order to isolate and define the emotional forces working on, and within, the dynamic of the scene.

The scene is the living cell, the hub of dramatic action, and serves two basic functions in the screenplay. One, the scene moves the story forward; or, two, reveals information about the main character. These two elements of story and character must be served in each and every scene, visually, if possible. Look at any scene in any screenplay, study any movie, and see whether this is true or not. It's very common to read the pages of a screenplay and find pages and pages of extraneous scenes devoted to incidents or encounters that have absolutely nothing to do with the story line.

By definition, a screenplay is a story told in *pictures*, in dialogue and description, and placed within the context of dramatic structure. This is something I never get tired of repeating, because for some reason we always seem to forget it. Each scene always has to move the narrative line forward, from beginning to end, beginning to end, even though it's not necessarily in that order, as illustrated by *Pulp Fiction* (Quentin Tarantino), or *Courage Under Fire* (Patrick Shane Duncan), or *The English Patient* (Anthony Minghella, beautifully adapted from the book by Michael Ondaatje).

The scene my student wrote, which she could only describe as being "soft and fuzzy," is really a key scene that moves the story forward. But the way she wrote it was not sharp enough; the dialogue was too nice, too direct; there was no tension, no subtext working, and it washed out. There was not enough definition or dimension in it.

So I had her redefine the character's dramatic need. In this particular scene the character's dramatic need is to find out any information she can about her mother's sudden and mysterious death. Was there any wrongdoing? A mistake of some kind? Why did the nurse suddenly quit and leave the hospital? Is there a cover-up going on? What's happening here?

These are all important questions within the context of the scene. And context, remember, is the *space that holds something in place.* It is the space inside the glass that holds the *content*—water, coffee, tea, milk, beer, soft drink, grapes, nuts or raisins, whatever—in place. The space inside the glass does not change: it *holds* the content together. It is the gravity of the scene; it is *context.*

I knew my student had to make the scene sharper, more defined, with more tension, and the only way to do that was by generating more conflict. So I made some suggestions: maybe the nurse is not at home when the main character arrives. Maybe the first thing she has to do is wait. Maybe in her car. Maybe a couple of hours. This provides a back story to the scene. It lets the character enter the scene with some built-in tension.

So let's add some more conflict. The main character has had to wait a couple of hours. So what else can we do to create conflict in the scene? What if the nurse has a boyfriend, and maybe the guy's not too bright and he lets the main character, the lawyer, into the apartment before the nurse arrives home. He assumes they're friends. So she could already be in the house when the nurse arrives home.

These elements would add a great deal of conflict to the scene. The nurse arrives home, she's pissed at her boyfriend for letting a stranger, the lawyer, in, and we can see by her defiance and attitude that she's frightened. For sure this woman knows what happened to the character's mother and does not want to say anything about it, for whatever reason. Maybe she's even preparing to leave town. But she's tough and doesn't want to give anything away.

What does that do to the scene? Obviously, it sharpens the dramatic forces within it. What had been soft now shows more potential for tension and conflict; there's an edge to it.

And there's a way to get even more out of the scene; throughout this book I'm going to be referring to the value of writing short essays about your story and characters, defining and expanding events and relationships. Even though the nurse is a minor character, she is important to the story, and therefore becomes an important scene in the story development and cannot be "fuzzy" in its execution.

I suggested that she sketch in the nurse's life. What exactly did she see in the hospital? How much does she know? What actually happened? I told her to create a step-by-step series of events from the nurse's point of view that led up to the death of the lawyer's mother.

Once that was done, I had her define the relationship between the nurse and her "boyfriend." There might be more subtext that could be mined for maximum dramatic value. So I had my student write a short *free-association essay* about their relationship. Simply to sharpen the elements of the scene. Where did the nurse meet him, how long have they been together, is it a serious relationship? Or maybe it's over; maybe they're getting ready to separate. The answers to these questions allow you to expand the dynamic forces working from within and without the scene.

These are steps that need to be taken so the dramatic elements that are necessary to drive the story forward can be heightened and defined.

She went back to the "drawing board," did the exercises I suggested, and began to see things from a different perspective. She created more possibilities for her screenplay by simply listening to her feelings of discomfort about what was wrong with these pages.

Throughout the cycles of history and literature, there have always been attempts to define the art and craft of writing, about what it is and how it works. To me, writing is all about asking questions and then waiting for the answers. The answers will always be there and in most cases will reveal themselves in a totally unexpected way. That's part of the wonder of the writing process.

Aided by these written exercises, my student was able to go deeper into the scene. She began to see it differently. She *saw*, for example, that when she first wrote the scene the interaction of her characters was vague and hazy, *soft*, and clarified that by redefining the dramatic need of the main character.

"What is character but the determination of incident?" Henry James, the great American novelist, wrote. *"And what is incident but the illumination of character?"*

So let's take this to another level. We all know that drama is conflict. Without conflict you have no action; without action you have no character; without character you have no story; and without story you have no screenplay. You only have a succession of incidents and events that flows to its conclusion.

It looks like a story, it acts like a story, but there's really nothing there but a bunch of hooks, gimmicks, or special effects.

Die Hard With a Vengeance (Jonathan Hensleigh) is a good illustration of that. The only thing we know about the Bruce Willis character is that we find him drunk in a van somewhere, and he hasn't seen his estranged wife for a year or so. And he's the one who's hauled out of his stupor to find and capture the "mad" bomber. Later, of course, we find out that a few years before, the Willis character was responsible for the death of the bomber's brother. Ho-hum. There's no focus on character here at all, only on the originality of the action sequences, which are simply strung together in a random and chaotic manner. Look at all those plot twists!

I wanted my student to sharpen her dramatic focus. In order to understand the forces of conflict working on the nurse in this scene, I suggested she do another exercise; that she write the scene from the nurse's point of view. In other words, if this story was about the nurse, if she was the main character, how would *she* react if she knew something about the incident, something she didn't want to reveal to anyone, and then the victim's daughter came snooping around, trying to find out information about what happened?

Changing the perspective of the scene like this, merely as an exercise, helps clarify and sharpen the character's point of view, and thus brings the dramatic conflict into bold relief.

That's what she did. And it opened up a whole new awareness in her writing. The rewritten scene became clean, sharp, and tight; there was subtext and context and it moved the story forward in a charged and highly dramatic fashion.

And it all started from her discomfort, from a little tug in her gut and her awareness that the scene was "soft and fuzzy."

There's an old adage in the film industry that states, what you try that doesn't work always shows you what does work.

The art of Problem Solving is the art of recognition.

Either you look at a problem as something that doesn't work, or you look at a problem as being a challenge, an opportunity to expand your screenwriting skills.

It's up to you.

2

So, What's the Problem?

How many times have you read something you've written and then gotten that strange feeling in your gut: you know there's something wrong but you just don't know what it is? You go over and over the scene or sequence, again and again, examining it, reexamining it, trying it one way, then another, and still it doesn't work.

What do you do? How do you go about trying to fix something when you don't know what's wrong with it? How do you go about isolating and defining the problem?

What is the problem? You may know something about it; the scene is too slow, too wordy, too boring, or the main character is a little weak, or there's too much action going on, or the ending may be a little slow, or a little too rushed, but you have no idea how to fix it. Are you able to *see* the problem? Can you define it, take it apart, articulate it? How do you go about sketching it out, isolating it?

Before you can solve any creative problem you've got to know what the problem is. And that means you've got to rethink and possibly reorganize whatever it is that needs to be fixed.

That means literally rewriting it. You've all heard the old expression "Writing is rewriting." Well, it's true. I tell that to writers all over the world and they panic: "You mean I've got to rewrite it?" they moan. The answer is yes. Yes, yes, yes. Sorry.

I've just been working with one of my students preparing a screenplay to submit to directors and actors, and he's gone through at least fifteen rewrites. He had to change almost the entire Second Half of Act II, altering subplots, removing some characters, and taking out a lot of fat that was really unnecessary to the story line.

The word *rewrite* means "to revise and correct," and that's exactly what must be done when you're hunting for a problem. Whether you're rewriting the entire screenplay, or an act, or a sequence, or just a scene or shot, the process of Problem Solving is the same; you're trying to recognize and define it, hunting for clues as to where it is and what it is. It becomes *The Problem*.

So, what's the problem?

There are times when you know what it is immediately, maybe the scene's too talky, or too "preachy," too specific or direct, but while you may know what it is, you don't really know enough about it to fix it.

That's where the process of rewriting comes in. The first thing you need to do to clarify and define the problem is to put it into a context, a window, so you can outline the parameters of whatever it is that's not working, whether it be a character, scene, or sequence.

The best way to do that is to do a *written exercise*. Sit down, take a piece of paper, or go to the computer, and in a couple of pages just throw down any thoughts or ideas you have about the problem. Free-associate; ask yourself the question "What is the problem I am looking for?"

It's important to remember to begin each question with the word *what*. Try to phrase the question in such a way that it begins with the word *what*. Not *why*. If you ask "why" something is not working, you'll get eighteen different answers and they'll all be correct.

But structuring a question that begins with the word *what* implies *a specific response*. And that's what you're looking for, something specific.

Check it out.

This is basically a kick-in-the-ass exercise; when you start throwing down thoughts and feelings about the problem area and *what you think the problem is*, you are beginning a creative process that sets you out on the path of the problem-solving mode.

It doesn't matter whether your thoughts and observations are correct or not. Just sit down and write this little free-association essay: *"What do I think is wrong with this scene, or sequence, or act?"* You don't want to get too general and ask yourself what's wrong with the screenplay. Let whatever comes up, come up. What *you* think the problem is, regardless of whether it's right or not. Just ask yourself some basic questions about the material. Free-associate by writing down any thoughts, words, and ideas about what you think is working and not working.

What do you think you can do to make your story stronger, to improve it, to make it more dynamic? What does your instinct tell you? Listen to it. There are many nights when I know something is wrong with what I'm writing but I can't put a handle on it, I can't really define it, so I may do a "dream assignment." Before I go to sleep, I ask my creative

Self to reveal in a dream something that will help clarify what it is that's not working. And most of the time I'll have a dream that night that illuminates something in *dream language* about what it is that is not working, and what I might be able to do to fix it. And there are times when I won't have any dream at all, and then a few days will pass, then I'll get a sudden insight into what the problem is and how to solve it.

I firmly believe that if you created the problem, you can solve it. Therefore, you have to look inside yourself for the answers.

Problems only exist so they can be solved. It doesn't really matter how you do it. The solution could come to you in a dream, or while driving the car, running in the park, or even cooking dinner. The answer will be there when you least expect it.

All you have to do is look for it. Trust yourself.

Let the answer come in its own time. Sometimes the answer comes easily, and sometimes not. That's the wonderful thing about it; you never really know when you'll get a solution, or what it'll be; just know you'll get it.

Problem Solving is part of the creative process.

So what's the problem? Read over the pages you think are not working and see if you can isolate or define the problem. Maybe your story doesn't follow one line of action, but goes off in several different directions at once. Or maybe too many things are happening to your main character. For example, your main character may be a cop, but you think you should show more about his partner, so you write some scenes about his partner, and pretty soon you'll find you've created an entire subplot that gets in the way of the story; or maybe you want to show the bad guy being "badder," so you keep adding scenes showing just how bad he is; that happened in *Die Hard With a Vengeance*. It's an easy way to "fill" the story but only succeeds in getting in the way. By spending so much time with other characters, you'll ultimately end up losing your main character and your story will probably end up going all over the place, in several directions simultaneously. The real problem is losing the focus on the main character, and that's who your story is really about.

Sometimes, when screenwriters don't know what to do next, or what happens next, they'll simply add a new character to the story line. Rather than working to develop the dramatic context of the scene, story, or character, or expanding the action, all they do is add a new character. But that won't work because it's really a problem of developing *story*, not character, although one always reflects and incorporates the other.

Or maybe you read your pages and decide that you have too many characters in the story, or that your main character is too passive, too reactive, and seems to disappear into the background while a minor character pops up and takes over the story line.

What is your story about? And who is your story about? That's what always has to be kept in mind.

So, do this little exercise where you free-associate about what the problem is. It's important to remember that when you do it, you're rereading pages with the awareness that you're looking for something that's not working. Just throw down any thoughts, words, or ideas in free association; you don't have to worry about grammar or spelling (nobody's going to see this but you), so just throw it down without regard to how good or how bad it is, or whether it's right or wrong. Don't make any judgments about your writing or what comes up; your judgments tend to censor and smother your creativity if you listen too closely.

So what are you looking for?

There are only three things you can be looking for: *Plot*, *Character*, and *Structure*. Those are the only three areas where you *can* have a problem. The entire story can be broken down into these three areas, and they become the hub, or means, of the Problem-Solving process. If you look at any problem in the screenplay—whether the script is too long and talky, or there's too much action and not enough character, or too much character and not enough action—whatever the problem, everything falls under the umbrella of *Plot*, *Character*, or *Structure*.

So, what's the problem?

Is it a problem of *Plot*, of *Character*, or of *Structure*?

That's the starting point in defining any problem areas in a screenplay—or all writing, for that matter. What is it that's not working? If a scene is not working, is it because of a problem of *Plot*, *Character*, or *Structure*? Is the material boring? Too talky? Does the scene, or action, move the story forward, or does it reveal information about the character?

If the line of action wanders too far from the story, a solution might be to add elements that keep the story anchored and moving forward; so that's an element of *Plot*. But in altering the plot you'll also find yourself forced to restructure the material. Changes to the plot and structure will affect your character's actions and reactions, requiring more adjustment. And that's how you'll fix it. All three areas will always be related to one another; only the approach differs.

When you can isolate and define what's not working in the screenplay, you'll see that any problem will have some kind of relationship to these three areas. And that shouldn't be so surprising. In life everything is related to everything else; nothing exists by itself alone, but only in its relationship to something else. So any problem in the screenplay will always exist in some relationship to *Plot*, *Character*, and *Structure*.

And since you're the one who identifies what's not working, you get to choose which it is. It's all the same ball of wax; we just pull it into three different parts so we can put it back together again.

Many problems can be identified as problems of *Plot*. For example, is the dramatic thrust of the story line clean, lean, and defined? Or does it seem muddled and unclear? Is there too much happening, is it too detailed or specific, or is there not enough happening to keep the tension taut and flowing, uninterrupted by a lot of talking heads? In other words, is the action believable?

Suppose you have a problem with the ending. Maybe it happens too fast, or maybe it's not dynamic or big enough. What do you do? You have to expand it, broaden the action—so in order to solve your problem, you have to open up the ending, create more incidents that will expand the action, which means focusing more on the main character; once that's done, then the material has to be restructured.

Plot, Character, Structure.

What happens if the character is too talky, and always seems to be explaining the situation, so it drags the action down? Are there too many characters that get in the way of the action? Does the dramatic line of action ring true, or does it rest on coincidence and contrivance? All of those flaws could be considered problems of *Character*. In defining the problem you might have to go back into the material and look for ways to make the character more active and energetic, and you can only do that by introducing some more dramatic elements. Then, of course, you would have to restructure the act and thread your character forcefully through the plot as if weaving him or her through a tapestry.

In Problem Solving everything can be reduced to a variation of *Plot, Character,* or *Structure.* They act and interact and react upon one another just like the juggler juggling his three oranges.

As soon as you are able to make a distinction, to isolate and define the problem as being one of *Plot,* for example, then you can begin to narrow it down. Suppose your ending, or a certain Plot Point relies on a particular story point or piece of information that seems contrived and predictable; if you think it's a problem of *Plot* you'll have to go back into the story line and introduce, or set up, an incident or event properly, an event that is naturally related to the story. In *The Shawshank Redemption* (Frank Darabont), the murder of Andy Dufresne's (Tim Robbins) wife is set up from page one, word one. The very first scene shows him sitting in his car, drinking whiskey and palming his gun, which is then intercut with the murder and his trial, and it's this incident or episode that drives the screenplay through the story line. The entire story is structured around this incident, and comes back into play during the Second Half of Act II, when a young convict tells Andy that a previous cell mate told him that he committed the two murders and it's the first time we wonder whether Andy really did kill his wife.

If that incident had not been set up from the very beginning of the screenplay, the ending would not be as powerful as it is. Incidents or events like this have to be carefully introduced into the story line so the ending can be paid off, and made believable, and be executed with maximum dramatic value.

The craft of screenwriting is a process of understanding

the relationship between the parts and the whole, the relationships between *Plot, Character,* and *Structure.* All the elements of a story, the action, episodes, characters, location, music, special effects, Plot Points, are related to one another, just the way an ice cube exists in relationship to water. An ice cube has a definite crystalline structure, and water has a definite molecular structure, but when the ice cube melts into water, you can't tell the difference between the molecules that made up the ice and those that made up the water. It is the same relationship that exists between a fire and its heat. The two only exist in relationship to each other. Each aspect reflects the other. It's the same relationship between the story and the screenplay.

Only after you've located the problem will you be able to define it. Can you determine whether the problem is one of *Plot, Character,* or *Structure?* That's the start point. If you are unable to separate the problem out, try to define it *as you see it:* e.g., the main character is too weak, the dialogue too direct or boring. Then write the free-association essay and it will lead you into determining the nature of the problem.

Only after you become clear on what the problem is, whether it's *Plot, Character,* or *Structure,* will you able to clarify and define the problem.

The next step is to locate the problem.

3

Locating the Problem

After you've determined *what* the problem is, the next step is locating it in terms of the dramatic story line to see exactly where it fits in the scheme of your story. That means locating it in terms of structure, where and when the problem occurs within the logical progression of events. It doesn't matter whether the problem is *Plot*, *Character*, or *Structure*.

Only when you identify the problem can you locate it. So identify it first, then locate it. Where the problem occurs becomes a major dynamic in terms of solving it.

What's the problem? Setting up and establishing your characters' dramatic need? Is the Plot Point at the end of Act I a function of the story, or simply an event of convenience? Is the relationship between the characters clean, strong, and convincing? Is your story line anchored in terms of progression, either physical or emotional, and what about the character arc and the sequence of events?

What's so important about locating the problem is that it allows you to create a perspective about it; you can see the forces working within and without the story. You can chart the story like a navigational map to see the overall structure and enable you to discover those forces working on it at that particular point.

So exactly where is the problem? In Act I, Act II, or Act III?

Which brings us to an overview discussion of screenplay structure. A screenplay is a unique form; it is neither novel nor play, but combines elements of both. Structure is the foundation of all screenwriting, the spine or skeleton that "holds" everything together. William Goldman (*Butch Cassidy and the Sundance Kid, Marathon Man, Maverick*) declares that "a screenplay is structure," and it's true. Structure is the gravity of story, the road map through the desert. It is both guide and support, and flexibility is its nature, for structure is like a tree in the wind that bends but doesn't break. The structural elements of a screenplay can be moved around and through the dramatic story line.

Why is structure so important in the screenplay?

The word itself means "to build, or to put together," and "the relationship between the parts and the whole." If you're building a story through action, characters, and events, those elements have to be structured into a definite beginning, middle, or end, though not always in that particular order. And each of those units, the beginning, the middle, and the end, is part of the story, part of the dramatic (or comedic) story line. It's the story that forms structure; structure doesn't form the story.

When you're developing a screenplay, and building and putting it together into a series of related incidents, episodes, or events, it should be leading you to the dramatic resolution, the solution of your story.

First you build it, then you structure it into its component parts, beginning, middle, and end, and it's the relationship between the parts and the whole that make it an organic whole.

Take a chess game, for example; that is the *whole:* but a chess game is composed of four individual and distinct parts, the *pieces*, the knights, king, bishop, queen, pawns, et cetera; the *player* or *players*, because somebody has to play the game; the *board*, because you can't play chess without it; and finally the *rules*, because that's what makes chess chess. Those are the four elements that make up the chess game. It is the relationship between the whole, *chess*, and its parts, the *pieces, players, board*, and *rules*, that makes a chess game what it is.

The story is also a *whole*, made up of specific parts, the characters, actions, Act I, II, III, scenes, sequences, locations, music, special effects, and so on. It is the relationship between these parts that gives a screenplay its strength and integrity.

A screenplay is a story told with pictures, in dialogue and description, and placed within the context of dramatic structure.

If we could see what a screenplay looks like, if we could hang it on the wall like a painting, it would have a particular form. To see what that *form looks like*, to see what its *nature* is, we use the *Paradigm* of screenplay structure. A paradigm is a model, example, or conceptual scheme. The paradigm of a table, for example, is a top with four legs. Within that paradigm you can have a small table, a large table, a narrow table, or a wide one, a square, round, rectangular, or octagonal one, a glass table, wood table, wrought-iron table, plastic table, or any combination thereof, and the paradigm of a table still holds firm; no matter how you bend it, change it, alter it, or twist it, it still remains *a top with four legs*. The *form* doesn't change.

Some people think the form of a screenplay is really a

formula. Nothing could be further from the truth. The difference between them is simple, yet unique. A form is a space, or context, that doesn't change. But the content that fills the form always changes. Take a glass. There is a space inside, and it's this space inside that holds the content in place; the water, tea, soft drink, beer, milk, juice, or raisins or nuts, or grapes, whatever, but the space inside the glass doesn't change; it holds the content in place, just as structure holds the different scenes, actions, locations, characters, and situations in place.

The form of a screenplay never changes; like gravity, it simply holds everything together, all the parts of your story, whereas the content is always changing.

That's what the *Paradigm* is; the form of the screenplay. If a screenplay is a story told with pictures, what is it that all stories have in common? As mentioned, a beginning, middle, and end (though not necessarily in that order). In dramatic terms the beginning corresponds to Act I, the middle to Act II, the end to Act III.

Here's what it looks like:

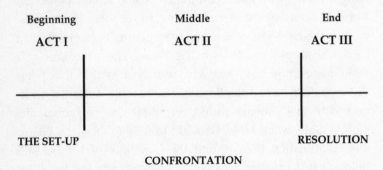

Act I is a unit of dramatic action that is approximately twenty to thirty pages long, and held together with the dramatic context known as the *Set-Up*. Act I sets up the story, establishing *who* and *what* the story is about, as well as defining the relationships between the characters and their needs.

Act II is a unit of dramatic action that is approximately sixty pages long, and held together with the dramatic context known as *Confrontation;* in this portion of the screenplay the main character confronts obstacle after obstacle in order to achieve his or her dramatic need. The *dramatic need* is defined as what the main character wants to win, gain, get, or achieve during the course of the screenplay. If you know the dramatic need of your character, then you can create obstacles to that need, and the story becomes one of your character overcoming, or failing to overcome, obstacle after obstacle in order to achieve his or her dramatic need.

All drama is conflict; without conflict there is no character; without character there is no action; without action there is no story. And without story there is no screenplay.

A Mid-Point occurs in the middle of Act II, about page 60, and it is an incident, episode, or event that breaks Act II down into two basic units of dramatic action; the First Half of Act II, and the Second Half of Act II. And it is the Mid-Point that connects these two parts of Act II. It is a link in the chain of dramatic action. A Mid-Point could be either a quiet moment, or a dramatic sequence; in *Witness* (Bill Kelley and Earl Wallace) it is a quiet moment in the barn when Harrison Ford and Kelly McGillis are dancing and cannot mask the attraction they feel for each other. In *Dances With Wolves* (Michael Blake) it is the dynamic action sequence of the buffalo hunt. The function of the Mid-Point is to keep the story moving forward; it is a *link in the chain of dramatic action connecting the First Half of Act II with the Second Half of Act II.*

This is what it looks like:

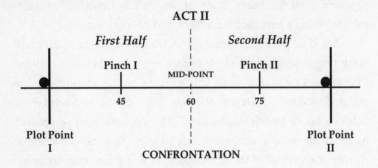

Act III is a unit of dramatic action that is approximately twenty to thirty pages long, and held together with the dramatic context known as *Resolution*. *Resolution* means "solution." What happens at the end of your story? Does your character live or die, succeed or fail, win the race or not, get married or divorced?

Set-Up, Confrontation, Resolution. Acts I, II, and III. But how do we get from the beginning, to the middle, from Act I into Act II, and then from Act II into Act III?

By creating a Plot Point at the end of Act I, and a Plot Point at the end of Act II; a Plot Point is any incident, episode, or event that "hooks" into the action, and spins it around into another direction, in this case from Act I into Act II, and Act II into Act III. There are many Plot Points in a screenplay, but the ones that anchor the story line in place are Plot Points I and II.

Act I is a unit of dramatic action that goes from the beginning of the screenplay to the Plot Point at the end of Act I and is held together with the dramatic context known as the *Set-Up*. Within this unit of action you've got to set up the story, establish the main character, and set up the dramatic premise. What is your story about? What are the forces working on the character to create the action? What are the relationships in your character's life? You have to *show* this, and it must all be set up in Act I.

Act I is a unit of dramatic action that can be broken down into three distinct sections; the first ten pages, second ten pages, and Plot Point I. Within the first ten pages three essential things have to be established: the *main character* (who your story is about), the *dramatic premise* (what the story is about), and the *dramatic situation* (the circumstances surrounding the action), all must be introduced and set up.

In *The Shawshank Redemption*, for example, the first ten pages go like this: We open with Andrew Dufresne (Tim Robbins), parked outside a house, drinking. A lively tune plays on the radio. He opens up the glove compartment and takes out a gun. Then we cut directly to the murder trial, where Andy is on the witness stand being hounded by the prosecutor. We cut back to Andy sitting in the car, smoking, drinking, waiting, then cut inside a house where a woman and a man are wrapped in an erotic embrace, then back to the murder trial, where we learn that he is being accused of murdering his wife and her lover in cold blood, then back to Andy, and the sequence builds until we set up his arrival at the Shawshank Prison. We've set up who the *main character* is—Andy; the *dramatic premise*—he's sentenced to "two life sentences" in Shawshank; and the *dramatic situation*—he claims he is innocent and didn't commit the crimes.

These three strands of narrative action (Andy inside the car, on the stand, and seeing his wife and lover) visually establish *the dramatic hook*, that incident or event that leads directly to Plot Point I, sometimes called the "inciting incident."

In *Shawshank* the dramatic hook is where he enters the prison, an incident that happens about page 10 in the screenplay. We don't know anything about him, but we meet Andy Dufresne through the eyes and the voice-over narration of Red (Morgan Freeman); he bets the other cons a pack of cigarettes that Andy will not last the first night in prison without breaking down. But it doesn't happen; someone else breaks down.

It's important to note that we enter the prison with Andy; we see it through his eyes and are introduced to the environment at the same time he is. Thus audience and character are bonded together in a dramatic connection; both learn what's happening in the story line at exactly the same time.

Andy's entrance into prison sets up the second ten pages of the screenplay, where the emphasis is on *following focus on the main character*. In this case we follow Andy's entrance into the prison through the voice-over narration of Red, so we *see* Andy's life in prison from *his* perspective. He is the main character (it's about him), even though Red has the larger part. So in these second ten pages we're focusing on Andy's entrance into prison, what his life will be like, and introduce the other characters who are part of his life during the course of the screenplay. We see the prisoners checking into prison, getting their clothes, hearing the lecture from the warden, being hosed down and deloused, then entering their cells.

After setting up and establishing life in prison, it's time to set up Plot Point I; about twenty-five minutes into the film, Andy approaches Red and says, "I hear you're a man who can get things done," then asks if Red can get him a rock hammer.

That initial conversation begins their relationship and is the cornerstone of the film. *That's why the Plot Point at the end of Act I is always the true beginning of your story.*

Plot Point I is the incident that moves the story forward, into Act II, a unit of dramatic action that is approximately sixty pages long and held together with the dramatic context known as *Confrontation*. Act II begins at the end of Plot Point I and continues until Plot Point II, and in this part of the screenplay the main character will overcome obstacle after obstacle after obstacle in order to achieve his or her dramatic need— *what the main character wants to win, gain, get, or achieve during the course of your screenplay.*

Everything in Shawshank Prison becomes an obstacle; whether it's the prisoner who sexually pursues Andy relentlessly, or whether it's just doing time, or the maggots in the food, or simply learning how to survive in the prison environment, the action of the story line continues to feed and develop the relationship between Andy and Red. Over the years they develop their own code of honor and become best friends.

When you're writing Act II, it's very easy to become lost in the maze of your own creation. That's why the Mid-Point becomes so important, for it connects the First Half of Act II with the Second Half of Act II, and is a link in the chain of dramatic action. The First Half of Act II deals with Andy learning "the ropes" of prison life, and the developing relationship between him and Red. And it is because Andy is a banker, an educated man, that he gains the trust of the warden and acquires the tools that will lead to his escape at Plot Point II. The Mid-Point, as mentioned, is either a quiet moment, or an active, dramatic sequence, that links the First Half of Act II with the Second Half of Act II. The First Half deals with gaining the trust of the warden, the Second Half deals with him having the trust that leads directly to the Plot Point at the end of Act II.

In *The Shawshank Redemption* the Mid-Point is that brief moment when Andy receives a shipload of books (after six years of letter writing) and is given permission to create a prison library. In his elation and exuberance he plays Mozart over the loudspeakers and ends up doing another stretch in solitary.

In order to build the First and Second Half of Act II, you need one major sequence to hold the action together. In the First Half it is a sequence that occurs around page 45, and in the Second Half of Act II it is a sequence that occurs around page 75; I call it the Pinch because it is an incident or event that keeps your story on track; it's a little "pinch" in the narrative action that keeps your story on line and leads to the Mid-Point, or Plot Point at the end of Act II.

In *The Shawshank Redemption*, Pinch I is the sequence where the warden has the prison guards strip Andy's cell, but in reality it's the warden's way of checking to see whether Andy can be trusted for any kind of future financial advice. Once the warden approves, Andy is moved to the library, and soon the prison guards are lining up for some sound financial guidance. It is this incident that moves the story forward and keeps the story on track leading to the Mid-Point, which occurs about page 60.

When you are locating your problem points you must find out where the problem occurs, and only then will you be able to find what the events leading up to the problem are and what the next story point is.

This is how the screenplay of *The Shawshank Redemption* is structured: On page 10 he enters the prison; at Plot Point I he establishes a relationship with Red, and obtains the rock hammer, which leads to his tarring the roof and winning the trust of the warden at Pinch I, which allows him to start the library at the Mid-Point, then introduce the new prisoner, Tommy, at Pinch II in order to reveal that Andy did not really kill his wife and her lover, leading to the warden refusing to help him, and to the warden's having Tommy murdered, and becomes the motivation for Andy escaping. Plot Point II.

Act III is a unit of dramatic action that is approximately thirty pages long (although in today's scripts it's more likely to be about twenty pages) that goes from the end of Plot Point II to the end of the screenplay and is held together with the context of *Resolution*. In other words, the story must resolve itself, and *resolution*, remember, means "solution." What is the solution of your screenplay?

In *Shawshank* Andy has escaped. The story focuses on Red: first we see with Red's voice-over narration how Andy escapes; then we see Red finally getting his parole and working for a while as a bag boy in a market. Unable to bear the constant fear, he decides that life would be better if he joined Andy in Mexico. He follows Andy's instructions to Buxton County, and then we watch as he finds the stone fence and large oak tree, spots the black rock "that should not be there," then digs until he uncovers the note and the money Andy has left for him.

We follow Red on the bus, and then the end comes when he is walking along the beach in Mexico and he and Andy are reunited.

Set-Up, Confrontation, Resolution. Acts I, II, and III. Plot Points I, II, Pinches I and II.

These incidents, episodes, or events are the structural anchoring pins of the story line. And this is the value of dramatic structure: it holds everything in place; it is the foundation, the skeleton, that *holds* the scenes and sequences, the action, in place. It is the *Paradigm* of dramatic structure.

This is how it looks:

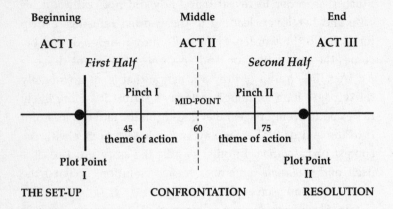

Beginning   Middle   End

ACT I   ACT II   ACT III

First Half   *Second Half*

Pinch I   MID-POINT   Pinch II

45   60   75

theme of action   theme of action

Plot Point I   Plot Point II

THE SET-UP   CONFRONTATION   RESOLUTION

When you know you have a problem with the script, when you can identify and locate it, you can place it within the structural story line of the story you are telling. And that means going back into the *Paradigm*, to identify and define it. Only then can you find the correct solution in order to build to that point by adding scenes, shots, or sequences to smooth out the action and keep it going. When you locate the problem on the *Paradigm*, then you can find out what you need to do to fix it.

Before any screenwriting problem can be solved, it has to be put into the context of story.

And that means locating it on the *Paradigm*.

4

Approaching the Problem

The only way to really approach the problem, whatever it might be, is to think of it as a rewrite. Writing is rewriting is the old adage, and it's true. You may not like the rewriting process, but *it is a process,* and that means it continually changes from day to day. What you write or conceive today may be out of date tomorrow, and what you write and conceive the day after tomorrow is out of date the day after that.

Screenwriting is a process, and it's larger than you are. It is a living thing, just like a relationship, and it changes and grows from day to day. That's just the way it is. Accept it and just do it.

When you're ready to deal with the problem, the first thing I suggest is to create an overview for yourself. Redefine and clarify your "take" on the material. See what you've written with objective eyes and try not be burdened with your subjective comments, or your likes and dislikes.

To unplug from the material and put you into an overview mode, I tell my students, whatever country they're in, to write three short essays, in free association, or automatic writing, not more than a page or page and a half, to see the material as a whole.

But before you do these essays, you need to read the screenplay through from beginning to end first, in one sitting, with no interruptions or phone calls or sudden desires to wash the kitchen floor. You want no distractions at all. Most importantly, lock up all your pens and papers in the drawer. This is an exercise.

As you're reading the screenplay, you'll notice some emotional shifts; you'll read a scene and wonder how could anybody write this drivel; or you'll think it the worst thing you've ever read, or see the incidents and events of the story as so outlandish that nobody would believe them. You'll feel totally depressed; just keep on reading. Then you'll read a scene you've written and think it's really not too bad, and then there's a scene that really works well. Certain scenes you'll suddenly be aware of are way too long and talky, but you know they can be cut and trimmed, and you'll swing on the pendulum of emotion between elation and despair. You'll simply experience a roller coaster of emotion as you read through the material.

When you finish your reading, take some time to think about the screenplay; contemplate your overall feelings about the story, the characters, and the action. As you begin to "cruise" through the progression of your story from beginning to end, you'll balance yourself out and start to move into an overview position to see the relationships between the parts and the whole, the relationships that exist between Act I, Act II, and Act III.

Think about what you've read. Is the story set up correctly? What about the relationships between the characters? Are they believable? Do the characters talk too much, explain too much? What about the conflicts and obstacles in Act II? Does the ending work?

You can do anything you want. What would you like to change?

Think about it. Just go through the story from beginning to end in terms of the action and the characters.

Now do the *three essays:*

The first essay. Answer the question *What was it that originally attracted me to the screenplay?* What was the idea that lured you to it? Was it a character that appealed to you, or was it the situation the character was in? Think about it. If you go back to that moment when you felt the first creative "tug," what was it that attracted you?

Then, in a free-association essay, throw down any thoughts, words, or ideas about what first drew you to the idea. Don't worry about grammar, spelling, or punctuation, just put your thoughts, words, and ideas down on paper. When I do this I write in fragments, just as it comes to me, without any logical order; it's a process of free association. Just try to capture and define what originally attracted you to the idea.

The second essay. Answer the question *What kind of a story did I end up writing?* In other words, we start out to write one kind of story and usually end up writing something different. For example, you may start out to write a courtroom thriller and it really turns out to be an action piece with a strong love interest. Or you may start out to write a strong dramatic piece with some humorous overtones and it ends up being both a drama and a comedy. James L. Brooks, for example, started writing *I'll Do Anything* as a musical comedy, and the music part of it didn't work, and when he removed the music it didn't work as a comedy either. During the process of writing it's very common to start out to do one thing and end up doing something else. So go into the story you have written and see how it relates to your original idea. Again, one or two pages, free association.

The third essay. Answer the question *What do I have to do to change what I did do into what I wanted to do?* In other words, the *intention must equal the result.* Again, this is free association. You may find that you have to strengthen several scenes in Act I, maybe add four or five new scenes, remove a few, set up and establish the dramatic premise a little earlier. What do you have to do to change the material into what you want it to be? You may have to focus on your character and maybe create more of a subplot; whatever it is, what do you have to do to make the changes?

It may be that what you've actually written is much better than what you started out to write. That's fine, but you still have to go back into Act I, and the First Half of Act II, and set up your story with the maximum dramatic value.

What's important is for you get clear on what you've written, and how to fix it. These free-association essays will do just that. Alvin Sargent (*Ordinary People, Julia, White Palace,* among others) once described the process this way: "Turn out the lights and close your eyes. Write what your fingers want to say. Be free, as free as you can be. To make no sense is to find sense. Sense will always appear. Trust it to arrive. It is the core of nonsense. It is not about anything but about everything. The glitter gets lost and the truth comes through. And then, when the lights are up, you will sift through it as would a sifter of gold. The mud will be gone and you will find at least a golden kernel or two has been stirred up. Close your eyes. Then write. . . ."

Once you've identified the problem, the best way to approach it is by working in sections, or units, of dramatic action. Each act is a separate, individual, and related part of the whole; Act I is a whole because it begins at the beginning, and ends at the end of Plot Point I and is held together with the dramatic context known as the *Set-Up*.

The First Half of Act II goes from the beginning of Act II to the Mid-Point, and is held together with the dramatic context of the *line of action*. The Second Half of Act II goes from the end of the Mid-Point to the Plot Point at the end of Act II and is held together with the *line of action*. And Act III is a unit of dramatic action that goes from the beginning of Act III to the end of the screenplay, and is held together with the dramatic context of *Resolution*.

Look at the *Paradigm:*

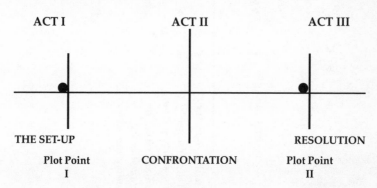

ACT I	ACT II	ACT III
THE SET-UP		RESOLUTION
Plot Point I	CONFRONTATION	Plot Point II

Each is a separate and complete unit of dramatic action; all are related in *Plot, Character,* and *Structure*. Because each unit is a whole as well as a part, it proves to be an ideal vehicle in approaching any problem you might have, whether it has to do with *Plot, Character,* or *Structure*.

So, what's the problem and where is it?

In Act I? If it is, then approach Act I as an independent

and separate unit of dramatic action, a part of the whole. Take a look in the overview:

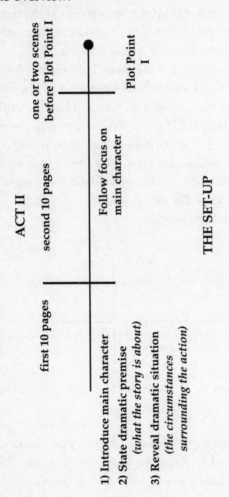

Since the context of Act I is the *Set-Up,* how are you setting up the story in terms of character and action? Is your script action driven, or character driven? If you're opening with an action scene, does it fully realize its dramatic function? What kind of sequence is it? A murder sequence, as in *Jade* (Joe Eszterhas), or a character-driven scene or sequence, as in *How to Make an American Quilt*, or a combination of both action and character, as in *Apollo 13*?

If you've located the problem in the first ten pages, you may need to rethink and redesign this first ten-page unit of dramatic action. It's here that you introduce your main character, state the dramatic premise, and establish the dramatic situation, the circumstances surrounding the action. Is the action strong enough, and the character revealed? How? Through an action or dialogue? In *Dances With Wolves* Michael Blake shows John Dunbar (Kevin Costner) stretched out on a table ready to have his leg amputated. But Dunbar, revealing an enormous sense of strength and courage, manages to force his way through the intense pain and pull on his boot. This one simple action, with minimum dialogue, shows us the very qualities of his character (strength and determination) that guide Dunbar's journey of discovery and lead to his transformation on the frontier. We see his character through his behavior, and as mentioned before, *film is behavior*.

As will be stressed throughout this book, everything is related to everything else in a screenplay; if you have to open up and redefine or restructure the story line and premise in these first ten pages, then you have to know that whatever changes you make, like sharpening and tightening the action or dialogue, will affect and change something else in another part of the script.

For every action there is an equal and opposite reaction is Newton's Third Law of Motion.

Whether your story is about a person caught in a web of extraordinary circumstances, or whether you're dramatizing an interior struggle, your character will be engaged in an emotional journey culminating in some kind of change in his or her thinking or behavior. You may feel your character needs to be better illuminated, so then you may find it essential to go back into your character biographies to define and redefine his/her relationships.

You must take the time to set up the foundations of your story line through the action and the characters in this unit of dramatic action.

If you feel the material in Act I is too slow, or not visual enough, check your physical location. Is there a strong visual arena? Are your characters talking, or explaining, more than necessary? Too much dialogue always slows the action down except when the story and situation play against each other, as in *Pulp Fiction*. Samuel L. Jackson is always spouting from the Bible in a way that is somewhat humorous, but then we learn he's a professional killer. And he can quote from the Bible and pull the trigger in the same breath. And it's this contradiction of character that makes the screenplay so effective and why Tarantino is such a gifted filmmaker.

If your problem is in the second ten pages, and you are following focus on the main character, do these pages show his or her relationships in a way that moves the story toward Plot Point I?

If you feel that the relationships are thin, or you introduce another character or characters, you may have to redefine those relationships by writing a one- or two-page essay on each character. This exercise allows you to bring a greater depth of character to the screenplay and establish stronger relationships between characters, because you now know these characters with a new and deeper understanding, "see" them in a new light.

Maybe you want to create two lines of visual action by intercutting a new character with the main character. When you have two lines of dramatic action operating simultaneously, this could possibly weaken the thrust of the story. Just follow the character. If that's the case, and the action is too weak for this opening unit of dramatic action, then you may have to cut out the other character and focus the action on the main character. Your story is always moving toward Plot Point I, so anything that does not further the action either has to be cut or rewritten. When you're writing a screenplay, you have to be ruthless, especially when you're in the process of solving a problem, even though you may feel you're cutting the best things you've written.

Just serve the material.

Have you set up the Plot Point at the end of Act I? Have you executed the Plot Point as effectively as you can? Does it do the job? Are you clear about what it is? If not, you have to define it to yourself clearly, so you can set it up and render it dramatically. Whether it's an action sequence, or a character decision, or even a change in locale, the Plot Point I is the true beginning of your story. That's why you have to take so much time and be so careful in writing Act I. You have to be totally clear on who these characters are and the story line and execute it properly, so you can move into the First Half of Act II riding the crest of the story wave you have been setting up from the very first scene.

In most rewrites in the Problem-Solving process it is not surprising to rewrite about eighty to eighty-five percent of Act I, either by sharpening or tightening the dialogue, or writing new scenes that bring the action into sharper focus, and being able to keep only a few scenes from the original pages.

What's most important in Act I is making sure enough visual and emotional information is given. If you need to do a major rewrite to solve a particular problem in Act I, then rethink this unit of dramatic action completely; take some three-by-five cards and restructure the story line on fourteen cards, writing one scene per card—though that is a contradiction when you are writing.

If you feel you have a problem in Act II, you have to go through the same process; first you have to identify the problem, then locate it in the proper structural framework of the story line before you can actually move into the Problem-Solving process.

First, where is the problem as you see it? In the First Half of Act II, or the Second Half of Act II? If the problem is in the First Half, where is it? Between Plot Point I and Pinch I, or Pinch I and the Mid-Point? If it's in the Second Half of Act II, does it fall between the Mid-Point and Pinch II, or between Pinch II and Plot Point II?

When you've isolated and defined the problem you need to be very specific, narrowing your perception so you can design a solution to the problem. It's very important to find out exactly where the problem occurs because then you approach it from a structural overview and thus uncover and refocus the dramatic elements that lead up to the problem. When you take the problem apart like this you begin to see very clearly what you need to do to fix it.

Remember, Act II is approximately a sixty-page unit of dramatic action that goes from Plot Point I to the end of Plot Point II and is held together with the context of *Confrontation*. The Mid-Point breaks Act II into two basic parts, the First Half of Act II and the Second Half of Act II.

Here's what it looks like:

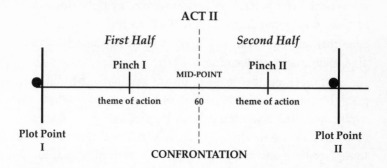

The best way to slide into the action of the First Half of Act II is to make sure you enter a story line from the character's *dramatic need;* what is it that your main character wants to win, gain, get, or achieve during the course of your screenplay? What is his or her motivation, or purpose, during the action of the screenplay? What is it that drives him or her through the action in Act II? These are questions you must be able to answer within the context of the entire screenplay.

What is the *theme of action* in the First Half of Act II? Clearly define it to yourself. It derives from your character's dramatic need. If your theme of action is *adapting to the frontier* as it is in the First Half of Act II in *Dances With Wolves,* then you can create obstacles to that need, and your story becomes your main character confronting those obstacles to achieve his or her dramatic need. The first thing that confronts John Dunbar is cleaning up Fort Sedgewick; once that is done, he begins adapting to the land; he begins his relationship with the Sioux, as it becomes essential here to expand and broaden the story line. This is his journey of discovery.

If your problem is with the main character, he might be

talking too much and slowing down the action, or the overall focus of the character may be too narrow or tight (for example, are you going from INT. to INT. to INT. in your scene construction?)—so you may need to open up the action visually, using different locations.

Approaching the problem means you have the ability to go right to that particular section of the screenplay where the problem is, and begin the process by modifying some scenes, or writing new ones. In many cases you'll find that you want to replace long and talky dialogue with a visual action, something that reveals character with just a little dialogue. That way you can keep the flow of the story moving forward, bridging both time and action from scene to scene, sequence to sequence. (More about this in Chapter 11.)

The structural story points of Pinch I, Mid-Point, Pinch II, and Plot Point II, hold the action of Act II in place so that it is clearly anchored and defined within the context of story. In this part of the process you get to make a choice: Do you need to open up the action to make it more visual? Or can you modify the dialogue and make it work? Remember that the purpose of every scene or sequence is either *to move the story forward or to reveal information about the character*.

So what do you need to do? Write it down. You may want to put this entire section of the First Half of Act II back on fourteen cards, card 7 being Pinch I. Or maybe you need to go into your character's life and redefine his or her relationships in a short, one- or two-page, free-association essay on the character's professional, personal, and private life; see if there's anything there that you can extract and add to the content of the screenplay to open it up a little.

The same principle applies to the Second Half of Act II, no matter what the problem is; whether it is *Plot, Character*, or

Structure, first locate it on the *Paradigm*. Where is it? Is it between the Mid-Point and Pinch II, or between Pinch II and Plot Point II? Once you determine the location, then you can approach from that particular unit of dramatic action. First, be clear about the *theme of action* for the Second Half of Act II. Where does the problem occur? Then break it down into its developing structural line; what events lead up to this particular problem? What do you need to do to restructure the material? If need be, put the action line down on fourteen cards, then go through the same process you did for the First Half of Act II.

The same thing with Act III.

ACT III

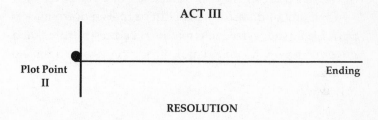

Plot Point II   Ending

RESOLUTION

Where in Act III does the problem occur? Does it deal with the resolution of the story? Or is the ending too thin, or too short, or too contrived, or too predictable? Do you have to expand or open up the action in Act III in order to effectively set up the resolution? And what about your ending? If that's the case, and you think the action's too thin, you've got to go back into your structure of the Third Act and rebuild the action in such a way that the ending becomes the payoff to the entire script. Again, that means writing new scenes, as well as tightening and sharpening others, possibly even changing the point of view, depending on the specific problem.

Is the ending believable? Does it happen too fast, or do

you need more of a Set-Up? It might be that you need to create an entirely new ending in order to resolve the action effectively. Finding a new ending is very common in the filmmaking process. Not only is it a Hollywood practice to gauge audience response toward a particular ending, but screenwriters from all over the world go through the exact same process. An ending either works or it doesn't; it either resolves the story line or it doesn't. And sometimes you don't know whether it works or not until you have gone through the entire screenplay.

The important thing to remember in approaching the problem is that the process is the same; it doesn't matter whether it's a problem of *Plot, Character,* or *Structure.*

Each unit of dramatic action can be broken down into its appropriate parts, effectively rewritten and restructured, and will provide a solid foundation in the process of Problem Solving.

Part I

SOME COMMON PROBLEMS

5

Talking Heads

Recently I conducted a screenwriting workshop in Rio de Janeiro. Screenwriters from Brazil, Argentina, Uruguay, Venezuela, and Chile had been chosen by their respective ministries of culture to participate, and they had all come to Rio to attend the three-week workshop.

It was intense. We met four hours a day, six days a week. The first week we spent preparing the material, and the second and third weeks we were writing up to ten pages a day. Sometimes more.

It was difficult. The one thing they needed, I told them, was something they didn't have—time. They didn't have time to contemplate their stories, and nurture all those nuances of character; the only thing they could do was write, to throw down all those thoughts, words, and ideas that came to mind. That way they could push aside the mind's resistance and limitations and allow the creative Self to emerge and guide them along the path of the screenplay.

Though Portuguese, Spanish, and English were all spoken, the language barrier proved to be no barrier at all; each writer wrote in his or her native language, the pages were then translated into English, and everybody read the pages in their native language.

My experience with the Latin American writers only reinforced what I've discovered in my travels and workshops; that no matter where you are in the world, no matter what language is spoken or what culture you're in, the language and grammar of screenwriting are the same, whether in Paris or Beijing, Rio de Janeiro, Mexico City, Tokyo, or Hollywood; writing is writing.

The way the screenwriters approach their material may be different, as it is in Europe and America. But some of the problems are the same. The European and Latin American screenwriters basically approach their screenplays in the same way. The Europeans come from a historical, intellectual tradition, and they base their material on the strength of the original concept or idea; this tradition has been laid down and followed since the fifteenth century in all the great universities.

This approach is still prevalent today. The European screenwriters (and Latin American writers) approach the screenplay from the idea of the story; it is this idea that pushes the story forward, dramatizes it, becomes its visual metaphor. The filmmaker will take the idea and dramatize it. Just look at the trilogy *Red, White,* and *Blue,* from the great filmmaker Krzysztof Kieslowski. Each story embodies a certain idea, like justice, and this theme is seen visually throughout the film, in the characters' emotions, as well as in the colors of the costumes and locations. The colors reflect the idea, the theme, and become an integral part of each story.

Recently I had the opportunity of seeing Michelangelo Antonioni's latest film, *Beyond the Clouds.* The opening image is of John Malkovich in an airplane high above the clouds, telling us he is a director, an observer of life; we then follow him through the four different episodes of the film and listen to his comments while observing the behavior of the characters.

The idea behind the film is the "search for love," and following this theme, we observe four different relationships. In the first segment, the girl is looking for a relationship through "words." It is the words of love that are important to her. In the second episode the director becomes involved with an exotic woman who searches for the "passion of love." In the third a marriage of many years is threatened by the husband's attraction to a beautiful woman, and finally the wife leaves him to search for the love he cannot give her anymore. And in the last episode a young man pursues a young woman on her way to church, and waits for her during Mass, only to learn that she is "afraid of life," and will enter a convent the next day.

Everyone is searching for love. It is this idea that drives the film forward. Dramatizing the idea creates the structure.

In a film like Wim Wenders's *Wings of Desire,* for example, the screenwriter begins with the *intellectual idea,* and then clothes it in a dramatic way. The story is about an angel (Peter Handke) who longs to know what it's like to be human. So Wenders shows us what it is to walk the path of a true human being. In the opening shots we *see* as well as *hear* the stream of consciousness of humanity as a parade of people passes in front of our eyes. Young and old, we witness their thoughts, their hopes and fears, their worries, their dreams. It's a wonderful opening. Finally, the angel descends and becomes a human being, and we follow his journey through life and love, through the joys and sorrow of walking the path of life.

But in the United States we approach the screenplay differently. Here, the screenwriter begins with an idea, then takes that idea and shapes it into a *story*, fashions it into a dramatic story line.

What's the difference?

Take a look at *How to Make an American Quilt*. It is a story about the fragile nature of relationships, the fear of commitment, the patterns of mother and daughter. During the story we learn about the lives of the women who make up the quilting bee. But the story focuses on the relationship between Finn (Winona Ryder) and her fiancé, Sam. We witness her doubts and feelings, and through her we see the stories of the other women, woven together just like the "quilt of love" they are making for Finn's wedding. It is a story, with beginning, middle, and end, and in the end her relationship is resolved. She follows the crow, who, just like the story in the quilt, leads her to Sam, and the last image we have is the two of them bedding down for the night in his VW bus. *Set-Up, Confrontation, Resolution*; beginning, middle, and end.

It is the story that drives this film, not the idea of commitment in relationships.

A few years ago I saw a short film by a French filmmaker. It was about a man who walks into a McDonald's restaurant on the Champs-Elysées and buys a huge order of french fries. He finds a strategic spot in the restaurant and suddenly begins throwing french fries all over; at the people, against the walls, on the floors, on the ceiling, everywhere. The people are furious. (It's a serious comedy.) Many of the patrons challenge him but the man pays no attention and continues throwing the fries. The police arrive. They warn the man.

But as soon as they leave, the man goes right back to throwing french fries. Soon, the entire restaurant is in an uproar. At the peak of their frenzy the man whips out a camera and starts taking pictures. Photograph after photograph is taken, and then in a blazing cut we see these same people as the subject of huge photographs now on display in a prestigious art gallery in Paris. It is only then that we understand that this man is a renowned artist, and the same people who were cursing him at McDonald's are now spending huge bucks to buy these so-called works of art.

Art is freedom of expression. That's the idea behind the film; the idea is dramatized.

The European screenwriter takes an idea and dramatizes it. The American screenwriter takes an idea and builds it into a story to dramatize it. If we took the idea that art is the freedom of expression, we would create a story. So we would search for a visual metaphor, a visual arena, to show our character, the artist, struggling for some kind of new art form, a new expression.

Who is this artist? What is his life like? What are the relationships in his life? Where is he in his career? What is his relationship to art? What about his friends, his family? Is he successful or not?

These questions all have to be answered to create a story. We take this information, the answers to these questions *(writing is really the ability to ask the right questions)* so we can structure this idea into a story line; we set up the artist's life in Act I, show who he is and what he does. The Plot Point at the end of Act I will be the particular incident or event which finally shows him that, in order to survive, he must change his artistic expression and seek out a new form, maybe even a new medium. We set up a crisis period in his life.

Act II would focus on his struggle to create a new form, and all the conflicts and hardships he has to endure in his professional, personal, and private lives. Gradually, we see him forging his first new form of expression, and then, at Plot Point II, he finds out what he has to do to generate a fusion of environmental and performance art.

Act III would show him executing his new "art form" in the McDonald's restaurant. Which is the entire French film.

Art is the freedom of expression—as seen from the European point of view and an American perspective.

The point to be made is that whether it's a European or Latin American or American film, the problems of screenwriting are the same; it doesn't matter in what language or culture the script is being written.

A screenplay is a story told in pictures, and there will always be some kind of problem when you *tell the story through words*, and not pictures.

It seems obvious, but I have had this experience over and over again: some of the writers I've worked with forget that a screenplay is a story told in pictures. They feel that if the characters can explain their particular thoughts, feelings, or emotions, the story line will somehow move forward through the characters' dialogue, not the action. Through words, not pictures. They think because the character talks a lot there will be insight and dimension; but the truth is that we must see the character in a situation that *reveals* his/her personality, no matter what the conflict or obstacle, whether it is an internal, emotional one, or an external, physical one.

Why is this significant?

Because at this period in our history, we are in a major communications revolution, and the screenplay is a form that is constantly evolving, for film is a combination of both art and science. It is a craft that drifts upon the growth of scientific technology. There are times when the screenwriter writes something and science has to create a technology to make it happen. Like *Terminator 2: Judgment Day;* the special effects had not been created when the script was completed. They *hoped* the special effects would work, and they did, and because of the science, film took a giant leap forward to making the art of film "more real."

Without the computer graphics created for *Terminator 2: Judgment Day*, we would not have been so affected by the dinosaurs in *Jurassic Park* (David Koepp) or the oddity of *Forrest Gump* (Eric Roth). Or all those morphing commercials that are flooding the television screens.

The computer technology of the nineties has literally exploded, creating a global revolution. The Internet, Web sites, all the on-line systems, connect the world. As of this writing over 50 million people in North America were on-line in 1997. *The Wall Street Journal* says that the number of people using the Internet is going to double and quadruple within a very short period of time.

That's only the beginning. Around the world people are using the Internet as part of their daily news-gathering ritual, and it is changing the ways we communicate with each other on a global scale. And this revolution is literally *changing the way we see things.* At this point in time we have become a visual society, and are no longer a literate one; the last fifty years have changed all that. No longer do we get our news and opinions from the written word. We get it from CNN, or the local news, and the Internet; we hear and see our music on CDs and video; and the latest study declares that the average person watches television on the average of three hours a day, more on the weekend; our children are computer literate by the age of six, and most of the time they are the ones who are teaching us to use the computer.

This evolution of science and art is creating a new language of film, a more visual way of telling stories for the screen. The language of film is becoming more visual; scripts filled with pages and pages of great dialogue are now considered "too talky." Two people talking in an office or restaurant, explaining things to each other, rarely works anymore.

This seems to be one of the most common problems in screenwriting. Over and over again, in country after country, most of the stories unfold through dialogue, not action. The characters talk and talk, and this only leads to a story that is dull and boring, developing through events that need to be explained.

Talking heads.

That's not screenwriting, that's stage writing. An essential part of all screenwriting is finding places where silence works better than words, finding the right visual arena, or image, to tell the story.

Today's films are much more visual, the character's emotional arc expressed through the character's actions and reactions. "What is character but the determination of incident?" says Henry James. "And what is incident but the illumination of character?"

How people react to the incidents and situations of the story tells us something about who they are: in other words, *what they do is who they are.*

When I first saw *Forrest Gump*, I thought it was a very, very talky film. Most of the story is told through dialogue along with the voice-over narration. Act I reveals who Forrest is, and his voice-over tells us things we need to know, but the dialogue and images don't contradict each other, they *complement* each other. Forrest tells us he has to wear leg braces because he has "a curved spine," and wearing them will make him "straight as an arrow." At first glance Forrest is dumb, maybe even stupid, as his IQ test states, but "stupid is as stupid does," he says, quoting his mother. And on the surface most people think he's some kind of retard, a "cripple," on the ocean of life. So we see by his braces that he's a "cripple," physically challenged, and this image is shattered when he is chased by the bullies and forced to run for his life. Voice-over and dialogue complement each other, and this technique keeps the story from becoming talky, or dull and sentimental. Forrest is a man who follows his dreams, then makes them come true.

Later, his behavior shows us something else: Forrest Gump is anything *but* a cripple. Though the words, pictures, and actions are different, they complement each other and move the story forward.

The same with *How to Make an American Quilt* (Jane Anderson). Before the story can truly begin, we need to know who this character is. So Finn's narration opens the film when she's a little girl, and tells us about the relationship with her mother, grandmother, and quilting friends, and then, in a beautiful cut to present time, visually tells us what her problem is: her relationship to Sam and how anxious she is about getting married. She tells us that she has trouble completing things; she's working on her third master's thesis because every time she's getting ready to complete it, she moves on to another subject and starts all over again. That, of course, is what her mother did with the men in her life. For Finn it is this fear of commitment that drives the story forward. In the end, however, she learns to follow her heart as the crow leads her to her understanding and final acceptance that Sam is truly her soul mate.

Both these screenplays are studies in character, but in order to reveal who the characters are, and what the obstacles are that confront them, we must see who they are, through their actions *and* their words.

Not through talking heads.

So if you have a problem in that you think your story is being told in words, look for places to illustrate your character's behavior. In *Thelma & Louise* (Callie Khouri) the title characters are packing for a two-day holiday to the mountains. Here's the way Thelma packs: She grabs everything in sight, then throws and stuffs it into the suitcase. She pulls open her cosmetics drawer and empties the contents into the suitcase. Pulls open another drawer of clothes, dumps it into the already bulging suitcase. And that, we see, is the way she lives.

Contrast this visually to the way Louise packs. They're going away for two days, so she takes two pairs of pants, two blouses, two bras, one bathrobe, two sweaters, two pairs of socks, throws in another pair just for good measure, closes her suitcase, wipes clean the single glass in her spotless kitchen sink, and leaves.

The difference between Thelma and Louise is the difference between night and day, an apple and an orange. Just from that simple action of packing a suitcase we learn a wealth of information about these two characters: one is messy, the other is neat, and it certainly reflects who they are in terms of their relationship with the men in their lives. Thelma married Darryl when she was seventeen, and the thought of growing old with him is not very appealing. "You get what you settle for," Louise comments.

Louise is not going to settle for the kind of relationship that Thelma settled for. As a matter of fact, this emotional decision of Louise's is what kicks the whole story of *Thelma &*

Louise into motion; in the back story Louise's boyfriend, Jimmy, a musician, has been on the road for three weeks and has not called her once. And she's pissed. So, "to get even," she decides she's not going to be home when he comes back in town. She's not going to let him treat her that way, and this decision sets up the whole story. By making the arrangement to be with Thelma out of town when Jimmy arrives home, Louise barrels down the road of fate that leads to her killing Thelma's rapist at Plot Point I.

Within the context of this story and these characters, the simple illustration of packing a suitcase reveals more information than dialogue ever could.

Instead of having your characters talk about their situation, let their behavior make the story line unfold in a more visual manner. Action is character; what a person does is who he is. Film is behavior.

Now, it may be that your characterization requires your characters to talk a lot. That's okay; just take a look at *Pulp Fiction.* The whole story is basically dialogue, and one long scene of dialogue leads to the next. The difference is in the quality of dialogue; Tarantino is a master at capturing the little quirks of character and behavior, like the discussion Jules and Vinnie have about McDonald's.

VINCENT
In Amsterdam you can buy beer in a
movie theater. And I don't mean in a
paper cup either. They give you a glass
of beer, like in a bar. In Paris you can
buy beer at McDonald's. Also, you know
what they call a Quarter Pounder with
cheese in Paris?

JULES

They don't call it a Quarter Pounder
with cheese?

VINCENT

No, they got the metric system there,
they wouldn't know what the fuck a
Quarter Pounder is.

JULES

What'd they call it?

VINCENT

Royale with cheese.

JULES

(repeating)
Royale with cheese. What'd they call a
Big Mac?

VINCENT

Big Mac's a Big Mac, but they call it Le
Big Mac.

JULES

What do they call a Whopper?

VINCENT

I dunno, I didn't go into a Burger King.
But you know what they put on french
fries in Holland instead of ketchup?

JULES

What?

VINCENT

Mayonnaise.

JULES

Goddamn!

VINCENT

I seen 'em do it. And I don't mean a
little bit on the side of the plate, they
fuckin' drown 'em in it.

JULES

Uuccchh!

On that note the scene ends and we cut to them opening the
trunk of their car and pulling out an arsenal of weapons. We
suddenly understand that these two guys are killers, and
they're on their way to a kill. The contrast between these two
characters talking about the seemingly ordinary events of life,
and their profession as hired killers, is what makes the scene
work so effectively. That's the brilliance of Quentin Tarantino.

It's easy to let your characters' dialogue explain your
characters and move the story forward. But a good screenplay
is much more than talking heads. It is a story told with pictures, in dialogue, and description, and placed within the context of dramatic structure.

It is the visual arena of action.

6

Dazed, Lost, and Confused

There may be times during the screenwriting process when you you experience a kind of a sinking sensation welling up inside and suddenly there is a cloud of negativity and confusion on the waters of your creativity. And it seems to come out of nowhere.

Most writers, including myself, try to ignore the feeling, to push it away, hide it under the carpet, and the more we try to dispel it, to pretend it's not there, to hover behind a false bravado, the more we realize we're stuck, lost somewhere within the maze of our own creation.

This is when we hit the "wall." Almost all writers, at some time or other, experience this wall, or block, and try to force their way through it. Sometimes it works, and sometimes it doesn't.

Most of the time it doesn't. And no matter where you are in the screenwriting process, the first words-on-paper draft or the rewrite, it doesn't take much to be overwhelmed by the writing process. We handle this kind of problem in many different ways, of course, like suddenly finding more important things to do; like cleaning the kitchen, or going to the market, or washing the dishes, or going to the movies. Whatever.

After all, some parts of the story are more difficult than others. And some scenes need more work than others. But after a few days struggling with these particular pages, struggling with some of these thoughts and feelings, you may notice some doubts about your abilities as a writer begin to surface. You may find yourself thinking too much, asking yourself questions like: What am I going to do? How am I going to get back on track? I wonder if I'm in *Writer's Block*? You'll question yourself, your talent, your ability to get the job done.

Then one morning you'll wake up and suddenly recognize that a heaviness of haze and uncertainty hangs around your neck, and the feeling that's been tugging at you for the last few days erupts and you know you really don't know what you are doing. You finally admit that you don't know how to help yourself or where to go and the only thing that makes any sense at all is surrendering to the state you are in—dazed, lost, and confused.

Welcome to the world of screenwriting.

It's one of those common problems that strike fear in the hearts of screenwriters everywhere.

In one of my recent screenwriting workshops, a student came into class one night with a strained and somewhat tortured look on her face. When I asked her what was wrong, her eyes welled up with tears and she became very serious, and said, "I don't know where I'm going. I'm totally lost, I'm confused, and my pages are pure shit. All that's happening is talk, talk, talk. I keep going around in circles and I don't know what to do. I'm so upset, I could cry."

It's a universal problem. How you get out of it varies

from person to person, script to script, but the first thing to do is to admit *you have a problem* and it's not going to go away until you deal with it, and confront it head-on. That's just one of the truths of life.

In my student's case she was so close to the material, she couldn't see it anymore, so the first thing I wanted her to do was just stop writing. When you reach this kind of crisis point, you're so overwhelmed and frustrated that you have to regroup. Just stop writing. Put down your computer, pen, and paper, typewriter, tape recorder, however you're working, and spend some time contemplating your story: What is your story about? What is the dramatic need of your main character? How are you going to resolve the story line? The answers to these questions are the key to getting back on track.

My student's story was about the reunion of four sisters after the death of their grandfather. In his will he had left them the house on the lake where they had all grown up. The main character had left this small southern town many years before to seek a professional career in New York. She had a lot of success in the city, but at the time the story begins, the company she has been working for all these years has just been purchased by a larger corporation and she's been informed that a major restructuring of her department is planned, and could possibly affect her position. That's the back story. When the story begins she is uncertain about the future, about her plans, about herself.

When she arrives, it is time for an emotional self-inventory, a time to clean up her life and renew her relationships with her three sisters. She's thrown into the cauldron of past and present, and must find her own way out. It is a dramatic and emotional situation loaded with dramatic possibilities.

So I started asking some questions. The writer explained

she was in the middle of the Second Act, so the first thing I asked her was if she was clear on her structural story points. She wasn't, she confessed; she was unsure about the Mid-Point, and felt so confused, she wasn't sure about Plot Point II either. She didn't know what to do.

So we went through the Problem-Solving process. Step by step. The first thing I had her to do was redefine the dramatic structure; so she went back to the story line and structured it on the *Paradigm,* identifying Plot Point I, Pinch I, the Mid-Point, Pinch II, and Plot Point II. She was still somewhat unsure about her ending, about whether the main character should stay and pick up the pieces of her life, or leave to go back to city and confront the uncertainty of change with a newfound awareness.

Then I wanted to know if she felt this was a problem of *Plot, Character,* or *Structure.* "Character," she replied, without hesitation. I didn't necessarily agree with that; I thought it might be a problem of both *Plot and Character.*

Look at it from both sides. From the *Character* side, the screenwriter had to deal with and know the inside, or emotional subtext, of the story; she had to trace the emotional arc that revolves around the relationships of the four sisters and whether they settle their differences or not. From the point of view of *Plot,* she had to be clear about the forces affecting the character from the *outside:* what happens to the house; if it's sold what are they going to do, and if they keep it what are they going to do? Questions, questions, questions.

We started from the character's emotional state at the time the story begins. What is she feeling when she leaves her home in the city to return for her grandfather's funeral? What's going on in her life? In her *professional* life with her career, and in her *personal* life, with her relationships, and then in her *private* life—what she does for herself, and how she feels about herself.

So we explored this a little. In the back story her company has just been taken over by a conglomerate, so how does she feel about it? How old is she when the story begins? Is there some kind of biological clock ticking, or already ringing? Is her grandfather's funeral going to get in the way of an important business decision? I wanted the writer to define the forces working on the character from the very beginning. What's going on with her relationships? Is she in a relationship? Is it a good relationship, is it beginning to unravel, or is she alone? Define it, from the beginning, when they first met. What would she do if she left her position and looked for another job?

These emotional questions needed to be answered and clearly defined before my student could go back into the story and confidently dig more deeply into the character.

Then I had her define her relationship with her sisters. I asked if she had gone back into the character's childhood and examined their feelings for one another, suggesting that she could even create some new incidents or events that might have happened. When she finished with that, I had her do an exercise in which she created a key experience in the life of the main character (her name was Abby), which might have happened between the ages of ten and sixteen, something that can reflect and become an emotional undercurrent of the story in present time. It may have been something that happened between her and her grandfather, or a traumatic incident with one of her sisters, something Abby still remembers and thinks about.

In *Thelma & Louise* it's the fact that Louise refuses to take one step in the state of Texas, even though it's going to cost her life; later we learn she was raped when she was a young girl living there. That's why she shoots Harlan in the parking lot when he's attempting to rape Thelma.

"What is character but the determination of incident?" Henry James asks.

I call this particular essay the *Circle of Being* (see Chapter 13). It is a specific incident that happens to the main character when he or she is between the ages of ten and sixteen. What it creates is an undercurrent that reflects a particular situation in the story in present time. In Abby's case it was her mother's early death and Abby's promise to look after her sisters. And though Abby made the promise, she resented it greatly because it was her dream to move away from the small town she'd grown up in.

I told the writer that she had to dive back into her characters' lives and redefine Abby's feelings when she returns and deals with the death of her grandfather, whom she had loved dearly; and how does she feel now that she is returning home? My student had not even considered these questions, or the emotional forces working on her characters. If you're writing this story, I told her, you have to know your characters' thoughts, feelings, and emotions; especially during the early years growing up at the lake, as young adults, and, most important, how they feel about each other now, in present time.

Another issue the *Circle-of-Being* exercise created was the influence of what the house means to each of the sisters. In terms of memories, cash value, and sentimental attachment, whatever. That house means something to each of the sisters; what is it? If you don't know, just read or reread Chekhov's *The Three Sisters.*

These emotional forces are working on the four characters through the entire screenplay; they are like the threads of color woven through the tapestry of your story line.

In *How to Make an American Quilt* the physical and emotional pasts of the characters are interwoven through the entire story line. The emotional life of the characters, their memories and *Circle-of-Being* experience, is structured in such a way that we can see the arc of the Winona Ryder character, see her understanding, awareness, and the change in her relationship to Sam.

If you are writing a story like this and do not know those emotional forces working on your character, it is very easy to run up against "the wall" and keep "going around in circles," ultimately falling into the well of *Writer's Block*.

Here's the way it usually works. You're totally immersed in the day-to-day process of screenwriting, but there may be one scene or sequence that does not work as well as it should and you might begin to wonder why it's not working. It's just a random thought and you probably pay no attention to it. But if the scene still does not work, you might become aware of a subtle shift occurring within yourself, maybe some doubts about why this scene or sequence is failing to come together. Then you might find that you're talking to yourself, having a little conversation about *The Problem*. The first thing that usually happens is you start questioning yourself: "If I weren't so stupid, I could do this," you might think to yourself. And the more you wrestle with the problem, the more your image as a screenwriter begins to erode, and then you might start making disparaging comments about yourself and your ability. That's when you begin sliding into "the pit," and soon an entire litany of negative judgments descends upon you.

"I knew I should have stayed away from this subject,"

you might think to yourself; or "I can't write worth shit." Soon you'll begin to expand and enlarge upon your own insecurities, thinking, "I don't know whether I should be writing this script," or "maybe I just don't have the talent to do this." or, "maybe I should just find a partner and write it with someone else." It goes on and on.

But underneath all these thoughts, comments, or judgments you're making is the common thread that somehow this is all "your fault." If you could do it, you would, and if you can't, it's because you don't have the talent or ability to do it. In short, we turn it inside and blame ourselves.

No wonder it's called *"Writer's Block."*

If you're in this particular dilemma, and your creative voice is smothered by this blanket of doubt and negativity, then it's time to *give the critic a voice.* That means giving that judgmental, critical, and negative voice that's roaming around inside your head the opportunity to speak his or her mind.

First, go to your screenplay pages—it doesn't matter whether you're writing on computer, typewriter, pad, or paper. Then take out a separate piece of paper and label it *The Critic's Page.* As you start writing, every time you become aware of a negative comment or judgment coming up, write it down on *The Critic's Page.* Number the comments, label them, just as if you were making a shopping list. For example, you might become aware that "these pages are terrible," or "I don't really know what I'm doing," or "This isn't working," or "Maybe somebody else should finish it for me." Maybe "These characters all sound the same," and it's apparent that "I've lost my vision," and so on. Whatever your thoughts and comments are about your pages, just lay them down; 1, 2, 3, 4, 5. . . .

The first day you're doing *The Critic's Page,* you may

write two pages of screenplay, and four pages of the critic. On the second day maybe you'll write three pages of screenplay and two or more pages of the critic. The third day maybe four or five pages of screenplay and a page or two of the critic.

At that point, stop writing. Take *The Critic's* pages, put them in order, and just read them; day one, day two, day three. As you think about these comments, mull them over in your mind. You'll discover something very interesting; the critic *always says the same thing.* It doesn't matter what kind of a scene it is, or who the characters are, or what you write, whether it's the pages from day one, two, or three, or whether it's a dialogue scene or an action scene, the critic says the same thing—the same words, the same phrases, the same expressions. It's all the same. No matter *what* you write, this is what your critic is going to be telling you. It stinks, it's no good, you should be doing something else.

That's the nature of the mind, to judge, to criticize, to evaluate. The mind can either be our best friend or our worst enemy. It's so easy to get plugged into judgments of right or wrong, good or bad.

Now, it could be that what the critic says is accurate. Maybe the pages *are* terrible, the characters *are* thin and one-dimensional, and you're going around in circles. So what? *Confusion is the first step toward clarity.* What you try that doesn't work always shows you what does work. As you struggle through any problem area, just get something down on paper. Just write shitty pages. You'll always be able to go back and make them better. That's the process all writers go through. So what if you've "hit a wall" and are going around in circles, dazed, lost, and confused?

Give the critic a voice. If you don't give the critic a voice, it will turn inside and begin to fester, getting worse and worse until it bursts. It's easy to let yourself become your own victim.

Until you become aware of the critic's voice running around at the back of your mind, you're going to become a victim of that voice. Recognizing and acknowledging that voice is the first step through the block; it's not necessary to act upon, or make a decision about, the judgments and evaluations the critic makes—whether the critic is right or not. No matter what stage you are at in the writing process, whether it's first words on paper, or rewriting, don't get too serious about what the critic tells you. One of the things we have to accept is that we always get lost within the maze of our own creations.

Many times the writer wants to use too many characters. In my student's story there were four sisters, but she hadn't done enough "creative research," she hadn't dug deeply enough into her characters, and she became lost in her story line. She did not know where she was going, had no idea of the emotional arc of each character, so she switched the point of view to different characters, and with four characters it becomes difficult to maintain an emotional progression through the story line. It's easy to lose sight of the main character if you do this, and that's why my student felt she was writing "in circles." She was. She had lost focus on the dramatic need of her main character, and thus lost sight of her story.

And when she reached that point in her script, it was all over. She had fallen off the map of her story line and the incidents that keep a story moving forward were leading nowhere. They were all dead ends. She didn't know what to do or where to go; her friends were no help, as they didn't understand the emotional circumstances of her writing experience.

As you sink deeper and deeper, the *Writer's Block* becomes bigger and bigger, hammering you into submission; the mere thought of writing turns you off; and because you're not writing you'll feel guilty, so whenever you sit down to work, you suddenly feel this "blanket of heaviness" settle over your head. You'll lose all objectivity, and fall into despair and ponder the meaning of life with thoughts of death and suicide.

Writer's Block. It happens all the time. To everybody. *The difference is how you deal with it. How you see it.*

There are two different ways to look at this "problem." One is to see your dilemma as a real problem, a real block, something to "overcome," or "break through," a physical and emotional obstacle that locks you into a creative straitjacket.

That's one way of looking at it.

But there's another way of looking at it. And that is to see the ordeal as *part of the writer's experience;* everybody goes through it. It's nothing new or unusual. If you recognize and acknowledge that, you've reached a creative crossroads. The realization becomes a creative guide to another level of your screenwriting craft. If you can look at it as an opportunity, you will find a way to strengthen and broaden your ability to create characters and story. It shows you that maybe you need to go deeper into your story, and strive for another level of richness, full of texture and dimension.

"A man's reach should exceed his grasp," the poet Robert Browning wrote.

If you understand that being dazed, lost, and confused is only a *symptom,* this "problem" becomes an opportunity to test yourself. Isn't that what life's all about—putting yourself on the line in a situation where you test yourself to rise to another level? It's simply an evolutionary step along the path of the screenwriting process.

If you accept this point of view, it means you're going to have to dig deeper into your material; you're going to have to stop writing, go back into your character's life and action, and define and clarify different elements of your character's life. You're going to have to go back and do new character biographies; define or redefine the characters and their relationships to each other that are the hub of your story line. In the chapters ahead there will be different exercises offered to deal with problems like this.

If you're working on a particular scene, for example, you may need to rewrite the scene, or change the points of view of your characters; you may need to change locations, or create new actions, new episodes or events, for your character. Sometimes you may have to restructure the action for a particular scene or sequence by restructuring an entire act!

If you're adapting a book, or an article, into a screenplay, at least there's a story line to follow, a thread of narrative that weaves itself through the incidents and events of the dramatic action. Sometimes there's a tendency to let the dialogue of the book, or play, whatever the original material is, dictate the story; if you rely on this too much it becomes an obstacle that will impede the screenplay. You may be trying to be too true to the source material.

That doesn't work at all. You've got to make the material your own, and that means breaking down the book, creating incidents or characters that complement the film's story line; so whatever you do, leave the book behind, and create whatever you need to make it work.

Whenever you feel lost, dazed, or confused, it only becomes a problem if you let it become a problem.

The things you try that don't work always show you what does work.

7

The Nature of Dull

Have you ever read something you've written and realized it's the dullest and most boring writing you've ever read? The pages seem worthless, trite, and your worst fears are confirmed: you have no talent, no ability, and the whole experience is like a bad dream. I mean, who cares, anyway!

It's not an uncommon feeling, and while it may be true some of the time, it's not true all the time. When you take a look at what you've written, and make the judgment that it's dull and boring, what can you do to fix it?

In other words, what is the *nature of dull*?

To really understand it, we have to explore the *symptoms of dull*—those traits in your writing style that may lead to writing dull and boring pages. And since this is a book about recognizing and identifying the *symptoms* of various screen-writing problems, we're going to take a look at what makes up the essence of dull writing.

That means examining the relationship between bad writing and good writing, since you can't define anything until you measure and compare it to something else; nothing exists in relationship to itself. And since *relationship* means a connection between two or more things, it means we can't define dull and boring writing until we know what makes up good writing.

When you read a well-written screenplay, "a good read," the words literally leap off the page at you. Part of it is style, yes, part of it is structure, yes, but the real dynamic of good screenwriting is creating strong and active characters, combined with a unique, stylized visual narrative that constantly moves the story forward. Many films reflect this very well: *The Shawshank Redemption, How to Make an American Quilt, Sense and Sensibility* (Emma Thompson), blend story with character, and a situation many people can relate to. *Twelve Monkeys* (David and Janet Peoples) blends a strong visual style with an interesting dramatic premise, but it's a "one-line" script (it lacks depth and dimension) that moves the story forward to its contrived and somewhat predictable ending. *Blade Runner* (Hampton Fancher and David Peoples) treats this same kind of theme more imaginatively, as does *The Fugitive* (Andrew Davis).

Strong action and strong characters. That's what makes good screenwriting.

One of the interesting things about a dull or boring screenplay is that nobody will tell you that it's dull and boring. People will say they didn't like it, or it didn't work for them, or they didn't like the characters or the premise, or maybe it's too serious, or too funny. But no one, not even wife, husband, lover, or best friend, will tell you that what you've written is a dull and boring screenplay. Go through your own experience and check it out.

In the long run, whether you've fallen into the pit of "dull and boring" is something you're going to have to determine for yourself. You might have to admit the possibility that you've written something that needs to be more active, more dynamic, something that will keep the reader turning pages. Because that's what good writing is all about—keeping the reader turning pages.

So, what are some of those qualities that make up good screenwriting?

Several things: perhaps the most important is to understand that the foundation of all good dramatic writing is *conflict*. All drama is conflict; without conflict you have no character; without character you have no action; without action you have no story. And without story you have no screenplay.

Dramatic conflict can either be *internal* or *external;* an emotional story like *How to Make an American Quilt,* or *Sense and Sensibility* has internal (and external) conflict. External conflict is a story where the conflict is outside the character, and the characters face physical (and of course, emotional) obstacles, such as *Apollo 13* or *Jurassic Park* (Michael Crichton and David Koepp). Creating conflict within the story, through the characters and events, is one of those simple, basic "truths" of all writing, whether it be novel, play, or screenplay.

In my seminars and workshops, no matter what the language or culture, I find that many screenwriters do not understand the importance of conflict in their stories. And their screenplays reflect that. So many times the characters seem listless, the scenes slow, taking too much time to develop; there is little or no direction, and it boils down to a screenplay that is dull and boring to read.

So what is *conflict*? If you look at the word it means to be "in opposition"; and the hub of any dramatic scene is having the character or characters be in opposition to some*one*, or some*thing*. Conflict can be anything, a struggle or a quarrel, a battle or a chase scene, internal or external, any kind of confrontation or obstacle, and it really doesn't matter whether it's emotional, physical, or mental.

Conflict must be at the very hub of your story, because it is the core of strong action and strong character. If you do not have this conflict, this foundation to your writing, you'll find yourself more often than not caught in the quagmire of dull writing.

If you wanted to examine "the stuff" that makes dull writing, what would you say? What is the *nature of dull*? What does it look like? What does it taste like, and what is its *essence*, the seed that sprouts into the tree?

There are *symptoms* that can be identified if you know what to look for, and they usually give a pretty good indication of what the problem is, whether the script is slow and heavy, or too long, or all the characters sound the same. If that's the case, then how do you fix it, or shape it, transform it from a "bad read" into a "good read"?

For example, if your dramatic premise seems weak and not clearly articulated and defined within the first ten pages, then the chances are that the *Set-Up* is weak and the material is going to wander around in different directions and lack a dramatic focus. That's a *symptom*; let it go on too long and you've got a dull screenplay; just as a scratchy irritation in the throat is sometimes the symptom of a cold or flu. Symptoms reveal things, and in the "art" of medicine, if you read the symptoms correctly, then you can find the cause, and heal the disease, whatever it might be. At least, in theory.

In screenwriting you cure the problem by knowing and understanding its symptoms. For example, suppose a writer wants to create a strong action line and, in so doing, sets up the story so fast, he or she simply skims over, or omits, necessary and essential character information? It won't take the writer long to realize the character's been sacrificed for action.

We can identify this because the character will be so busy reacting to the events or the situation that we don't have an opportunity to learn anything about him or her. That's a *symptom*. And it always seems to lead to a dull and boring read. When I see a script unfolding like this, with the character simply reacting to his or her situation, I'll give the writer thirty pages to see whether it works or not. If it doesn't, I'll stop reading, because I don't need to read any more to see the story's not working.

Screenwriting is a craft; one scene builds upon another, and the visual information we receive is cumulative; it is that relationship between the scene and the dramatic need of the story that keeps it moving forward. As mentioned before, each scene must fulfill one of two major functions in the storytelling process: *A scene either moves the story forward, or reveals information about the main character(s).* And if that doesn't happen, and you wander off in some side directions that are unrelated to the main narrative line, then the *gravity of dull* will gradually drag your story to a standstill.

Sometimes the *symptom* of a dull read begins with a situation that is not believable; the characters or the situation seems too farfetched, or too predictable; events happen too easily, and we know that people would not act or react to the situation the way they do in the screenplay. Just look at the ending of *Waterworld*. To have a character discard what has driven him through the whole movie, and then go back to the way he was before the story began, is totally unbelievable. It's a pose, an image. Within the context of the story it doesn't work. No matter how far out the story is.

In the lexicon of literary criticism this concept is known as the "willing suspension of disbelief." The English poet Samuel Taylor Coleridge stated that when you approach a work of art, you must leave your perception of reality behind and approach it on its own merits, on its own level. In other words, you must willingly suspend your disbelief no matter how far the subject matter strays from what you know to be true, or not true. No matter how outrageous the premise, no matter how unpredictable the characters, the situations, reactions, or plot developments are, all thoughts have to be left behind when you approach "the work."

Terminator 2: Judgment Day is a perfect example. The dramatic premise of a world self-destructing in August 1997, creating an age of machines, who have sent back through time a "terminator" to destroy, when he is ten years old, the person who will lead the future rebellion is pretty far out. Is it believable? Logically, of course not, but we believe the film experience because of the strong action, strong character, and incredible special effects. The same with *Blade Runner*.

If the action and characters do not make a story line believable, then there is no "willing suspension of disbelief." We believe the Ace Ventura movies or *Dumb and Dumber* because they're *so* ridiculous they couldn't be real, so there's nothing we can't believe within the dramatic context.

Contrast this with what we see on episodic television or on some of the MOWs that grace our television airwaves; usually, it's unreal people in unreal situations.

That's because writing for television and writing for film are two different things; one's an apple and one's an orange. One is a radio soap opera with pictures, where everything has to be explained, and the other is a story told through pictures, finding places where silence works better than words. In episodic TV, for example, you're writing characters that have already been created, so writing for series television means the writer has to focus on how these people react in certain situations.

In many of the MOWs, the basis of the story, whether it's taken from a real-life experience or not, is diluted and watered down into a predictable and convenient story line; the focus is on the commercials, not the show. "Television is an advertising medium where the shows fill up the time between commercials" is the way one television executive described it. Dramatic choices are made because there's not enough time to dig deeper to get underneath the character's skin—to find a bridge to the character's inner country. So, if the reader does not believe the dramatic premise and situation, then you've had it; there is no "willing suspension of disbelief."

It is a major *symptom* in the nature of dull.

I remember talking with Oliver Stone, and he told me that *Platoon* had languished on the shelf for more than ten years, and he had really given up hope of seeing it made during his lifetime. When I asked why, he told me that most of the people who read the first draft of the screenplay were captivated by it, while others were afraid that the war in Vietnam was not a commercial subject. And this was after he had won the Academy Award for *Midnight Express*. But there were a few friends who told him that when they read the material they didn't "get" it, that it really didn't hold their interest.

That's the kiss of death. So he went back to reread the script and suddenly realized he had introduced some twenty-six characters in the first ten pages of the screenplay. That's just too many characters for the reader to follow. No wonder it didn't hold their interest. When Stone understood the problem, he went back and rewrote the opening by cutting out several characters and focusing more on the main character (Charlie Sheen); we see the war through his eyes, share his experience, even though he is surrounded by all those other characters.

In *Nixon*, which Stone directed and cowrote along with Stephen Rivele and Christopher Wilkinson, his directorial use of cross-cutting between the many different characters is very much like "surfing" the tube, or "surfing" the Net, and the way he goes from one character and situation to another, from one scene to another, is brilliant. We live in the world of multimedia now, and our attention spans are brief, so we can see and understand things as we do on television, with our remotes clicking from one channel to another, or clicking from one Web site to another. That's the style of *Nixon*, the way it's written and structured.

Besides the lack of conflict and material being unbelievable, what are some of the other *symptoms* of dull screenwriting?

Sometimes incidents and events are *too contrived* and *too predictable*. Things happen too easily. This is usually because the dramatic need of the main character is not defined or sufficiently well thought out; the obstacles become too predictable, the conflict too shallow. The dramatic needs of the story are being satisfied too easily, and that tends to dilute the narrative drive. What do you get? Dull and boring.

Other screenplays rely on *subplots* to move the story forward. This dilutes the focus of the main character and gives rise to a thin and one-dimensional characterization. Most of the action is spent *cross-cutting* between the scenes of character that are needed to move the story forward, and scenes of the subplot. The story jumps back and forth between one thread of the subplot and the main story line, and if you set up your First Act this way, then the two stories come together at Plot Point I. Other times the stories will merge together late in the Second Act, and that makes it more confusing because you don't really know *what* the story is about, or *who* it's about.

Cross-cutting between the story line and the subplot makes the reader work too hard trying to figure out what the relationship is between the two or more threads of the story. Sometimes a subplot is necessary, but if the essential story points have not been set up and introduced properly, the story become so complicated that it's difficult to understand what's going on.

An easy way to spot one of the *symptoms of dull* is through the main character. As mentioned, good screenwriting always shows itself in strong character and strong action. So, if you use your main character as an indicator, and feel that he or she is not strong enough, or there's too much dialogue and not enough visual action, you're probably right in assuming the character is weak and reactive. In this case the character appears to ride the surface of the story line, and there's not enough information to go deeper into the psyche of the character to see what's really going on.

Think about creating an incident that works upon your character in such a way that his or her reaction reveals a more forceful and illuminating dimension of character.

This creation of incident will be reflected in the scenes you choose to write, for the screenplay is revealed through the scene; it is the cell of dramatic action. A scene is composed of shots, what the *camera sees*, and it can either be a single shot, or a series of shots, held together by a specific *location;* where the scene takes place, and the *time* when it takes place.

If you change either place or time, then you have to change the scene. Moving from the kitchen to the living room to the garage means three different scenes, because there are three separate locations. If you had a scene in the kitchen in the morning, then have one in the afternoon, it's two different scenes. Why? Because you have to change the light; morning light is totally different from afternoon light, so if you change the time, that means making a lighting change and you must therefore write a new scene.

Basically, there are two ways to create a scene: one is to write the scene in the *direct* or *obvious* way, in which the characters do what is expected and natural. Since the primary ingredient of drama is the unexpected, you try to play against the grain of the scene, that is, take the unexpected approach.

In *The Shawshank Redemption*, when Tommy, the young man, tells Andy and Red a former cell mate had revealed to him that he had murdered a banker's wife and her lover, "and the banker got blamed for it," we know for the first time that Andrew (Tim Robbins) is innocent. When Andy goes to the warden and tries to convince him of his innocence, the warden refuses to listen, and throws him in the hole for a month.

The next scene shows Tommy being called outside to have a "heart-to-heart" talk with the warden. The warden wants to know "the right thing to do" and wants Tommy's help to verify if what he told Andy is true. Would Tommy be willing to "swear before a judge and jury . . . having placed your hand on the Good Book and taken an oath before Almighty God Himself?" "Just gimme that chance," Tommy replies. The warden nods, understanding, puts out his cigarette, looks up at the guard tower, then turns away, and in that instant Tommy is gunned down.

The obvious way to do that scene would be to have the warden tell Tommy that he's never going to get a chance to testify, that he knows he's lying, and nothing Tommy would say or do could convince the warden to open up Andy's case for a retrial. Normally, we'd expect the warden would help Andy reclaim his innocence, and count on Tommy to help him do it.

And that's the way Frank Darabont, the screenwriter, sets us up; then he turns everything around when he has the kid gunned down by the prison guard. Now we know who the *real criminal* is. Then, to rub it in, the warden goes to Andy in the hole, and tells him the boy was shot trying to escape. And just to let Andy know who's really in charge here, he keeps him in the hole for another month. That action sets up Andy to escape at Plot Point II. We expect one thing, then something else happens. It's the indirect approach to the scene that makes it work so effectively.

Another symptom of dull screenwriting is when the screenwriter *enters the scene too early* and too much time is spent talking about something totally unrelated that will move the story forward. For example, entering a scene too early usually results in the characters talking about something totally unrelated to the purpose of the scene. Enter the scene just before the purpose is revealed; Enter late and get out early is the general rule.

The art of screenwriting is in finding places where silence works better than words. Recently, one of my students told me that after he had completed writing a scene, the thought occurred to him to go back and take another look at it. Something was bothering him about it and he didn't know what it was. So he read and reread the scene, and suddenly understood how he could make it work more effectively with just *two lines of dialogue*! That's just good screenwriting. You don't need pages and pages of dialogue to set up, explain, or move your story forward; just a few lines will do, if you enter the scene at the right point.

In *How to Make an American Quilt* past and present are woven together by questions and answers. And even though there are many different stories, they are all connected with the theme of the film: "Where Love Resides." Each story deals with an affair of the heart, and each reflects another aspect of Finn's dilemma regarding her commitment to Sam. The quilt is the metaphor for the entire film.

Another symptom: having the character always react to situations or events. If that happens too much, the character becomes passive and reactive. An important ingredient of good character creation is finding the best way to *introduce* that character. If your character is too egotistical or uncaring, he or she will be unsympathetic. Just look at *Diehard 3;* we meet the Bruce Willis character drunk, in a van, not having seen his wife in a year. We don't really care too much about him.

Sometimes a screenplay starts off too quickly, and if the action happens too fast, the reader doesn't know who or why the character is participating in this action or event. If the story starts off too slowly, then everything has to be explained through dialogue, so there is no dramatic tension to pull the reader through the story line. It leads to a dull screenplay.

One of the things I've discovered about the nature of dull is that while scenes may be structured well, with the dialogue clean and sharp, there is no payoff to the scene. We don't see the natural conclusion of the scene because the screenwriter cuts away before the purpose of the scene is fulfilled. I've read so many screenplays where the writer seems to forget why the scene is in there in the first place. Each scene is related to every other, and you've only got 120 pages to tell your story, so you can't waste time writing scenes that are not paid off. Characters, incidents, events, decisions, all need to be set up at some point in the story. It doesn't have to be in the scene before, or in the same scene, or in the scene after, it can be anywhere, because all aspects of a story line are related to one another and therefore information can be planted anywhere. It can be set up in the first ten pages, then paid off in Act II or III. What really matters is when you set something up in the screenplay, you have to pay it off, either visually or verbally; either through pictures or dialogue.

Another aspect to the *nature of dull* is overwritten scene description. People across the world ask me how long a descriptive paragraph should be, and I reply that any descriptive paragraph, whether it's action or character, or any combination of the two, should not be longer than four sentences.

Why four? There are many reasons. First, when you're writing a screenplay there has to be a lot of white space on the page. Long, bulky, single-spaced paragraphs that take up a half page or more are just too difficult to read. I tell my students that I don't care what the particular action is, they just can't put it all into one descriptive paragraph. Break the paragraph up into four or five sentences. A reader reads the screenplay as if he or she is seeing the movie on the screen. So pages have to be lean, clean, and tight, and not bogged down with a lot of descriptive comments that will never make their way to the screen.

The quickest way to make a reader put down a screen-play is to stop him with a lot of thick and bulky paragraphs that fill up the page. It turns the reader off, and becomes another symptom in the *nature of dull*.

Part II

PROBLEMS OF PLOT

The Problem Sheet

The *Problem Sheet* is an abbreviated guide that is meant to be used as an interactive tool. It lists a number of screenwriting *symptoms* that can help you identify and define various problems. If you have a problem, and you match it with some of the symptoms listed, the contents in that chapter can offer various ways of solving it. Some *symptoms* listed will be the same for several chapters. That's because the same symptoms are relevant for different kinds of problems; it really doesn't matter whether it's a problem of *Plot*, *Character*, or *Structure*. A problem is a problem, no matter how you label it.

The Problem Sheet

TOO MUCH, TOO SOON

- THE STORY IS TOLD IN WORDS, NOT PICTURES

- THE ACTION DOES NOT MOVE THE STORY FORWARD

- THE DRAMATIC PREMISE IS NOT CLEAR

- WHO IS THE MAIN CHARACTER?

- CHARACTERS ARE TOO EXPOSITORY

- MAIN CHARACTER IS TOO PASSIVE AND REACTIVE

- THERE ARE TOO MANY CHARACTERS

- EVERYTHING HAS TO BE EXPLAINED

- THE FIRST ACT IS TOO LONG

- THE STORY LINE IS TOO CHOPPY AND DISJOINTED

- TOO MUCH HAPPENS TOO FAST

8

Too Much, Too Soon

What happens when you read a screenplay and you have the impression that something's wrong with it, but you don't really know what it is? If you think about it, you might be able to trace your awareness, or discomfort, from the very beginning of the script. And if you examine that feeling a little further, then go back and take another look at the material, you'll probably see that the problem has been present right from the beginning.

As a general rule, if you want to find the origin of any problem you have to start looking for it at the very start—from page one, word one. If you do that and analyze the material, you may begin to notice some things. For example, there may be too many characters, or you don't really know who the main character is, who the story is about. Or maybe it just feels like the script is too talky and the action progresses more through dialogue and exposition than the visual image. Or so much seems to be happening that the focus of the story, what it's really about, seems choppy, sloppy, and disjointed.

Look at the material again, and you will probably realize

that there is so much information being given and the story moves so fast, you might not really know what's going on.

All these elements are symptoms of too much information being given too early in the story; too much is happening too soon. The result: not enough depth or insight into the characters and not enough conflict or drama in the narrative line. And it's definitely a problem.

If you want to look for the cause or the source of this particular problem, it will almost always be found in Act I and, more specifically, in the first ten pages of the screenplay.

A good screenplay is set up from page one, word one. Act I is a unit of dramatic action that begins with the opening scene and continues until the Plot Point at the end of the act. It is held together with the dramatic context known as the *Set-Up*; because all the elements of the story, the characters, the dramatic premise and situation, the relationships between them, must be established within this particular unit of dramatic action. Act I is a unit of action in which all the elements of the story must be carefully integrated and set up; all the incidents and events in this unit of action must lead directly to the Plot Point at the end of Act I, the true beginning of your story.

If the script is not set up correctly, then there is a certain tendency to keep adding characters and events to the story line to make it move faster. The story seems to skate on the surface of the action without penetrating its layers of texture and depth, creating the feeling that the story is trite, contrived, and predictable.

Why does this happen? It seems like many writers approach their screenplays without enough preparation; they're so anxious to begin writing the script that they don't take the time to explore and develop the relationships between the action and characters. So they begin from the smallest kernel of information and then feel their way through the First Act. Most of their time is spent trying to figure out what the story is about and what happens next, so they throw down as many story points as they can in the First Act, hoping the story will manifest itself.

It doesn't work. Seeds are planted, but not cultivated, watered, or nourished. The writer tells his or her story in the first ten pages, then is lost and doesn't know what to do next.

Preparation and research are essential to the screenwriting process. It is the responsibility of the screenwriter to know and clearly define who the *main character* is, what the *dramatic premise* is—what the story is about—and what the *dramatic situation* is—the circumstances surrounding the action. If you don't know the story well enough, if you haven't spent enough time doing the required research, then you run the risk of inserting more incidents and events into the story line just to try to make it work, and then the narrative thread of the story usually goes awry; the stuff just isn't working.

Sometimes the problem exists because the story line is too thin, and more "plot" has to be found, but the solution is not creating more interesting incidents or characters to put into the screenplay. Creating more "things" to happen, more obstacles to confront, doesn't do anything except expand the problem.

The trouble is often traceable to a writer's impulse to get the script off to a fast and provocative start. If you've only got ten pages to grab the attention of the reader or audience, then the tendency is to make sure the story captures the reader's interest. And often that means dumping the characters, their obstacles, and their relationship with the other characters into this ten-page unit of dramatic action.

It's too much, too soon. More is not necessarily better. If you take great screenplays like *Shawshank Redemption, Thelma & Louise, The Silence of the Lambs,* or *Apollo 13,* all the major ingredients of the story line are either there in place, or referred to, within the first ten-page unit of dramatic action. That's why the context of Act I is the *Set-Up.*

The Shawshank Redemption is a great example. Since the story deals with Andy in prison, we have to set up the murder of Andy's wife and lover, as well as the trial and verdict, before he enters the prison. We have to know why he's there and what *crime* he has committed. The three threads of the story line—murder, trial, and verdict—are brilliantly intercut, so we *see* the events leading to his conviction even though we don't actually see him committing the murders.

Many screenwriters would approach the story from the perspective of dialogue; they might begin with Andy entering the prison, and then, during his relationship with Red, he would tell the story in bits and pieces. As Red informs us in voice-over, Andy didn't seem to belong in the prison population; when he walked "he strolled, like a man in a park without a care or worry." During their first few scenes together he could explain to Red about the murder of his wife. In terms of setting up the story this approach would work, but then the tendency might be *to explain* rather than *reveal.*

In *Apollo 13* the first ten pages set up all the narrative threads that are needed to establish the situation. After newsreel shots of the fire that killed the three astronauts of Apollo 1 (the transition from newsreel to present time, TV to TV, is very much like the flashback transitions in *How to Make an American Quilt,* except the quilt is used as the visual motif), the script opens with a friendly partylike gathering watching Neil Armstrong's first walk on the moon. In just a few words we learn these people are astronauts in the current NASA program and the dream of Jim Lovell (Tom Hanks) is to land on the moon. In just a few pages we know everything we need to know, including the suspicion that his wife has some deep fear about his going into space again.

The dramatic hook occurs on page 10, when Lovell returns home and surprises his family with the news that his space mission has just been moved up to the Apollo 13 position. (Originally, a scene had been written showing Lovell with the NASA officials getting the assignment, but it slowed everything down, so it was cut.)

Once he gets the assignment, we can focus, in the second ten pages, on his training and preparation for the mission, so we can see what the astronauts had to go through to prepare for their flight. Plot Point I is the lift-off into space.

Apollo 13 is an excellent example of classic screenwriting that sets up character and story from page one, word one, both through action and dialogue. The script could easily have started with Lovell and his crew being informed their mission was being pushed up, and if it had been written that way, most of the expository information would have to be established in this first ten-page unit of dramatic action.

In *Sense and Sensibility*, based on Jane Austen's nineteenth-century novel, it would have been very easy to put in too much too soon. In the first few pages we could set up the back story, the relationships within the family, the death of the father, how it affects the three sisters, but this normally would be too much information for Act I. Nevertheless, it's got to be there for us to set up the story correctly.

How did Emma Thompson handle this? In voice-over we hear about the family, see the father on his deathbed, and we learn the fortunes of the family are to be automatically inherited by the son. And he promises his dying father that he will take care of his three sisters. But after the funeral the son's wife has other plans for her husband's inheritance.

That's a lot of information to present in the first ten pages. But it's been set up in both narration and pictures, so we see the father's widow and his three daughters are literally without the roof over their heads. The rest of Act I deals with how the family is going to cope with this new situation, and we see them play it out in scene after scene. The girls have to be married, of course, for in those days women needed husbands to take care of them. And when the possible match between the Emma Thompson character with Hugh Grant doesn't happen, the girls give up the house to their brother and move to the country. Plot Point I.

If all this back-story information had been executed through dialogue, there would have been way too much explanation in the story. It would have been too *wordy*, the characters *passive* and *reactive*, the *scenes too long* and *expository*, with the result that the narrative action would not *move the story forward.*

Take a look at the *Problem Sheet.* It's all there.

That's why each element of the story line must be carefully laid out before you even begin writing. Believe it or not, most problems in screenwriting are there because not enough research was done; the story, the characters, and all the dramatic forces working on the story have not been thought out enough.

The inclination to put too much, too soon, into your story line is, I find, usually the result of a number of different things, but the primary cause is that most writers don't spend enough time doing character research. A biography of the main character may not have been written, or maybe not enough was written, with the result that the character seems thin or unsympathetic. The result: a weak character so busy reacting to all the incidents and events of the plot that he or she becomes passive and seemingly disappears off the page. The main character will have no point of view, and some of the lesser, or minor, characters take over. The main character becomes lost in the background.

If you examine the *Problem Sheet* you'll see that almost all the symptoms seem to stem from the writers not knowing the characters well enough. Too many plot twists and turns have to be explained, and the action wanders—as in *Diehard 3*—the dramatic premise forgotten or unclear. This happens in *Broken Arrow* (Graham Yost), the John Woo film in which character is sacrificed for action. What carries the film, of course, is not the story or the characters, but the action.

This particular problem of too much, too soon, is defined as a problem of *Plot*, but the symptoms we've been analyzing stem from *Character*. Why is that?

Because to fix this kind of problem you've got to open up, develop, and enlarge the incidents of the story line, adding new *Plot* elements even though the problem evolves from *Character*.

For example, a woman was writing a story that takes place in the sixteenth century about a band of traveling musicians. The main character is a young woman, deeply in love and recently married, whose husband, when the story opens, is accidentally killed in a river accident. Right after the funeral, her father is determined to marry her to an old man, a very rich and respected merchant, but she refuses and will not obey his commands or honor his wishes. She doesn't know what to do, but when she's invited to a lord's estate to cure his young son (she's set up to be a natural healer), she allows

herself to be seduced by him. Her action permits her to get
out of the unbearable situation with her father, but sets her
apart from the others in the band. She is filled with pride and
independence and no one is going to tell her what to do.
Especially when it concerns her feelings.

The nobleman is enchanted with her, but when he learns
she has used him (he was only a solution to a problem, after
all) he vows that if he can't have her, no one else will either.
So he sets into motion a plan that will keep her as a prisoner
in his castle. And we know that if she ever goes to prison, this
free spirit will literally wither and die.

That's basically the story, and it works well. When my
student began writing the screenplay, she began hurrying the
action, putting in too much information because she thought
she had to explain how the musicians lived, what their society
was like, and their interrelationships within this musical clan.
She structured Act I this way, opening with the group crossing a raging river, when suddenly the husband falls into a
swirling eddy and can't swim against the mighty current and
drowns. The young wife rushes to him, but it's too late. The
funeral follows, and immediately following the ceremony her
father tells her that he has sold her to the old man, the merchant, and she must marry him. She can't deal with it and
flees, but after a few weeks the young widow is summoned to
the nobleman's estate to cure his son. The son recovers, the
nobleman becomes infatuated with her, and she determines
that he is the answer to her prayers and lets herself be seduced.

Being seduced by the nobleman is the Plot Point at the
end of Act I. It gives us enough time to set up the death, the
relationships within the band, and establish the dramatic

premise. The dramatic and visual possibilities are strong, the emotional opportunities rich. The narrative flow of events gives us a good insight into the arena of life of the traveling musicians.

But the woman was still insecure about the story and wrote everything that should happen in Act I into the first ten pages. She literally shoved everything together so the main character meets the nobleman by page 10. As a result, everything happens so fast that nothing is really developed; all the insights that could give us a full and rich portrait of the characters were omitted. In terms of story, there was too much information being given too soon. Everything was mashed together and the events simply rode on the surface of the story like a leaf floating on the water.

When I explained that she had too much information in these first pages, she did not really know how to fix it. I told her she had to go back into her characters in order to get more material, so as to develop Act I more completely. So I gave her an exercise: I had her write a free-association essay about the main character's emotional state; what her feelings were for her husband/lover during their courtship and marriage.

Then I had her develop an emotional back story to her character; what happened between wife and husband immediately before the story begins. Maybe they had an argument the morning before crossing the river; maybe they had just finished making love and vowed their love for each other. I had her describe the character's feelings of grief and loss, her anger at being left behind without him, and her fury and frustration at being bound by the constraints of this unwritten law.

The exercise helped the woman approach some of those

emotional bridges that have to be crossed in order to develop character. When she became more familiar with her character's emotional life, I had her take each one of the events she had written in those first ten pages, and separate them into individual sequences with a beginning, middle, and end. I had her write them all out, in a page-or-two essay; when she finished, she could add and create new material that would allowed her to open up the fertile landscape of her story.

A *sequence, remember, is a series of scenes connected by one single idea with a definite beginning, middle, and end.* A funeral, a wedding (*Four Weddings and a Funeral* is really five sequences strung together), a chase, a shootout, and so on.

Here's how we broke it down for Act I: The band moving toward the river then crossing the river is one sequence; being swept away and the chase leading to the young husband's death, another; her reaction to the loss, her mourning, the funeral, another. All these sequences are complete within themselves and can be structured individually into beginning, middle, and end. Because the new material has to be expanded, structured, and woven into the story line, it brings more depth and dimension to the emotional needs of the character.

That's why it's a problem of *Plot,* though it encompasses elements of both *Structure* and *Character.* The solution to this particular problem is more easily approached from the perspective of *Plot;* that is, we add events to the story line in order to develop the dramatic action more fully. I'm sure it would be easier if we could clearly and conveniently separate each problem into its own little category complete unto itself, but that's not the way it works. In life, as in screenwriting, everything is related to everything else.

Because *Plot, Character,* and *Structure* are the foundations of screenwriting, they will always be interrelated, though certain problems can be approached more easily via one category than another.

You could also solve this kind of problem by approaching it from the category of *Structure* or *Character*. It really doesn't matter how you approach the problem as long as you identify and define it.

What's most important is to find the right way to set up your story; find the picture, or the scene, that best illustrates the story *and* the character. As mentioned, in *Apollo 13*, the script opens with Jim Lovell (Tom Hanks) and other astronauts at a party, watching Neil Armstrong's landing on the moon. The picture on TV and the simple comments by the characters let us know immediately that these people are involved in the space mission to the moon. Within the first ten pages we know that Jim Lovell's dream, his dramatic premise, is to return to the moon.

All this information has been set up simply and economically by the screenwriter's knowledge of who these characters are, what their dramatic need is, what the story is about, and the circumstances surrounding the action. What's set up in Jim Lovell's case is that he knows he may never fly to the moon again because of the accident in the Apollo spacecraft.

This is just good screenwriting. Everything we need to know, we know within this first ten-page unit of dramatic action. It sets up the story so that Plot Point I, the true beginning of the story, is the blastoff into space for the Apollo 13 mission. And thus the temptation to set up the story through dialogue has been avoided.

When you think you have a problem, go back into the material and reread it from the point of view that *maybe too much is happening too soon.* Is the front end of your screenplay, the first 10 pages, overloaded with information, characters, or events? Is so much happening so fast that the reader becomes lost or does the major focus of the story line seem lost?

The Problem Sheet

THE NEED TO EXPLAIN

- VISUAL ARENA IS TOO STATIC

- STORY SEEMS TOO CONFUSING, TOO COMPLEX

- EVENTS ARE CONTRIVED, PREDICTABLE

- THE STAKES ARE NOT HIGH ENOUGH

- NOT ENOUGH VISUAL ACTION

- THE STORY BUILDS TOO SLOWLY, AND WANDERS OFF IN TOO MANY DIRECTIONS

- CHARACTERS ARE NOT DEFINED

- CHARACTERS ARE TOO INTERNAL

- EVERYTHING HAS TO BE EXPLAINED

- THE MINOR CHARACTERS SEEM TO TAKE OVER THE ACTION

9

The Need to Explain

Recently, I read a screenplay about a boat builder on the coast of the Yucatán who is forced out of business by an unscrupulous politician demanding bribes and he reacts by floundering in a lifestyle of drunkenness and bankruptcy. He becomes his own victim. Since the story is about his redemption, we see him go through his transformation by joining a rebel action to help bring about the fall of a Central American dictator.

It is a good action piece, has great visual locations, and has the potential to be a good vehicle for the character's growth, change, and development. But the screenplay didn't read that way and the story's potential was never realized. And here's why.

The writer opens the screenplay with a scene where the main character delivers a boat, which he has been commissioned to build for the politician. Everything seems fine; there are nice visuals but no real conflict as the scene is meant to reveal the extraordinary design abilities of the main character, the builder. The boat he has built is literally a piece of art.

And, the way the scene is written, both characters seem satisfied with the transaction.

Cut to five years later. The main character is now struggling for work, has the reputation of being unreliable, an alcoholic, and we see him lose several jobs. And his design abilities are never again mentioned or play any significant part in the rest of the screenplay.

At Plot Point I, needing money, he accepts a job as a crew member on a large fishing boat, and during a severe storm the boat is shipwrecked farther up the coast. Forced to remain in this thinly populated area while they repair the boat, they discover a band of guerrillas who enlist them in their cause to overthrow the local political dictator, a man groomed and supported by the same unscrupulous politician that ran the main character out of business. He joins them and takes the first steps along his journey of repentance that leads to recognizing his own self-worth and regaining his dignity as a person.

That's the story. During the first part of my read things seemed okay, but around page 30 I began to notice that my attention was wandering, and the more I read the more aware I became of it. So I knew something was wrong; something was not working as well as it should. I started looking for the source of the problem. What I began to see was that the main character was constantly reacting to the situation, and somehow he seemed to be lost on the page in relationship to the other characters. He was involved in every scene, yes, but he seemed bland and uninteresting, and just seemed to disappear off the page.

The first symptom.

I went back to the very beginning of the screenplay, and started looking. When I examined the opening scene between the builder and the politician, I saw there was no conflict at all between the two men, either internal or external. And in the next scene, when the writer cuts into the story five years later, we see the *reaction* to the man's plight. What I saw immediately is the main character was always explaining his actions, his situation, his life, to the other characters. That stopped the forward flow of the story as the character has to justify why he is here, what he is feeling, what his dramatic need is. Because the reader isn't shown the character falling into the pit of hard times during those five years, he or she has to be informed what happened. If you don't show it, you have to say it; you have to explain it for the story to move forward. And when that happens your character is lost on the page, caught in the web of talking heads.

We don't have to explain everything in a screenplay; we just have to know what happens. It's not a question of not explaining anything, it's a question of how the explanation is written. In *Apollo 13* the very first shot under the credits is the actual newsreel footage of the first Apollo astronauts caught in the fire in the space capsule. Three lives were lost, and if we didn't see this, we would have to explain it, because it is the spark that ignites the whole story, moving Jim Lovell's crew up to the Apollo 13 slot in the NASA schedule.

Many times during the screenplay the screenwriter will have the urge, or the need, to explain things—things about the character, things about the situation, things about the story—because if something is not clear, it has to be explained. It is one of the most common problems screenwriters encounter. The process of screenwriting always remains the same, but the creative problems are always different. If there is an action scene, and we don't know what's happening, it has to be explained at some point in order to keep the story moving forward. That's the only way to hold the reader or audience's interest.

Exposition is a key element in the craft of screenwriting. The word itself is defined as the "information necessary to move the story forward."

There are two ways to write exposition; set it up through dialogue, or dramatize it through pictures. Exposition is the easiest, yet the hardest, dialogue to write. It states the obvious, which makes it easy, because the screenwriter simply puts down what needs to be said in order to move the story forward; hard, because the dialogue is usually so obvious, it's embarrassing.

How do you solve this? By finding ways to dramatize the exposition. By finding the right visual image, or metaphor, to serve the story line.

Broken Arrow opens with a fight scene in which Deke (John Travolta) is boxing with his air force copilot, Hale (Christian Slater). Who these characters are, and the forces working upon them, are revealed by their actions. Deke doesn't hesitate to use any maneuver he can to defeat Hale. Hale believes in the rules, fighting hard to win, but never sacrificing his humanity. There is a dialogue between the two men within the riveting action of this scene, and it reveals everything we need to know about their characters throughout the film. And, in the end, the motivation, or purpose, behind Deke's plan to steal two nuclear weapons only needs to be explained in a few lines of dialogue.

In *Jurassic Park* we create the explanation of the story, the premise, in the little interactive presentation that the Sir Richard Attenborough character puts on for his visitors. In his demonstration that is part animation and interactive live action, he explains that mosquitoes in the Jurassic Park era would feed off the dinosaur's blood, then get trapped in tree sap, which would fossilize to amber. Now, millions of years later, the amber is pierced and the mosquito fossil's blood siphoned off, and through the advancement of genetic technology we have been able to create dinosaur clones.

That's the entire premise of the movie. If we don't believe that, then "there is no willing suspension of disbelief" and the story becomes a joke.

So, how do they set this up? They explain it, sure, with both pictures and images. But first you have to grab the reader or the audience's attention, so the script opens with an action sequence that reeks of mystery and suspense. That's Spielberg's great gift as a filmmaker. We don't yet know what's going on, but we know something really big and mean is inside that cage of steel and it's very, very dangerous.

Take a look at this sequence again. Nothing is explained. All we can do is watch as one of the technicians is yanked and hurled around like a piece of lettuce in a tossed salad. And at the end of the sequence we still don't know what's going on. But we're hooked; that's why in action-oriented films, or certain types of mysteries or thrillers, the writer opens with an action sequence that needs to be explained at some point during the story. It's called the *"inciting incident."* A primary rule in screenwriting is that we discover what's going on at the same time the character does. The main character and the reader or audience are connected by the mutual effort of trying to figure out what's going on.

Things have to be explained; sometimes through words, sometimes through pictures. It all depends on the type of screenplay you're writing.

The premise established, we meet the main characters, Sam Neill and Laura Dern, in the Badlands of South Dakota, working the dinosaur digs, using the latest computer technology to isolate the fossil remains of some prehistoric animal. A helicopter lands, bringing the Attenborough character, who convinces the two scientists that if they come with him and "sign off" on his project, he will fund their research digs for the next three years. They can't say no to that. They do need funds to continue their research project. So, they cannot "not" go.

That's the first ten pages of the screenplay; nothing is explained, but it's all been set up, the situation demonstrated.

Now the second ten pages of dramatic action begin, and here it becomes necessary to establish exposition; there is the need to explain. As the characters drive through the open landscape, they see their first dinosaurs, living and breathing and roaming as they were during the Jurassic Period. It's like being lost on an island in time. Again, as we see the explanation, we don't need to explain it through dialogue.

And this is where the questions of "how they do it" and "why they do it" become important and do need to be explained. That's when we have the little interactive presentation explaining the science and technology, set amid the activity of the high-tech laboratory. The other characters are introduced and now we're ready to begin the "true" story.

At Plot Point I they enter Jurassic Park and the massive gates swing shut. Everything has been set up and explained, the characters introduced. Some explanations are part of the visual arena; for example, when they enter the park they see a cow being hoisted into a compound. The young girl is appalled as we hear a vicious roar, then witness a lot of activity within the trees and then we see the empty harness, broken and bloody, being lifted out. Nothing needs to be said; no words are necessary. It's feeding time. We see the same thing with a goat chained to a post. Sitting. Waiting. A short time later, after the storm hits, we see only the chain swinging back and forth, empty. Then the T-rex is upon them.

A screenplay is a story told with pictures, so we have to create the pictures that reveal the story and keep it moving forward; then exposition and the need to explain are kept at a minimum.

The problem with so many screenwriters is that they rely too heavily on dialogue to move the story forward. In some screenplays, like the one mentioned at the front of this chapter, scene after scene deals with some kind of explanation about something that's already happened.

The result: the story moves too slowly, and seems to wander in several different directions. And despite the characters' constantly seeming to explain themselves, the impression is that they are not well-defined, are passive instead of active. Washed out on the page. In the story about the boat builder in the Caribbean, it became necessary for the screenwriter to explain everything because *certain scenes had been omitted in the story line.* That makes it a problem of *Plot.*

In *Jurassic Park* the exposition is presented with a combination of visual elements in order to move the story forward; the introduction of the Sam Neill and Laura Dern characters on the fossil dig in the South Dakota Badlands shows us who these characters are, so the story doesn't become bogged down in explanations, as the writers weave the threads of the story line.

When you're writing a screenplay you have to explain things, that's part of the nature of the medium, but the real question is in *how you do it.* Whether through dialogue or pictures.

Think about it. If you feel there's something not quite

working in your script, take a look at the *Problem Sheet* and see whether you're explaining too much. Here's what you can do.

First, you're dealing with an action and a character, and then you're creating conflict, so we have to know what your character is thinking and feeling in this particular situation. If you start explaining too many things, your story line becomes *confused* or *complex*, because you always have to explain what's happening to your main character. To fix it you have to add elements to the story line *(Plot)*, and many times these dramatic events seem somewhat *contrived* and *predictable*. And if your story is moving forward mainly through dialogue, it becomes *talking heads*, and when that happens some of the *lesser characters start taking over the action.*

To solve this kind of problem you need to rethink your story from two points of view, from the visual as well as the character aspect. Do your scenes have enough of a visual dynamic? Or, do they take place in offices, rooms, and restaurants? In other words, does your screenplay go from INTERIOR to INTERIOR to INTERIOR to INTERIOR with hardly any EXTERIORS anywhere? If you are explaining things too much, one of the first symptoms you look for is whether the story is too closed or too narrow, and if it is, then you have to open it up visually.

Here's an example from a script that one of my students wrote. The story, a period piece set in the forties, is about a woman pilot who wants to compete in an aerial race flying a World War II fighter plane that has only been flown by men. During the story she has to battle the prejudice against her, her own fear that she may not be able to do it, as well as other obstacles. And because there is a lot of information that has to be given about the main character, the writer started to explain too many things.

First, I have to say that this entire exercise is taken out of context and is totally speculative. The scene I'm going to excerpt is between the main character, Kate, and her boyfriend, Holt, also a pilot, who reluctantly supports her in her quest to be the first woman to fly this plane in competition.

> **KATE**
> I'm a little nervous, that's all. Whatever possessed me to think I could do this?

> **HOLT**
> This . . . meaning, the race? How is this different from mounting an exhibit at the museum?
> *(where she works)*
> You plot, plan, research, study, talk to a lot of people, and the day the thing opens, you're a wreck.

> **KATE**
> Do you think of Chris? Ever?
> *(a friend who died flying the same plane)*

> **HOLT**
> Sure. He was my best friend. I think of him a lot. Especially today. He'd be real proud of you.

> **KATE**
> You think so?

HOLT

I know it.
(He hugs her)
You scared?

KATE

A little.

HOLT

Good. A little scared is good. It keeps
you alert. . . . Hey, if you're not good
enough, you won't qualify here either.
But if you do qualify, you're as good as
any man up there.

KATE

(grinning)
Maybe better.

HOLT

Maybe. You'll enjoy it, once it starts.
You'll see. I love you, Kate, I don't want
you to do anything you don't want to
do. We can quit now. Just tell me what
you want to do.
(She looks at him)
That's what I thought.

He lifts her from her perch and carries her to the bed.

HOLT

We have plenty of time before your
briefing.

And, then we cut to the next scene at the airport.

Words and phrases like *nervous, scared, Do you think about Chris? I love you,* all explain feelings, they don't show them. When that happens, the dialogue becomes too direct and tells us what the characters are thinking and feeling. That seems to empty the lines of conflict, and the scene becomes bland and somewhat dull. There is no subtext in the scene; the subtext is what is not said during the scene, all those hidden thoughts or feelings that are the core of what the scene is really all about.

What's the best way to fix this?

I think to really be effective, this particular scene has to be structured from the very beginning of the scene. It should be mentioned that this kind of problem can be solved either through *Plot* or *Character.* I am approaching it through *Plot* because we have to *see* Kate in her environment to know that she can actually compete and hold her own in the flying race. That means we have to see her flying the plane more, so we can learn how she handles it, and the ideal way to do that would be to show her flying the plane and being unable to control it on some level; maybe she finds it difficult to land, or she loses control of the plane and finds it very difficult to regain control in the air. We need to create some conflict with her, something that might put her in jeopardy. This is missing in the screenplay. To show that also means showing her in various stages of her professional, personal, and private life. (That's why this solution is approached from the category of *Plot.*)

For example, Holt says that in an exhibit at the museum (Kate is assistant director), ''you plot, plan, research, study, talk to a lot of people, and the day the thing opens, you're a wreck.'' All true, but we've not seen this side of her character yet in the screenplay. We've only seen bits and pieces of her at the museum, and never under any kind of stress or pressure. In order to really open up the script, we have to show her in some kind of emergency situation, which she handles. All drama is conflict. As I like to say, without conflict there is no action; without action there is no character; without character there is no story. And without story there is no screenplay.

What makes *The Silence of the Lambs* so effective is that Clarice Starling (Jodie Foster) is a student at the FBI Academy and over and over again we see her in the training environment. We see her skill with a gun, in hostagelike situations, on the firing range, in the library, and she discovers the severed head of a murder victim, so we know that when she comes face to face with the serial killer in the basement, she can hold her own. We know that she can take care of herself, and this has carefully been structured into the story line from the very beginning. The first time we see her she's running the obstacle course, and we learn in the next scene that she ranks in the upper quarter of her class, comprised of both men and women.

If we had not seen that she could take care of herself in dangerous situations, then the ending of the film would have been totally unsatisfying; there would be no "willing suspension of disbelief" and we wouldn't buy it at all.

In the story about the woman pilot, a possible way to approach the scene and make it more visually effective without explaining things is to *add new scenes* to set up this scene. Then you can use the emotional currents to make it more potent and energetic. That's why the problem can be solved through *Plot*.

We can also approach it from *Character*, and that means going deeper into the relationship between Kate and Holt. In this particular draft of the script Kate and Holt have been together a little over two years. We don't know much about this relationship, other than what has been explained through the dialogue. He's there for her, supportive in her need, but there's no *past* to this relationship. It has to be created by the writer, with written essays about how they met, their past relationships; who they were with, how long it lasted, what happened that led to their breakup. These things have to be known, otherwise they will not be defined and will have to be explained.

There's another part of the scene that can be explored, and that's the relationship with "Chris," the friend of Holt's who died in a plane crash before the story begins. So far, he's only been talked about, never shown. That's the kind of scene that would affect the present scene directly; Chris's crash was not included in the script, but if we had seen it, and its effect on the characters, we might have been able to set up the relationship between Holt and Chris as well as between Kate and Chris. If we knew this relationship, we could get deeper into the emotional context of the scene at hand. Both characters could be struggling with their feelings in this scene; Holt with his memory of Chris, and his fear for Kate, and Kate in her relationship with Chris, her own fear she must confront, and her relationship with Holt, the man she loves. Remember *Top Gun;* it's this element of the Tom Cruise character conquering his own fear that drives the entire screenplay. It would add a much deeper dimension to the scene.

Instead, all the emotional nuances of the scene are approached through dialogue, explained rather than seen or felt. Because the emotional forces working on the scene were not prepared deeply enough, the presentation seems confined to the surface, lacking in depth. We don't know what Kate's thoughts and feelings are except what she says.

It's true that this is only one scene in the entire screenplay. But look how indicative it is; the whole screenplay is written in this tone, and it lacks a force and an energy that should be driving a story like this. Film is a visual medium and it must be approached both through its action and its character.

Otherwise, you just have to explain everything.

The Problem Sheet

SOMETHING'S MISSING

- STORY LACKS TENSION AND SUSPENSE

- THE STAKES ARE NOT HIGH ENOUGH

- THE STORY LINE IS TOO PLOTTY, TOO COMPLEX, THINGS HAPPEN TOO FAST

- STORY IS TOO THIN, TOO VAGUE, TOO CONTRIVED

- TOO MANY PLOT TWISTS AND TURNS

- DIALOGUE IS TOO TALKY, TOO DIRECT

- CHARACTERS ARE FLAT, ONE-DIMENSIONAL

- MAIN CHARACTER IS NOT VERY SYMPATHETIC

- CHARACTER ALWAYS REACTS TO THE SITUATION, AND HAS NO REAL POINT OF VIEW

- MINOR CHARACTERS STAND OUT MORE THAN THE MAIN CHARACTER

10

Something's Missing

When I'm reading a screenplay, I'm always look-
ing for a story line that's lean, clean, and tight. I want the
characters to move through the narrative landscape with a
strong dramatic need and strong point of view. I want to be
surprised and don't want the story to seem contrived or predictable, and I want all scenes and sequences to be related to
one another, where nothing, neither a throwaway action nor a
line of dialogue, is tossed in just to keep the story moving
forward.

It's what I call "the good read." Unfortunately, I'm disap-
pointed most of the time. The same goes for almost all the
readers in Hollywood, no matter if it's a studio executive,
producer, director, development person, or reader. Person-
ally, I'm directly involved in the reading and writing of about
a thousand screenplays a year; either I'm commissioned to
read them by various producers and production companies,
or I'm working with my many students and helping them
design and develop their screenplays. Over and over again I
find certain tendencies within the screenplay that lead directly to a particular problem; as mentioned in Chapter 8,

either there is too much material fueling the story, or not enough; something is missing.

Many times during the screenwriting process the screenwriter is faced with the creative choice of whether to write a particular scene or not write it. Sometimes a tendency develops where writers will skip scenes that they think are unimportant and unnecessary, scenes they think they could do without. If you find that you start asking yourself "whether I really need to write this scene or not," you begin a *critical process* of *making a judgment*. And while that is a positive and necessary step in the screenwriting process, if overdone it can lead to a creative decision that results in your *not* writing the scene. And once this process has been formed as part of the writing process, once you get into the pattern of saying, "No, I don't need to write this scene," for whatever reason—you establish the habit of saying no.

Then you're in trouble.

Inevitably, something will be missing in the screenplay; most of the time it will be something important or significant to the action, a key scene or sequence that must be there for the story to move forward. When I was a consultant on *White Palace* (Alvin Sargent), with Susan Sarandon and James Spader, there was a significant transition at the end of the Second Act. The James Spader character makes a decision to follow Susan Sarandon to New York. But the way the script was written did not give us any clue that the character was going to leave; there was a scene, and then the next scene showed him arriving in New York. How he got there, when he made the decision, why he made the decision, was never addressed during this particular draft of the screenplay. Just that he goes.

When I first read this section of the script, I was very

confused. It just didn't make sense, especially in light of what happens between the two characters when they encounter each other again. It was a major omission; without this key scene of the Spader character making the decision to leave and follow Sarandon to New York, there was a big, gaping hole in the action. It had to be filled. Such a scene was not only important, it was a structural necessity, for this scene is really the Plot Point at the end of the Second Act.

When something is missing in the screenplay, either a scene or sequence, a character's decision or reaction, it will always get in the way of the action, because we can intuitively feel something is *not there* that should be.

One of my students was writing an action-adventure script about the rescue of an American airman who had been shot down and captured by a guerrilla force in North Korea. And while there were many action scenes, literally one after the other, the writer had omitted saying anything about this character, about what his life was like before his capture, or his family, or what information he had, or his hopes and fears; even in *Crimson Tide* we see the Denzel Washington character at his daughter's birthday party just before he receives the phone call about the Russian threat. And in the setup of the Gene Hackman character something is said about the navy being his "real family." We also *see* his relationship with his dog, and that reveals a great deal about him. It's not just action scene after action scene.

Most of the character dynamic that makes a screenplay really effective, no matter if it's an action-adventure, or thriller, or relationship story, was clearly missing in my student's pages. And it was pretty obvious.

Good screenwriting is a *blend of strong action* and *strong character*. They go hand in hand.

How can you correct something like that? In this case I had my student stop his writing and go back and do more character work. First I had him write several essays about the main character, then suggested some character elements that might be woven into the screenplay. In my student's story the main character is a loner; shot down behind enemy lines, captured, no one to talk to—this creates a situation where a flashback, or what I like to call a *"flashpresent,"* would work very well. For example, as the character's plane is plummeting to the earth we could possibly see, in very quick cuts, various elements of his life. As he yanks his ejector seat, we could possibly see bits and pieces of his life; a scene with his mother, maybe a shot of his wife, or a child playing with a little dog, or a beautiful sunset. These are just some visual suggestions that could open up the script so as to incorporate some character elements into the action. He parachutes into the trees, then there's an action scene of him being hunted down and captured. The screenwriter had become so totally involved in the action elements of the screenplay that he had completely neglected the character.

Something was missing. It was a real problem.

Any creative decision you make about whether to write a particular scene or not is a necessary and essential step in the screenwriting process. But following the *question* about whether or not you need the scene, instead of following what's needed for the *story* to work, leads to a screenplay that reads "thin," with no tension or suspense, and obvious *plot holes* that need to be explained in order for the story to move forward.

And failure to take care of and fill these particular *plot holes* will often lead to stories, and characters, that are thin and one-dimensional. We call this type of screenplay a "one-line" film.

Sometimes, a one-line film works very effectively: *Speed* (Graham Yost) and *Broken Arrow* are good examples of an idea pushed to its extreme, with just enough character delineation to make it interesting. *Il Postino* is brilliant.

But *The Englishman Who Went Up a Hill but Came Down a Mountain* is a good example of a "one-line" script that doesn't work. The story, about an English surveyor and his partner, assigned to reclassify a hill into a mountain in Wales right after the First World War, is a cute premise, cleverly laid out, but extremely simple in terms of style and execution.

The title says it all; that's what the entire script is about, and there's nothing more to it than this particular situation. That's what this movie really is, a situation, not a story, and for that reason the conflict and tension inherent in the story seem lost; is this mountain really a hill, or is this hill really a mountain? That's the only real tension that powers the story forward.

The stakes are not high enough—that is, the emotional stakes. What's at stake in this story? Not much of anything. The people here have nothing to lose. To make it work more dramatically, more effectively, the emotional intensity has to be higher; that means the conflict has be increased. Something of value, whether emotional or physical, internal or external, has to be at stake, or at risk. A character's strong dramatic need will generate more conflict only if there are obstacles that must be overcome. If this is the case, you've got to go into the character's life and find the element or elements that can raise the emotional stakes of the situation.

Why? Take a look at Anson, the Hugh Grant character; he is weak and passive and always seems to be reacting to the situation and other characters. We really don't know too much about him, and he literally disappears into the background of the story. There is nothing about his character, or in his character, to draw and focus our attention on him. He has nothing at stake. The barkeeper, Morgan, on the other hand, is a much more dynamic character. Even the character of the Reverend is portrayed with more gusto and life, and stands out more than Anson. The love relationship with the Betsy character seems predictable and contrived, as if it's just thrown in because there has to be a "love interest" in every script. And why she's attracted to this shell-shocked wimp is, at least to my mind, a total mystery. We know he was shell shocked, but we don't know anything about *him*, and how this has affected him. She is a strong and attractive woman. Why would she consent to be with this kind of a man? Is she his savior? A rescuer? A distraught mother? We don't know, we can only guess.

So, what's the problem?

Something's missing. First of all, the main character is never really defined. The conflict itself is weak and results in very little tension or suspense because the characters are always reacting to the situation; except for Morgan they are not driven by their passions and emotions, only by their need to make this particular hill fall into the category of being listed as a mountain.

Why is that so important? This is the first hole that needs to be filled. It's never really explained. They talk about it, yes, they discuss it, yes, but there is no underlying reason, or motivation, to take this simple conflict seriously. As a result, the story is thin and contrived, the plot line weak. Why these Welsh people of Fynnor Gawr cared so much whether the "British" declared their summit a hill or a mountain is never really established. This might have been a fierce struggle, storywise, for the Welsh are a proud and independent people. Couldn't there have been some kind of conflict spawned the English forcing their laws and their way of life upon the Welsh? The natural rivalry inherent in the story could have been the natural abrasion that might have added more depth and dimension to the story line.

If you feel your story is too thin, or missing something, or if the stakes are not high enough, or if you feel the characters are talking too much, or they all sound alike, or nothing happens, go back over the material and determine whether you've spent enough time setting up the conflict in the story. You can also add color, or create conflict and texture to your characterizations. In *The Englishman* . . . the Hugh Grant character is weak because we don't know enough about him. We don't know much about his background, about how his shell-shock experience has affected him; we don't know whether he longs for a secure and loving relationship, or must overcome a long and deep-seated conflict of prejudice against the Welsh. These are all potential areas of character conflict that might have been explored and expanded to offer a more interesting and dramatic dimension to the story. If these areas had been explored, the film would have been much more than a "one-liner." Sometimes, when the material is thin, and something seems to be missing, look for a *subplot* to weave into the action. A subplot is an additional plotline that becomes a secondary branch of the story line. Adding a subplot is a good idea *sometimes,* and sometimes not, depending on the story. Many writers I know are convinced that every story needs a subplot, so they always try to find a way to inject one.

There are two ways to approach creating a subplot; either adding another element to the narrative line of your script through the *action*, or building it from *character*. That's your first creative decision, because all subplots are a function either of *action* or of *character*. The purpose of a *subplot* is to add more solid dramatic possibilities to your story line; to open up the action so the script becomes more visual, and to fill in any pieces of missing action to sharpen and define the conflict.

Because the subplot springs from *action* and *character*, it means you have to create the particular incidents and events and then structure and weave them through the dramatic action. That's why you solve this particular problem by approaching it from *Plot* as well as *Character*.

If you build your subplot based on the *Character*, you will have to create more obstacles to the story line. For example, if your character is a doctor who's searching for a cure for AIDS, and he's almost found it, you might think about creating a subplot about another doctor who is competing with the main character and possibly has found another cure for the same disease. In medical terms it's important to be the first to discover a cure, because that's what attracts the funding and research dollars. So, maybe the character's dramatic need might be to be the first person to discover the cure. This sets up an additional conflict where the main character is racing against, and challenging, this other character, to be the first to find the cure for AIDS. A subplot like this becomes a very effective way to add and build more dimension into the story line.

How would you go about building this particular subplot? First, you have to create the other character, in this case a doctor doing research with AIDS, and then find out who he or she is by writing a character biography. Maybe these two doctors have had some contact in the past, either before the story starts, or through various research publications; maybe they even went to school together. You can establish this information through the character biography by writing various essays clarifying and defining the dramatic forces working on these two characters. This secondary character will be a major figure in the story, even if he or she is in only a few scenes in the script. Setting up a situation this way allows you to select scenes that will add depth to the plot.

By clarifying and defining what brings a new character into the conflict, and how the main character reacts to this new situation, you generate a whole series of actions and reactions that will hook into the main story line. You are creating additional action to the story, a *subplot* that will give the script a new look and feel. Many writers actually develop the subplot as a separate story, then structure it on the *Paradigm* and then weave it through the dramatic action. That's why it's listed more as a problem of *Plot* than of *Character*.

Whenever you feel you need to cut away from the main action, you can now insert scenes from the subplot and create a much stronger narrative line.

If you want to build a *subplot* based on *action*, here's the perfect example: *Ransom*, the Ron Howard film with Mel Gibson and Rene Russo, from an original script by Alexander Ignon, and rewritten by Richard Price *(Clockers)*. The script is about the kidnapping of a child of a wealthy family and the physical and emotion toll it takes upon them.

In the first draft of the screenplay the action concentrated on the family and how they dealt with the ordeal, how it affected their relationship. The kidnapping was only the "hook" to focus on the characters during the time of their emotional ordeal. And the point of the story was that people are all the same; rich or poor, man or woman, black, white, brown, or yellow, when the lives of children are at stake, the emotional reality experienced is really the same for everybody. Feelings are feelings.

Which is basically the point of the story. But when Richard Price came onto the project, he became aware that, while it was a great situation as written, something seemed to be missing; the script wasn't as strong as it could be. Ron Howard agreed. When they reread the original material from this perspective, they became aware that during the entire screenplay there was nothing about the kidnappers, nothing about the kidnappers' point of view. Who are these people? Why did they kidnap this particular child? How does the kidnapping affect the parents *and* the kidnappers? This is a bizarre and unique relationship that, if explored, could provide another dimension to the script.

So Price started developing the kidnappers' side of the story, and in the subplot we're able to see who these people are and why they've chosen to commit this crime.

The *subplot* opened up the entire screenplay, giving it a richness it had not had before.

If you want to build and develop a subplot based on *Character*, go back into your character's life and redefine it; you're looking for elements of his or her life that would lend themselves to the story and add another facet to the conflict. You can find them by going into your character's *professional* life, his *personal* life, and his *private* life.

What does your main character do for a living? What is his or her profession? What are the relationships between your main character and the people he or she works with? Good? Bad? Are there any conflicts between your character and the people he or she works with? What are they? Has a particular project gone astray? A payment that wasn't made?

Does your character socialize with her office mates after work? What does she do? Is she having an affair? Are her parents alive? Is she sick, or healthy? Write an essay of two or three pages laying this all out. Free-associate and just throw all your thoughts and ideas down; again, don't worry about grammar or spelling or writing fragments. Just toss the words down on the paper. This is automatic writing, and you'll be amazed at what you discover. Writing is always an act of discovery, and you never really know what's going to come out. That's what makes it such an exhilarating experience. It's an incredible high.

If you define these elements of your character's *professional* life, you will find some kind of incident or event you can *hook* into to build the subplot.

What about your character's *personal* life? What are the relationships your main character has during the course of the screenplay? Is he married, single, widowed, divorced, or separated? Can you define these relationships? If your character is single, is he or she in some kind of a relationship when the story begins? What state is the relationship in? Is it good, or falling apart? *Think of conflict here;* it's much better, at least dramatically, to have a relationship that's not in the best shape. Two people who are happy together have very little dramatic value. So create some conflict: perhaps the passion has fallen away, or he's having an affair, or she feels that she's being taken for granted.

If your character is married, what's the relationship like? Is it strong and stable, or is one of the partners questioning his or her commitment? How long have they been married? Are there any children? How many? Define your main character's marriage in a two- or three-page essay and see if you can pull any elements out that may help you build and structure some kind of a subplot. Look for those specific elements that will expand the boundaries of the story line.

You can also do it through your character's *private life*. *Private life* means what your character does when he or she is alone. What hobbies, or interests, does your character have? Taking a class in cooking? A writing class? Looking for "buys" while surfing the Net? Working out three or four times a week? What kind of workout? Yoga? Weights? Dance classes? All these areas can be explored and easily offer a variety of creative choices in terms of developing subplots.

Pets are another way you can add incidents and elements to your screenplay. Does your character have any pets? If so, what kind? As mentioned, in *Crimson Tide* the Gene Hackman character comes on board his submarine with his little dog. The serial killer Jame Gumb, in *The Silence of the Lambs*, has a little fat poodle, "Precious." Pets are a wonderful way to add depth and sympathy to your character.

You can even use this dramatically in the story. I had an experience one night a few years ago. I had a very important dinner meeting. But about an hour before I was to leave, I suddenly noticed my cat, about seventeen years old, was not well. She had great difficulty breathing and was unable to move. I dropped everything and immediately took her to receive emergency treatment. I knew I was going to be late for the meeting, but as far as I was concerned, I had no choice in the matter. The cat was my first priority. So, I took her to the animal emergency center, the vet examined her, gave her some shots, and kept her overnight. I went on to the meeting, and while everything appeared normal, at least on the surface, my thoughts and feelings were with my cat. And it was that situation or incident that could create a dramatic *subplot*. If I was looking for some kind of incident or episode to bulk up my screenplay from the function of *Character*, this kind of incident or event would be a perfect vehicle.

As I recall, I had a very tough time that night. My cat was given an injection and some pills, and came home the next day. But an incident like this can add depth to your characters and fill in some of the missing holes in your story line.

Just remember that you can approach writing a *subplot* either through *action* or *character*. Each is an effective way to build substance and dimension to the story line, and provides information that moves the story forward visually, rather than verbally. If you have set up the elements of the *subplot*, and they are clearly established and defined, then you can follow them easily as they surface through the story line, like dolphins breaking the waves.

The Problem Sheet

ANOTHER TIME, ANOTHER PLACE: BRIDGING TIME AND ACTION

- THE SCRIPT IS TOO LONG

- STORY IS EPISODIC, TOO EXPOSITORY

- TOO MANY THINGS HAPPEN, WITH NO FOCUS IN THE STORY LINE

- THINGS HAPPEN TOO FAST

- TOO MANY CHARACTERS

- THE MAIN CHARACTER IS TOO WEAK, OVERPOWERED BY OTHER CHARACTERS

- SCENES ARE TOO LONG, TOO COMPLICATED

- TOO MANY SUBPLOTS

- THERE SEEM TO BE TWO STORIES IN ONE

- TOO MANY THINGS HAVE TO BE EXPLAINED

11

Another Time, Another Place: Bridging Time and Action

A look at the *Problem Sheet* reveals a lot of common problems that plague screenplays. Many times I'll read a screenplay and within the first ten pages I can make a fairly accurate "read" of the material. I look for a lean, clean, visual style, with an economy of story, the characters and their actions clear and concise. If there are too many characters, or too much action, or too many long-winded scenes, the chances are the script will be overlong, say more than 145 pages. If that's the case, the story line might be too broad, too expansive, too big in scope, resulting in the main character's not being clearly defined; or there may be too many characters, or too many scenes where the main character is not involved, or a story line that covers too much time and too much action.

Scripts that span a number of years, like *The Shawshank Redemption*, are very difficult to write because the time frame is very long and there may be too many incidents that have to be covered and explained. There's too much going on. So when you're working on a subject that covers a long period of time, you have to know what problems you're going to be confronting.

Apollo 13 is a script like this. The story is a chronological time line that covers seven days, and what makes it difficult to write is that a series of events must happen that includes a multitude of details, and each one is contingent upon the others. I understand that the first few drafts of *Apollo 13* were more than two hundred pages long. So what do you have to do to make it work effectively? If you're not true to the "history" of the story, the circumstances and events, you're bound to break the "willing suspension of disbelief," and nobody will buy it. It's just not "real" or believable, and this becomes apparent immediately. The music is there, but that's about it.

So how do you approach the *historical film* or the period piece? A script based on actual characters and events? There are many ways to approach the *historical screenplay*. First, of course, you have to do the textual research, reading books, magazines, or newspapers of the time and subject, finding out all you can about the period, as well as the people and the forces of the times. Personal diaries or novels of that period are also a good source. Once you've done the research, then you can place the historical facts into a progression of events that become the structural foundation of the screenplay.

Then you have to decide how you're going to end it. What incident or event will resolve your story line most effectively? Is it based on an actual incident whose ending we already know, like *Apollo 13*, *All the President's Men* (William Goldman), or *Nixon*? Or will you base the ending on some kind of commentary using a scrawl over the end credits, as in *Dances With Wolves*? In other words, how true do you have to be to history? And the answer is simple: Be true to the facts, and the events of history, but the motivations that drive the characters can be created and entirely fictional.

Immortal Beloved (Bernard Rose) is a script like this: if you know anything at all about Beethoven's life, you'll know that the events shown were obviously fabricated; if you look for "the real" Beethoven in that script, you'll have a hard time finding him.

If you happen to be writing a script like this, a historical or period piece, and you find that your script is too long, and too episodic, or you have too many characters, or too much seems to be going on, the first question you have to ask yourself is not "What do I keep in?" but *"What do I leave out?"*

It's *the* major creative decision that must be made before you even begin to approach the story, or the rewrite. If you don't ask yourself this question, it often leads to difficulties and raises many problems, most notably *selectivity*. What events *do I need* to tell the story in the most visually effective way, and then, what can I leave out?

One of the ways to solve this particular problem is by using *transitions*. The passage of time and the link between the scenes and sequences has to be conceived visually, for moving the action from one scene to the next requires a visual transition. *Transitions* bridge time and move the action forward quickly, visually. Whether you're writing an original screenplay, or adapting a novel, play, magazine, or news article, each piece of film, each scene or sequence, must bridge a particular *time* to a particular *place* in order to move the story forward. To go from Point A to Point B in a screenplay requires making transitions that connect the two. If you don't make those transitions, then you may wind up with many of the symptoms that are on the *Problem Sheet*.

There are four major ways to make *transitions:* cutting

from *picture to picture, sound to sound, music to music, or special effect to special effect.* There can be *dissolves, fadeouts,* and *smash cuts.*

It wasn't too long ago that the screenwriter depended on the director or film editor to create these visual transitions, but at the present time most of the working screenwriters know that it is the writer's responsibility to write the required transitions from scene to scene. One of the recognizable traits of the screenwriter in the nineties is his or her ability to write good visual transitions. And at the present time there seems to be an evolution in the style and sophistication of the art of transition. Even a script like *Pulp Fiction,* which is sequential and episodic, uses effective transitions so the five episodes that make up the screenplay seem to be connected into a single story line. The title page even proclaims the script is really "three stories about one story." If Tarantino and Avary had not created those transitions, the script would have been disjointed and episodic and not worked as well as it does.

As far as I'm concerned, it is the screenwriter's responsibility to write these transitional scenes that move the story forward and bridge time and action. Writing good transitions is also a very good way to solve a number of problems.

Transitions have always been an integral part of the screenwriting process. From the earliest days of silent movies the craft of filmmaking has always been the same: to tell a story in pictures, building it from beginning to end with little bits and pieces of film. That's what a screenplay is: a story told with pictures.

In *The Shawshank Redemption,* for example, the passage of time is handled incredibly well. Only one shot is needed to tell us the passage of time: the large posters of Rita Hayworth, Marilyn Monroe, and Raquel Welch visually indicate that several decades have passed by. That, and some music on the soundtrack. In *How to Make an American Quilt* a young woman of twenty-six is kneeling down looking at a book and we hear her in voice-over narration: "How do two separate people fuse into this thing called a couple? And if your love is that strong, then how do you still keep a little room for yourself . . . ?" That's what the whole film is about, and when Finn stands up, we match-cut to her as a little girl of five or six years standing up looking at the women in the quilting bee as her narration leads us directly into the story line.

Why are transitions so important? Because when you're reading a script, or seeing a movie, it has to flow smoothly across a time period that is usually not more than two hours. The story line has to be a seamless parade of images across the page or screen, and time becomes a relative phenomenon; days and years and decades can be condensed into seconds, a few seconds stretched into minutes, as a leap is made from one image to another. That's one of the things that make *The Shawshank Redemption* such a remarkable movie; the passage of time does not draw attention to itself. It becomes an integral part of the fabric of the screenplay.

Transitions can be as varied and as multiple as the colors in a kaleidoscope. In *The Silence of the Lambs*, for example, the screenwriter, Ted Tally, generally plays the last line of one scene over the first line of the next. The dialogue is used to bridge time and action and shows one way that *sound* can be the link connecting two different scenes. Tally ends one scene with a question, then opens the next scene by answering that question.

This kind of overlapping transition scene has been done many times before, of course, most notably in *Julia*, Alvin

Sargent's Academy Award–winning screenplay adapted from Lillian Hellman's *Pentimento*. But the way Tally approached his transitions pushes the boundaries of the medium in such a way that we're not even aware of them. If you're watching a movie and become aware of the visual transitions, or feel the "arty" influence of the director in each scene, chances are it's not a very good film.

The style and sophistication of the transition is evolving all the time. In *Lone Star* John Sayles makes his transitions bridging time and action in a very unique way: he has the characters remain in present time, then pans the camera over to a character or a place and suddenly we have moved across time, either forward or backward. It's very effective, extremely visual, and I think shows the remarkable versatility of Sayles as a writer and director.

Apollo 13 is a film based on an actual historic event, and the screenwriters bridge the action by simply cutting back and forth—a technique called *cross-cutting*—among the three astronauts in the spacecraft and the Mission Control team in Houston. The story moves forward by action/reaction, and is held together by the events and circumstances. *Thelma & Louise* also moves forward by cross-cutting between the two women on the run and the policeman searching for them.

Every screenplay has its own particular style and form in terms of transitions. An action film usually has short, quick transitions, because the film moves forward at a very rapid pace and we have to be swept up into the action. But in a character-driven piece the transitions could possibly come from silence, or looks between the characters, or dialogue. There is never *any one right way* to make transitions. *The only criterion is whether it works or not.*

There may be times when you're so engrossed in putting

the story down on paper that you don't even think about the transitional flow of the script. But when you finish the first or second draft, you find that you've written a screenplay that may be 145 pages or longer. During the actual screenwriting process that's okay, but afterward you're going to have to do a lot of work to cut it to a proper length. A 140-plus page screenplay is only accepted if it's by William Goldman, Quentin Tarantino, David Koepp, or Eric Roth.

If your screenplay is too long, and you feel there's too much going on, too many things happening, or too many characters, look for ways to bridge the time and action. Transitions solve so many problems in screenwriting and sometimes the bridge to another time, or another place, can be as simple as changing the character's clothes, or using match cuts, or changing the weather, or using holidays to condense the time and action.

One of the most interesting films to use transitions as an integral part of the story is *Pulp Fiction*. This is a unique film in many respects, but what's especially interesting is the way Tarantino and Roger Avary created the transitions to keep the film flowing smoothly in one single time line.

As the title-page reads, *Pulp Fiction* is really "three stories about one story." The first page of the screenplay is "The Table of Contents," and states that there is a prologue, where the holdup begins (with Tim Roth and Amanda Plummer) then a story called "Vincent and Marcellus Wallace's Wife," another called "The Gold Watch," and the last story, "Vincent, Jules, Jimmie, and the Wolf" (in the film the title's been changed to "The Bonnie Situation"), which leads us into the Epilogue and the conclusion of the robbery. The use of a Prologue, which opens the script, and the Epilogue, which closes it, is called a *"bookend"* device; the opening scene or sequence leads into the story and the last part of the scene or sequence closes it. *The Bridges of Madison County* (Richard LaGravenese) is another example of the use of a "bookend" opening and closing. Despite all the five specific episodes that make up the script of *Pulp Fiction*, it really seems like one story. Why?

Because of the transitions.

All the transitions in this screenplay are character driven, and the reason the film works so effectively is that the three stories are woven together with these characters. Even though it is "three stories about one story," the focal point always seems to be Vincent, the John Travolta character.

The film opens in the restaurant with Tim Roth—Pumpkin—and his girlfriend, Honeybunny (Amanda Plummer); they pull out their guns and the robbery begins. We freeze at this point, then cut to Vincent and Jules driving somewhere having one of their many weighty and lengthy discussions about the difference between McDonald's restaurants here and abroad. They seem like two nice guys until they open the trunk, pull out several guns, and make their way inside an apartment building. Their actions seem to contradict their dialogue, which makes them interesting and colorful characters. They walk up the stairs, stake out a room, all the time continuing their discussion about the moral and ethical complications of a "foot massage." Especially Marcellus's wife Mia's foot massage which left the "masseur" with a very "severe speech problem."

It is this attitude of casual nonchalance that is so effective in the film. There have been all kinds of essays and comments and literary debates about *Pulp Fiction*, and they reveal the extent to which movies have become the social fingerprints of our time.

The two hit men force their way inside the room and

confront the four young men who tried to rip off Marcellus Wallace and not deliver what they said they were going to deliver, the mysterious briefcase with the light inside, and the combination 666, the devil's numbers. (In Hitchcockian terms, the briefcase and what's inside would be called the "McGuffin.") As Jules quotes from the Bible (another nice character touch), Vincent and Jules kill three of the four guys in a very explosive scene. When Brett, one of the four, leaps out of the bathroom with his gun blazing, *missing* Vincent and Jules, it becomes "a fucking miracle," and then we cut to:

Marcellus's bar, where the "boss" is telling Butch (Bruce Willis), a boxer, to take a fall in the fifth round of his fight. Butch agrees, reluctantly, to deliberately lose the fight, then goes to the bar for a pack of cigarettes and is joined by Vincent, who has just arrived (wearing the funny clothes he wears in story #3), and the two exchange some words. They don't like each other. Vincent is called in to the boss, Marcellus, who gives him an order: take his wife out to dinner.

At this point we have a choice; in terms of story we can either follow Butch, or Vincent. We follow Vincent. We set up the encounter between Vincent and Mia when he scores some "great" heroin, and then follow him as he takes Mia out to dinner in a long and bizarre sequence, ending with her overdosing on heroin. Vincent saves her, they say their goodbyes to a "memorable" evening, and we go into:

The second story, titled "The Gold Watch." The transition between these two stories is simply to Fade Out at the end of the Vincent/Mia sequence, and Fade In on a flashback sequence of a young Butch being told the story of his father's gold watch that he had carried up his ass for more than six years in a Vietnamese POW camp. When the young boy reaches to take the watch, Butch wakes up in his dressing room just before the fight. We know Butch was supposed to take a fall, but we actually don't see the fight; we cut to the taxi driver listening to the results. We hear on the driver's radio that a fighter has died, then we see Butch leap into a Dumpster, then into the cab, and make his way to a motel, where his girlfriend is waiting for him.

She has forgotten the gold watch at his apartment. Furious, he realizes he must go back and retrieve it, even though it may cost him his life. He has double-crossed Marcellus and he knows there will be a contract on him (executed by Vincent and Jules). Sure enough, when he returns to the apartment, and retrieves the sacred watch, Vincent emerges from the bathroom and Butch blows him away. Which is perhaps the most arresting moment in the film, because the scene is out of its normal time frame. It's a nonlinear action. And, occurring as it does in the middle of the script, it breaks the normal linear thread of the story line. This "nonlinear" structure is what has been so instrumental in the success of the film, and become the inspiration for many others coming up in the latter part of the nineties.

Butch escapes in his little VW and at a stoplight sees Marcellus and literally runs over him in his efforts to get away. In the ensuing somewhat comedic escape, both men are captured by two goon brothers, Ned and Zed, who lock them up in order to sodomize them. Butch escapes, but decides he cannot let Marcellus remain in the hands of these two goonies. He rescues him, again at the peril of his own life, and when Marcellus grants him a pardon, he promises to leave with his girlfriend, never to be seen again. As Mia and Vincent have agreed to reveal nothing about what happened at dinner, Marcellus and Butch make an agreement not to say anything about this incident. Life is a compromise.

Which then brings us to the third story, "Vincent, Jules, Jimmie, and the Wolf," though in the film the title's been changed to "The Bonnie Situation." Bonnie is Jimmie's wife, the nurse who is expected home within the hour. And Jimmie (played by Tarantino) is not going to jeopardize his marriage by his wife finding a dead man in the garage. It's a situation that needs to be handled by the Wolf, the Harvey Keitel character whom we heard Marcellus mention at the end of the previous story.

The story begins at the end of the opening section after the Prologue, in what is really an overlapping scene from another point of view. When Jules kills the first man, the character Brett, whom we have not seen before, has been in the bathroom, a gun in hand. He listens to Jules spouting the Bible in the living room and then we hear gunshots. Muttering to himself, Brett leaps out of the bathroom firing six times at Jules and Vincent and misses each time; the bullets thud harmlessly into the wall. As Jules says, "It's a fuckin' miracle," and he becomes obsessed with the fact that they're still alive. "This is some serious shit," he says as they drive away, the other character, Marvin, being held "captive" in the backseat. They become engrossed in an illuminating conversation, Jules declaring that they've survived "only by divine intervention"; Vincent disagrees, and when he turns to get Marvin's opinion, the gun he's holding accidentally fires and Marvin's head is blown all over the car.

In a panic Jules calls his friend Jimmie and they go there to clean up the car and get rid of the body. A quick call to Marcellus produces "The Wolf," and he comes to their rescue and saves the day. The job done, the body and the car both disposed of, the two of them are hungry and go get some breakfast.

That, of course, is the transition that leads to the coffee shop that Tim Roth and his girlfriend are going to rob. As they are having breakfast and continuing their discussion, Vincent goes to the bathroom, and when he's gone the robbery begins, so we begin this action a little bit before it ended in the Prologue. Another nice use of nonlinear structure. The two of them thwart the holdup, permit Pumpkin and Honeybunny to leave, and then leave themselves. The end.

This nonlinear structure works very well within the framework of the three stories, Epilogue, and Prologue. It is really what makes the film so interesting and appealing. Just for the sake of an exercise we could put these three stories, along with the Prologue and Epilogue, into a linear story line. We might open with Vincent and Jules on their way to kill the kids who were trying to rip off Marcellus. They leave, accidentally kill Marvin, go to the "Jules, Vincent, Jimmie, and the Wolf" sequence, which would be followed by their breakfast, leading to the Prologue and Epilogue. We follow them to the Marcellus bar scene of the first story, where Vincent and Butch meet; we would follow Vincent to Mia and their night out, then end with Butch and the gold watch, with Vinnie's death and Butch's escape. Yes, it would work, but it certainly would not be as effective as it is now.

It is the transitions between these stories that really hold it all together; they make the screenplay work, bridging both linear time and narrative line. All the characters are introduced and set up from the beginning, and these characters are the links that connect the three stories, even though they are told in a nonlinear way. The "wackiness" of the characters (their discussions and the dialogue are wonderful), along with the bizarre humor of the stories, makes *Pulp Fiction* the entertaining and highly influential film it is and, I think, will continue to be.

Different kinds of films require different kinds of transitions. An action or action-adventure film like *Apollo 13* or *Mission: Impossible* (David Koepp and Robert Towne), requires swift transitions, sharp, dynamic bridges that keep the pace flowing fast and smooth, so the reader and viewer are swept into a torrent of movement. Look at *Twister,* simply a one-line story of storm chasers; it is the four storm sequences that really hold the film together. So everything in the story acts as a transition leading into the next storm.

A character piece, like *Pulp Fiction* or *The Bridges of Madison County,* requires a different kind of transitional connection, a smooth and careful sculpting of transitions. In a comedy the transitions from one scene to the next might be capped with one-liners, but they must be character driven or humor driven in order to move the story forward in a funny and seamless way.

Transitions in a biographical or historical screenplay present a problem of selectivity. How do you weave what might be a number of historical incidents into a 120-page screenplay? If you simply string the character's life story, or a series of events, in chronological order, it becomes nothing more than a filmed essay; first this happens, then that happens, then this other thing happens, and so on until the character dies or something significant takes place that leads to an ending we already know. As in *Nixon,* or *Apollo 13,* or *Gandhi.*

Recently I had the opportunity of working with a Brazilian writer-director on a screenplay about the famous Brazilian composer Villa-Lobos. The writer did not want simply to show a biographical chronology of events, so he chose to write the screenplay like a free-association collage, fragmented bits and pieces of the composer's life presented in a nonlinear fashion like some kind of visual jigsaw puzzle. That way, he explained to me, he hoped to make the composer's life both visual and interesting. But, he confided, he felt very insecure about the script; he didn't know whether it worked or not.

When I first read the material I thought it an interesting presentation, but unfortunately, the script didn't work; it was a hard and difficult read because I didn't know *what* was going on; I didn't know what the story was about and it was hard to get a grasp of the main character.

My problem was "how to fix it," how to keep the writer's style and subject matter intact but also to tell the story of the composer, the subject of the script. At first I thought this was a structural problem, but when I went back over the material, trying to isolate and define the historical moments of the character's life, I realized that the main character seemed to disappear off the page; that's when I realized that it was really a problem of *Character*, because the events of his life seemed to overshadow him. The women in his life seemed to dominate him, the smaller characters seemed larger than he was, and there seemed to be too many events going on.

When I took it apart, I saw the screenplay really focused on five major periods of the composer's life, and it was these "parts" that were broken up and placed in various sections of the screenplay. I had the impression that *the main character got lost on the page,* for he literally disappeared from the action, even though it was his story and he was the main character. The main character always seemed to be reacting to the events of his life, and not creating them. The main character in a screenplay always has to be active; he or she must *cause* things to happen.

A biographical film like *Gandhi,* for example, covers only a few events of his life, yet the conflict the character confronts and endures is encapsulated in two or three events and they become the structural foundation the script is built upon. The film covers only three major periods in Gandhi's life: as a young attorney fighting for social causes; then formulating and embracing his philosophy and practice of "passive resistance"; then trying to mend the Hindu-Muslim disputes. Gandhi's murder and death "bookend" the film, very much like the bookend Prologue and Epilogue in *Pulp Fiction.*

The Brazilian script, as fragmented as it was, really dealt with these five periods of the composer's life: his childhood, his struggles to get his music performed; the two women in his life; his world fame; and his final acceptance of old age.

As I started going through the script again, I found that I could isolate and define these five areas of his life, but there seemed to be several key scenes missing, scenes needed to highlight and accent those periods of the composer's life. And it was these key scenes, I felt—discovering the source of his inspiration, meeting his second wife, overcoming those incredible obstacles to get his music performed, and so on— which became the Plot Points, or anchors, the basic glue that held the script together.

Good transitions in a screenplay should never really be noticed; they should disappear into the visual narrative like the individual threads that make up a piece of cloth.

Transitions become an essential tool in the Problem-Solving process. If your script is too long, look for whole chunks of action, or full sequences, to omit and then find some kind of transition to tie the remainder together and bridge the action. Sometimes you can cover a longer period of time by using a *montage*.

A montage is a sequence, a series of scenes connected by one single idea with a definite beginning, middle, and end. The purpose of a montage is to cover a lot of time, or a lot of events, in a very short period of time. In the Brazilian screenplay we used several montages in order to move the story forward quickly. We numbered the shots: 1) walking along the beach; 2) at dinner alone; 3) working hard at the piano, sheet music spread all around him on the floor; 4) walking into an office; 5) in another office arguing violently with a short, fat bureaucrat, wearing different clothes from the previous shot; 6) walking angrily out of another building, on another day, wearing the same crumpled suit with a different tie, and so on. The montage served a very specific purpose within the screenplay, yet conceived as one single action carried out over a period of several days.

Perhaps the best transition ever put on film was the marriage montage in *Citizen Kane* (Orson Welles and Herman Mankiewicz). The sequence starts after the marriage of Kane and his first wife, as they sit at the breakfast table having an intimate conversation. There is a *swish pan* (the camera swishes out the frame) and we see them in different clothes talking and reading the paper. *Swish Pan* and we see them at a slightly larger table having a very heated discussion. *Swish Pan* to them having a more vocal argument about him spending so much time at the office. *Swish Pan* to them at a much larger table, both silent, both reading the paper; she asks him something and he simply grunts a reply. *Swish Pan* to them at a very long table eating in total silence. It tells us so much in so little, using pictures instead of words. It's an incredible sequence that is probably the best portrait of the disintegration of a marriage ever conceived.

Part III

PROBLEMS OF CHARACTER

The Problem Sheet

WHAT IS CHARACTER?

- THE MAIN CHARACTER EXPLAINS TOO MUCH ABOUT HIMSELF/HERSELF

- MAIN CHARACTER IS NOT VERY SYMPATHETIC

- THE MAIN CHARACTER IS TOO REACTIVE, TOO INTERNAL, SEEMS TO DISAPPEAR OFF THE PAGE

- I AM THE MAIN CHARACTER

- ALL THE CHARACTERS SOUND THE SAME

- MINOR CHARACTERS ARE MORE INTERESTING, STRONGER, THAN THE MAIN CHARACTER

- RELATIONSHIPS ARE TOO VAGUE, NOT CLEARLY DEFINED

- DIALOGUE IS TOO LITERARY, TOO FLOWERY, TOO OBVIOUS

12

What Is Character?

The problems of creating real people in real situations can be so varied and challenging that trying to define them is like trying to capture infinity in a glass. Generations of noted writers, from Aristotle to Ibsen, Eugene O'Neill to Arthur Miller, have struggled valiantly trying to articulate the art and the craft of creating good characters.

It is difficult to capture a "true human being" on paper, and more difficult in screenwriting, because we're dealing in pictures, not words. Great writers have always had this need to explain how they create character. One of the most profound literary theorists was Henry James, the great nineteenth-century American novelist. James was fascinated with the art and craft of writing, and approached it like a scientist, the same way his brother, William James, the famous psychologist, was occupied with the dynamics of the human mind. Henry James wrote several essays trying to document and capture the intricacies of creating character. In one of those essays mentioned earlier, James posed a literary question: *"What is* character *but the determination of incident? And what is* incident *but the illumination of character?"*

It's a profound statement.

Does that mean the character determines the incident? Or the incident creates character? This is something that should be analyzed and understood, especially when dealing with character. If you're trying to solve a problem relating to character, whether an action, reaction, or dialogue, it's essential to understand the dynamics of *Character*. If you examine the *Problem Sheet*, most of the symptoms described could apply to any number of problems or situations found within the characters. Most of the problems listed deal with defining and articulating the actions and dimension of the character by relating to his thoughts, feelings, and emotions.

Waldo Salt, the great screenwriter of *Coming Home* and *Midnight Cowboy*, among others, when asked about how he went about creating characters, replied that first he chose a simple dramatic need and then added on to it, and colored it until it became a universal chord common to Everyman.

What is the dramatic need of your character? Do you know it? Can you articulate it? Can you trace it through the events of the story so it reflects a depth, and a change in the character? First of all, how do you determine whether you have a problem? Look at the *Problem Sheet:* do you feel your character is talking too much, or explaining too much about the story or characters? Do the characters sound the same? Do you think that you're the main character? Does your character seem to disappear off the page? Do other characters seem to overshadow your main character? This is a common problem and applicable to all sorts of situations. Remember, there's no *one way* to approach the problem of creating better character; there are many ways. The only rule you have to follow is whether it works or not.

The first thing you need to do in solving a problem of

Character is determining what the problem is. Identify it. Define it. As you read through the material looking for any telltale signs or symptoms, you have to trust yourself and your instincts; if you feel this little "tug" of discomfort, that's usually an indicator that something is not working as well as it should.

What's the best way to approach solving the problem of *Character*? Start at the beginning; ask yourself the question *What is Character*?

That's the question Henry James explored when he began his inquiries into the nature of character. In a screenplay the story always has to move forward, from beginning to end, whether in a linear or a nonlinear fashion. The way you drive your story forward is by focusing on *the actions* of the *character*. As mentioned before, every scene in a screenplay should fulfill one of two functions: Either it moves the story forward, or it reveals information about the character.

So what is *Character*? *Action is character; what a person does is who he is, not necessarily what he says.* Film is behavior. Because we're telling a story in pictures, we must show how the character acts and reacts to the incidents and events that he or she must confront and overcome. If you read your script again through the eyes of your character, and you begin to sense and feel that your characters are not as sharp or defined as you think they ought to be, and you want to make them stronger, more dimensional, and universal, the first thing you must determine is whether they're an *active force* in the screenplay; do they *cause* things to happen, or do things *happen to* them? It's one of the more prevalent problems of *Character*.

Take another look at the *Problem Sheet;* you'll see several symptoms common to main characters who seem to react to the events of the story. It's so important to remember that when you're writing the screenplay, the main character must always *cause things to happen;* not that she doesn't react to incidents or events some of the time, but if she is *always* reacting to events, she becomes passive, weak, and that's when she seems to disappear off the page. Lesser characters appear more interesting than the main character, and seem to have more life and flamboyance.

James's observation that character is determined by incident and that the incident determines character is really at the heart of the writing of screenplays, especially now, in the nineties. Just take a look at the films being done in Hollywood today; at this point in time there's a trend called the "event movie," in which the character or characters are placed in extraordinary situations, and then we see how they react. In this scenario the word *story* may be a little too generous. Most of these characters seem to be just an idea of character, and the incident, or event—the *special effects,* actually—have become the star attraction. Look at *Twister, Speed, Mission: Impossible, Jurassic Park;* the art and technology of computer generated images (CGI) is expanding so rapidly that the studios are actively seeking projects in which the event, or the incident, becomes greater than the story or characters. Subjects like volcanoes, earthquakes, floods, firestorms, or any other kind of natural disaster have become the star vehicles for "event" filmmakers. As the science progresses in moviemaking, the story lines, the subject matter, will adapt themselves to the times. Water rises to its own level.

Character is character. When executed properly, James's comment is an epiphany; just look at *Thelma & Louise.* The script sets up these two people by showing who they are. Louise, unmarried, a waitress, has a boyfriend, Jimmy, a musician, who's playing a gig on the road and hasn't called her once in three weeks. She's pissed, and resolves that she's not going to be home when he returns. So she decides to go to a friend's cabin in the mountains without telling him where she is. When he does arrive home, she just won't be there. That's the back story.

Thelma, on the other hand, appears to be a "ditzy" housewife; her kitchen is a mess, and her "breakfast," a little nibble from a frozen candy bar, which she puts back in the freezer only to whip it out for another bite, reveals an aspect of character; we *see* who she is by what she does, her actions.

Her husband, Darryl, an arrogant, egotistical fool, is a high-school hero whose best years are behind him. He treats her with so little respect that she has to lie to him just so she can go away for the weekend with her friend. "You get what you settle for," Louise remarks to her on the road.

Her personality is revealed by the way she packs her suitcase. She's going away for the weekend, and this will be the first time she's been away from her husband, but she doesn't know what she needs to take with her, so she takes everything. In contrast Louise only takes two each of the things she needs. Film is behavior.

Act I sets up their relationship, so when they pull into the parking lot of the Silver Bullet, the "dramatic hook," we get to learn more about their relationship with the men in their lives. By the time Harlan tries to rape Thelma, their characters have already been established. When Louise interferes, Harlan tells her to "suck my dick," and Louise totally loses it; she pulls the trigger, kills Harlan, and in that one second their lives and destiny have changed. Plot Point I. It is this *incident*, of being two fugitives on the run, that will alter and define their character. The impulse to pull that trigger came out of an experience in Louise's past. This past event and how it affects present time will be covered in more depth in Chapter 13.

That change is what the whole script is about; it is the incident that really determines their character. Their flight to Mexico becomes a journey of self-discovery that eventually leads to their death; and this awareness of only a few choices left reveals that they have nothing in their "past life" to go back to; they have burned their bridges and have literally "run out of world," as screenwriter Callie Khouri says. Their destiny has been determined by their actions, and those actions have revealed who they really are. It is a journey of self-discovery. They now understand there is no way back. You can't step into the same river twice.

"What is character but the determination of incident? And what is incident but the illumination of character?"

What is the particular incident or event that triggers the action of your screenplay? Once you know this key incident, then you can measure and evaluate how your character acts or reacts. In *Twister* the situation is set up in a back story situation where the two main characters (Helen Hunt and Bill Paxton) have filed for divorce, and when the script opens the papers are ready to be signed. The little opening sequence, in which a family races to the storm cellar to outrun a twister, shows us the dramatic need of the Helen Hunt character. Because she has lost her father to a twister, she has grown up and become a noted storm chaser. The Bill Paxton character wants to be free so he can marry his girlfriend, Melissa (Jami Gertz), and get on with his life and become a TV weatherman. From that point there really is no story; it's simply the storm chasers racing after the four twisters that becomes the subject and structure of the screenplay. These four encounters are the glue that holds everything together.

So what kind of problem do you see with your character? Is he or she too talky, too passive, or does the dialogue all sound the same, or do the other characters stand out more? Find out what it is. Locate and define it on the *Problem Sheet.* Can you define what you think the problem is? Imagine how it would look to you if the problem were already solved. Are your relationships clear, the emotional dynamics planted, and the character's arc charted? It doesn't matter whether you're writing an action, thriller, love story, or comedy. Character is character.

What makes good character? Four things: *dramatic need, point of view, attitude,* and *change.* In order to really solve the problems of *Character,* it's essential to go back into your character and rebuild the foundations of his or her life.

What is your character's *dramatic need?* That is, *what does your main character(s) want to win, gain, get, or achieve during the course of your screenplay?* Can you define it? Articulate it?

The *dramatic need* is what drives your character through the story line. In most cases you can express the dramatic need in a sentence or two. The dramatic need of *Twister,* for example, is to find a way to release all those little weather balls into the heart of the twister. In *Thelma & Louise* the dramatic need is to escape safely to Mexico, and that's what drives the two characters. Or, in *Apollo 13* the dramatic need is to return the astronauts safely to earth.

But it didn't start out that way. When the story began, the dramatic need was to walk on the moon, and that changed when the oxygen tank blew. The dramatic question then became not whether they were going to land on the moon, but whether they'd be able to survive and return to earth safely.

Many times the dramatic need will change during the course of the story. If your character's dramatic need does change, it will usually occur at Plot Point I, which is, as mentioned, the true beginning of your story. Louise killing Harlan at Plot Point I forces the action in a new direction; instead of spending a weekend in the mountains, Thelma and Louise have become fugitives from the law. They must escape safely. Or, in *Dances With Wolves*, John Dunbar's dramatic need is to go to the farthermost point of the frontier. But when he finally reaches Fort Sedgewick, Plot Point I, his dramatic need is now to learn how to adapt to the land and create a relationship with the Sioux.

What about your character's *point of view—the way he or she views the world?* This is usually a belief system, and as the psychologists say, "What we believe to be true, is true."

There's an ancient Hindu scripture titled the *Yoga Vāsistha*, which states that *"the World is as you see it."* That means what's inside your head—your thoughts, feelings, emotions, memories—are reflected outside, in your everyday experience. It is our mind, how we *see* the world, that determines our experience. Inside and outside are the same. So how does your character *view* the world? Is there some kind of moral code, a sense of right or wrong, that determines his or her actions? "I believe in God" is a point of view. So is "I don't believe in God." And so is "I don't know whether there's a God or not." All three positions are true. You can express a character's point of view through his or her behavior, or through dialogue; for example, being a vegetarian is a point of view, because your character might believe that "I would never eat something that was killed for me." It doesn't mean it's right or wrong, it's just the person's belief system. You can show it, say it, or have another character say it, it doesn't really matter; but you, as writer, have *to know it.*

Point of view creates conflict. The entire screenplay of *Crimson Tide* is constructed around the way two people see the world. In the story a group of Russian rebels have taken over the missile base and a U.S. submarine, the *Alabama*, carrying live nuclear warheads, is sent out to either launch a war, with a "first strike," or to retaliate against any Russian missiles that may possibly be sent. The captain, the Gene Hackman character, believes that "war is an extension of politics," and it is his duty to carry out his orders even if it means a nuclear holocaust. The Denzel Washington character, on the other hand, the executive officer, believes that because of nuclear weapons, war has become out of date, an outmoded concept. The purpose of war is to win, and if both sides launch nuclear weapons, there will be no "winner," only losers. War is no longer a viable option.

That's when the *Alabama* receives emergency orders to launch a first-strike nuclear attack against the Russian rebels. As they are preparing to launch the weapons, they receive another emergency message that is cut off before the entire text can be transmitted. What do the orders say? Should they continue to follow the first orders and launch first strike? Or do they delay the launch to confirm or deny the first order?

These two differing points of view, these two *belief systems*, generate the conflict that drives the script forward. That's classic Henry James. Both points of view are right within the framework of character. There is no right and wrong, good or bad. Hegel, the great German philosopher, maintained that the essence of tragedy derives not from one character being "right" and the other "wrong," or the conflict of good against evil, but from *both characters being right*, and the story becoming one of "right against right" carried to its logical conclusion.

Both characters in *Crimson Tide* operate from that sense of truth within themselves. The captain maintains that the situation demands he follow the first orders received. The XO does not agree and claims the second order, even though not completely received, overrides the first and must be confirmed before they can launch their first-strike missiles. Nobody's right or wrong in this conflict because their actions are determined by their *point of view*, the way they see the world.

As I'm fond of repeating, *all drama is conflict*; without conflict you have no action; without action you have no character; without character you have no story, and without story, you have no screenplay.

It's as simple as that.

In *The Shawshank Redemption*, after almost twenty years in the Shawshank Prison, Red has acquired a cynical point of view because, through his eyes, *hope* is simply a four-letter word. His spirit has been so crushed by the prison system that he declares to Andy, "Hope is a dangerous thing. Drive a man insane. It's got no place here. Better get used to the idea." And it is his emotional journey that leads to him to the right understanding, which is that "hope is a good thing," as Andy tells him.

Andy, of course, has a different point of view; he believes that "there are things in this world not carved out of gray stone. That there's a small place inside of us they can never lock away. Hope." And that's what keeps Andy going in prison, that's what made him sacrifice a week of his life in "the hole," just so he could hear the two opera singers singing an aria from Mozart.

Here's the way it's written in the script:

INT. WARDEN'S OFFICE—AFTERNOON

Andy is reclined in the chair, transported, arms fluidly conducting the music. Ecstasy and rapture. Shawshank no longer exists. It has been banished from the mind of men.

> **RED (VO)**
> I have no idea to this day what them
> two Italian ladies were singin' about.
> Truth is, I don't *want* to know. Some
> things are best left unsaid. I like to think
> they were singin' about something so
> beautiful, it *can't* be expressed in words,
> and makes your heart ache because of it.
> I tell you, those voices *soared*. Higher
> and farther than anybody in a gray place
> dares to dream. It was like some
> beautiful bird flapped into our drab little
> cage and made these walls dissolve
> away . . . and for the briefest of
> moments . . . every last man at
> Shawshank felt free.

That's what drove Andy to play the aria. For that "briefest of moments" he was free and showed us the force and power of the human spirit. It's a beautiful scene.

The third thing that makes good character is *Attitude.* *Attitude* is defined as a "manner or opinion," and is usually an intellectual pose or decision. Being "macho" is really an attitude. I'm tough, see, I'm better than you are, it's all attitude; it's what Dennis Rodman is all about. He's made a career out of attitude and it far surpasses his basketball prowess. Have you ever gone into a store to buy something and found yourself dealing with a person who does not want to be there at all, or a person who looks down on you? Have you ever walked into a fancy restaurant not wearing the "right" clothes? It's that kind of judgment where someone is convinced "they're right" and "you're wrong"; judgments, opinions, evaluations, all stem from attitude. Understanding your character's attitude is allowing him to reach out and touch his humanity.

The Truth About Cats and Dogs (Audrey Wells) is a delightful romantic comedy that is entirely based on the character's attitude. Abby, the character played by Janeane Garofalo, is a woman who lives *by her opinion, her attitude;* the decision she's made is that all men really want in a woman is a pretty face and a great body. This attitude governs her behavior through the entire film. And Nora, the Uma Thurman character, just takes it for granted that she's not very bright. You know, the "dumb blond" with the heart of gold. Marilyn Monroe is a legend because of her attitude expressed through the parts she played. Both Abby and Nora have to learn that their attitude is "not who they really are." Their journey through the film is to accept themselves for who they really are.

An *attitude*, as differentiated from point of view, can be right or wrong, good or bad, positive or negative, angry or happy, cynical or naive, superior or inferior, liberal or conservative. Do you know anybody who "thinks they're better than everyone else"? Or people who feel the world owes them a living; or "it's really who you know" that determines your success factor in this world.

Sometimes it's difficult to separate the *point of view* from the *attitude*. Many of my students struggle to define these two qualities, but I tell them it really doesn't matter; when you're creating the basic core of the character, you're taking one large ball of wax and in this case, pulling it into four separate pieces. The parts and the whole, right? Who cares whether one part is the *point of view* and another the *attitude*? It doesn't make any difference; the parts and the whole, as mentioned, are really the same thing. So, if you're unsure about whether a particular character trait is a *point of view* or an *attitude*, don't worry about it. Just separate the concepts in your own mind.

The fourth element that makes up good character is *change*. Does your character change during the course of the screenplay? If so, what is the change? Can you define it? Articulate it? Can you trace the emotional arc of the character from the beginning to the end? In *The Truth About Cats and Dogs* all three characters undergo a change that brings about a new awareness of who they really are. Abby's final acceptance that Brian really loves her *for who she is* completes the character arc of change.

In *The Shawshank Redemption* Andy endured prison life only until he learned that it could be proven someone else had committed the murder of his wife and her lover. Only when the warden refuses to help him get a new trial and Tommy, the witness, is killed does he refuse to serve any longer. When he entered the prison he considered himself guilty, even though he hadn't pulled the trigger, but now he has served "his time" and realizes the moment has come for him to escape. As we learn later, he has been preparing this for years.

Having a character change during the course of the screenplay is not a requirement if it doesn't fit your story. But since change is a universal constant of life, if you can impel a change within your character, it creates an arc of behavior and adds another dimension to the material.

These ingredients are what make up the foundation of good character; if you know these four elements, *dramatic need*, *point of view*, *attitude*, and *change*, you can approach any problem that deals with character.

The Problem Sheet

The Circle of Being

- The main character is dull, boring

- The characters lack depth, dimension

- The character's emotional arc is too thin and undefined

- There's not enough conflict

- The emotional stakes are not high enough

- The dialogue is stilted, awkward

- All the characters sound the same

- The main character explains too much

- The dramatic need of the main character is vague, undefined

- There seems to be a lack of tension

- Story goes off in too many directions

13

The Circle of Being

There are times during the screenwriter's journey when the story works well, with a tense and dramatic plot, and all the characters seem to have interesting backgrounds, but there's a nagging sense that the dialogue is thin, maybe "tinny," filled with clichés, and doesn't seem to go anywhere. Something seems not to be working, and you really can't put your finger on what it is; maybe you've had the script read by a few friends or associates, and they tell you they "like it." When you press them further, more often than not they point to the dialogue and say it may need polishing.

You hear this quite a bit in Hollywood, especially among development executives, and when they encounter this problem their solution is to bring in another writer to rewrite the dialogue. Writing is rewriting, and sometimes as many as twelve writers are brought in to "hone and polish" the project.

Sometimes it works, and sometimes it doesn't. *The Rock* is a case in point. The original screenplay, written by David Weisberg and Douglas Cook, was a really strong screenplay in terms of plot and character, it was just the dialogue that seemed to be flat and one-dimensional and didn't seem to be working as well as it could. It had an exciting premise, good characters, interesting backgrounds, and pretty obviously had the potential to be a good "thump-and-pump" movie. Another writer, Mark Rosner, was brought in to rewrite the material. He did a draft and that is what attracted the director, Michael Bay. But when Bay came on the project he thought the dialogue needed more of a "spin," so he brought in Jonathan Hensleigh to make it more contemporary and bring it up to date.

Hensleigh worked hand in hand with the director for months, honing and polishing the dialogue, and was on the set every day just in case he was needed. When the film was completed the credits were established, and then the screenplay went to the arbitration panel at the Writers Guild of America. The panel consists of three screenwriters, independent of each other, who read the screenplay from the inception to the final draft. Each writer's contribution is measured and analyzed. In some cases the arbitration panel will read fifteen different drafts of the screenplay, contrasting and comparing each one with the final product. Then they'll award the screenwriting credits based on how they see each writer's contribution. In the case of *The Rock* it was determined that the original writers should get the screen credit, and not Jonathan Hensleigh.

That decision sparked a real debate within the creative community. The director was outraged, as were a number of other people in Hollywood. He insisted that Hensleigh receive a credit, and rightfully so. Didn't rewriting the dialogue warrant a screen credit?

Yes and no.

The Writers Guild of America, the WGA, has determined

that a screenwriter can only receive a screenwriting credit if he or she has rewritten fifty percent or more of the screenplay. So when a new writer is brought in he or she, in most cases, will alter the structure, add new locations, create new scenes and characters, while trying to keep, hopefully, the *idea* of the screenplay that was originally purchased by the studio or production company.

What's the point of all this? Dialogue is a *function of character*. It's true that some writers have a better ear for writing dialogue than others; they're just born with a natural talent and ability, and it's really a gift. But if you know your character well enough, if you feel comfortable inside his or her skin, the dialogue will be individual and appropriate and capture the "essence" of that character. The dialogue may not be that great, but it'll still work. The function of dialogue, remember, is simple; dialogue either moves the story forward or reveals information about the character. You can say things, explain things, or show things in order to reveal character.

If you look at the *Problem Sheet*, most of the symptoms listed there deal with dialogue. After all, dialogue is one of the most striking qualities about your character. It tells us who he or she is, sets up the exposition, moves the story forward, adds humor, and can be one of the elements used in transitions. If you think your dialogue is too thin, or your characters all sound alike, or if you explain too much, the best way to solve the problem is to go back to the beginning and rethink your character.

One of the ways to accomplish this is by doing an exercise I call the *"Circle of Being."* It's a process, really, a process that allows you uncover some kind of an incident or event in your character's life that emotionally parallels and impacts the story line; it's an event that happens to your main character when he or she is between the ages of ten and sixteen. This is an age period where some kind of traumatic event could conceivably occur that would affect the entire course of your character's life. It might be the death of a parent, or of a loved one; it could be physical abuse that results in a deep emotional scar; it could be a physical event or injury, or quite possibly a move to a new city or country.

Thelma & Louise is a very good example. As Louise was growing up in Texas she was raped and discovered she was unable to get justice. It was this incident that "formed" her behavior and ultimately led to the incident that powers the entire story line, the shooting of the rapist Harlan in the parking lot. It explains why she pulled the trigger in the first place, and why she wouldn't set one foot inside the state of Texas.

If you think about it, the *Circle of Being* is a valuable exercise, or a tool, that you can use in crafting, enriching, and enhancing your character. If you go into your character's life and ask yourself what traumatic incident might have occurred to him or her between the ages of ten and sixteen, see what happens.

Why ten and sixteen? Because it happens to be a very important age in a person's life. The noted behaviorist Joseph Chilton Pierce states that there are four major growths, or spurts, of human intelligence in our lives. The first occurs when the child is about a year old, when he or she learns to walk. The second spurt occurs about age four, when the child learns that he or she has an identity, as a boy or a girl, *and* has a given name; when the four-year-old acts, there is a response, and at that age he/she belongs to a family, and these are his/her parents and he/her lives in this house in this city. At this age, the child is able to communicate his or her needs.

The third stage, or spurt, in the growth of human intelligence occurs when the child is about nine or ten; that's the age when he or she understands that he has a definite personality, a singular and individual voice. The young person is learning to question authority, forming his or her own opinions, and starting "speaking his mind." This is a very vital time in the life of the child.

The fourth stage in the growth of human intelligence, and the most important developmental spurt, according to Pierce, occurs when the person is about fifteen or sixteen. The teenager. That's the age when the teenager rebels against everything and tries to find his/her own voice, suddenly understands that his parents are no longer the center of the universe, and looks outward into the world for role models, seeking forms of behavior, like clothes or hair, that are acceptable to his peers and express who they are. They have an identity. Just look at your own kids, or your brother's or sister's kids or your friends' kids, and look at how they dress, how they act and react, what kind of music they're listening to, their slang and manner of speaking. It's a period of life that is so influential in a person's life that it will form a subconscious identity, or impression, for the rest of their life, much as furniture leaves impressions in the rug. Take a moment to see how strong this impression is in your own life; close your eyes and go back to that time when you were about fifteen or sixteen, and see what incident or event affected you the most. What was the incident or event that springs to mind? If you want, play some music from that time and see what memories it brings up, and then take a moment to see how some particular incident from that period has affected you and possibly changed your life.

The *Circle of Being* is a wonderful tool that lets you dig into the emotional substance and dimension of your character. Just look how it affected Louise; when Callie Khouri wrote the screenplay, she did not refer to the incident at all except to state that Louise had no intention whatsoever of stepping one foot inside Texas, no matter what the reason. But the director, Ridley Scott, thought the audience should know about this event and how it triggered Louise's actions, so he had Khouri make a few references to the incident; Hal, the Harvey Keitel character, even told her, "I know what happened in Texas," and Thelma guesses that "it happened to you, didn't it?" referring to the rape attempt. To the very end Louise never responds to this.

This incident is the reason for Louise to stubbornly insist that they're not going to cross the Texas state line. Because the only way to get to Mexico without going through Texas is to go through Oklahoma, the decision ultimately costs them their lives. This *Circle-of-Being* incident is relived in the parking lot when she sees Harlan attempting to rape Thelma, and she totally loses it.

Thelma & Louise is an extraordinary film, but many writers I've talked to didn't like it for this very reason; they say Louise "overreacted" by shooting Harlan, and could not "willingly suspend their disbelief" enough to get into the story after that. But I think they didn't get that it was really the sixteen- or eighteen-year-old rape victim Louise who pulled that trigger, not Louise in present time.

If you can go back into your character's life and create an incident or event that becomes an influence or a force working on your character, you can enhance the texture of any character you're writing. By creating the *Circle of Being* you can generate a plot complication that will expand the depth and dimension of your character and literally drive the story forward. In *Twister* the *Circle-of-Being* incident is shown in the opening sequence, when Helen Hunt's father is swept out of the storm cellar; it is the incident that motivates her to become a "storm chaser."

One of my students, a well-known and working playwright, wanted to make the switch from writing for the stage to writing for the screen. He had an interesting story that involved the reconciliation of two sisters after an absence of many years. The story opens when the main character, who happens to be a dentist, accidentally injures her teeth, and to correct the problem she must undergo a dental procedure. While she's under the influence of the anesthesia she flashes back to the time when she was a young girl and witnessed her sister being raped by their uncle. Fearful of being seen, she runs away and in her flight trips over a rock, falls, and hits her front teeth, the same teeth that are *acting up now*. She had totally repressed the memory of this incident and it leads her to pursue a reconciliation with her sister. It was the *Circle-of-Being* event that sparked the entire story. By forcing herself to confront and deal with this incident that took place in her past, she begins to look at her life and sees that she must mend her relationship with her sister. It's a powerful moment during the screenplay, and I suggested to the writer that we see visual bits and pieces of this incident throughout the story as it unfolds, so he began to weave and incorporate this visual memory throughout the body of the screenplay. It turned out to be very powerful material.

I call this process the *Circle of Being* because if you picture your character as a circle and then section him/her off, as you would divide a piece of pie, you section off the physical, emotional, mental, and intellectual incidents or events that make up the fabric of your character. In this way you can create a well-rounded portrait of your character, and then everything

you do—all the emotions, thoughts, and feelings you dramatize—works to expand your characterization.

One of the most powerful examples of the *Circle of Being*
and the way it can be used is the incident that powers the
action in Arthur Miller's play *Death of a Salesman*. Now, even
though it's a play, and is explained through dialogue, it is this
Circle of Being that makes the character of Willy Loman so
powerful. The story, about an aging salesman forced to come
to grips with the loss of his dream, is a masterpiece and one of
the greatest American plays of our time.

Sometimes, depending on your story line, you might
want to verbally express the *Circle-of-Being* incident, but in
other stories, like *Thelma & Louise*, it's stronger because it's not
explained. You, as writer, don't necessarily have to explain it,
but—and it's a very big *but*—you have to know it. Because if
you don't know it, who does?

In this particular scene from *Death of a Salesman*, Willy
Loman has come to see his "boss"—actually, the son of the
man he worked for over thirty-four years—with his dreams
and the American dream shattered to pieces. Now, with the
last vestige of his dignity, he has come to ask the son of his
boss if he can give up the road, literally his way of life, and
work at the main office. Willy Loman is a salesman, and he
doesn't know anything else.

Willy is asking Howard, the son, for a job on the floor,
and first he asks for $65 a week, then drops his request to $50
a week, and then, in his final humiliation, he is literally forced
to beg for $40 a week. But this "is a business, kid, and every-
body's gotta pull his own weight," and Willy Loman's sales
figures have not been the best lately. Willy responds by re-
treating into his memory and tells Howard what drew him to
become a salesman: "When I was a boy—eighteen, nineteen,"

he says, "—I was already on the road. And there was a question in my mind as to whether selling had a future for me. . . ."

He pauses for a long moment, then continues on. [That's when] "I met a *salesman* in the Parker House. His name was Dave Singleman. And he was eighty-four years old, and he'd drummed merchandise in thirty-one states. And old Dave, he'd go up to his room, y' understand, put on his green velvet slippers—I'll never forget—and pick up his phone and call the buyers, and without ever leaving his room, at the age of eighty-four, he made his living. And when I saw that, I realized that selling was the greatest career a man could want. 'Cause what could be more satisfying than to be able to go, at the age of eighty-four, into twenty or thirty different cities, and pick up a phone, and be remembered and loved and helped by so many different people? Do you know when he died—and by the way he died the *death of a salesman*, in his green velvet slippers in the smoker of the New York, New Haven and Hartford, going into Boston—hundreds of salesmen and buyers were at his funeral."

That's Willy Loman's dream; that's what drives him to get up every morning and hit the road, and when that dries up, the dream is dead and life is not worth living. That's the *Circle-of-Being* experience in Willy's life. Remember Andy Dufresne's line in *The Shawshank Redemption*. "Hope is a good thing, maybe the best of things, and no good thing ever dies." But if the dream collides with reality, as in the case of Willy Loman, and all hope is lost, then what's left? The death of a salesman.

That's the force and the power of the *Circle of Being*. Once you've created an experience or an incident that affects the life of your character, then you can base the emotional arc on that incident and have the character confront and resolve (or not resolve) the experience. It becomes a way of embellishing the depth and dimension of character, to create a strong and defined point of view and attitude, and contains within it the spark of conflict.

Recently, I was commissioned to oversee the writing of a screenplay about a Native American warrior from the Oneida Nation, one of the six member nations of the Iroquois Confederacy, called the "Longhouse," and their divided loyalties between the American colonists and the British Crown during the American Revolutionary War. The main character is forced, literally against his will, into a situation where he has to align himself with the colonists in their war against the British. The immediate result, which is historically accurate, was a situation in which brother fought against brother, family against family; the ultimate result, unfortunately, was the confiscation of the Indian lands, the entire Northeastern part of the U.S., by the American government. It's a story of divided loyalties, a story of fate and destiny, and based on a historical incident.

But the facts of this warrior's life were thin, almost nonexistent. What was known was that he sided with the colonists, but why he did so was never answered, and that was a question that had to be answered dramatically.

This was the situation: It is well known historically that the Iroquois Confederacy wanted to remain neutral in this conflict; the elders declared that a war of this kind, a war of rebellion, was like an argument between a father and son. And anyone who takes sides in this kind of conflict becomes party to a no-win situation. If the Confederacy sided with the British, in this case the father, and the son was defeated and lay broken and bleeding on the battlefield, the father would hate the people who had done it. On the other hand, if the Confederacy sided with the son, the colonists, and the father was vanquished and suffering in defeat, the Indian nations would alienate all their British friends. So the best thing to do, they decided, was to stay neutral.

So that's what they did. Until the British army, bearing gifts of rum and trinkets, persuaded a prominent member of the Mohawk nation to join them. He then convinced several of his brothers to side with the British. And, when the British army started their march toward Albany, they were aided by these Mohawk warriors. In their first battle they attacked a colonial fort where the Oneida women and children, their cousins, had taken refuge. Historically, that's correct. Again, would that action alone make the Oneida warrior align himself with the colonists?

Not necessarily so. My partner in this project didn't really know how to solve this particular situation, so I suggested that she create a *Circle of Being* for the character. I told her to start from the character's life and the known historical facts. The warrior was born the son of an Oneida woman and a German settler. So what event might have happened to the main character during his youth, say, around the age of fifteen?

If you look at the significance of the *Circle of Being*, it can be a defining incident that embraces all those internal, external, emotional, physical, and background forces working on the character's life. What kind of incident would make the warrior turn against his own friends and relatives? There are many answers to this question, of course, but one particular solution (a created, dramatic incident) worked very well; when the warrior was a young man, say about fifteen, he watched his father die at the hands of some drunken British soldiers, and then they burned their meager crops and the houses they were living in. Contrived? Yes, but historically, it was not all that uncommon for an incident like this to happen, especially at that time. In dramatic terms it worked very well, and it's an incident that really doesn't have to be explained during the screenplay, as long as the writer *knows* it. In this case the *Circle-of-Being* incident is referred to only once, and all the emotional choices and decisions the character makes follow from that significant event.

Some films use the *Circle of Being* as the basis of the entire story line, and it becomes the subject of the film. I was at a prerelease screening of a film entitled *Loved* (written and directed by Erin Dignam), starring Robin Wright and William Hurt. It's the story of a young woman who had been entangled in a mentally and physically abusive relationship some six years before the story began. She was sixteen then and it was her first "serious" relationship. She managed to extricate herself from her lover, but in the years following the relationship, the man became involved with two other women, and in one of these relationships the woman suffered a broken leg and hip at the man's hands. In the other relationship, in the scene that opens the film, the man and woman are in a heavy discussion next to a crowded highway. The man turns and walks away, and the woman races directly into the path of a speeding car and is killed. The DA's office wants to bring a charge of manslaughter against the man, and to fortify their case they want the Robin Wright character to testify, so a preliminary hearing is held. During the time she is on the stand, she has to relive the relationship, confront it, and deal with it; in the end she accepts her share of responsibility for the abuse she suffered and frees herself from it, and the last scene shows her ready to resume her life and hopefully enter into a more positive and loving relationship. Sometimes a bad or abusive relationship is better than none at all. From the character's perspective the physical abuse she received from this man demonstrated how much he loved her.

It's a good illustration of how the *Circle of Being* generates an entire screenplay. If you take a look at the problems described on the *Problem Sheet*, many of them can be directly solved by creating a strong *Circle-of-Being* incident for the main character.

In *The Silence of the Lambs* the *Circle of Being* plays a prominent role in generating the transformation of the character Clarice Starling, played by Jodie Foster. *The Silence of the Lambs* is the story of a young FBI trainee tracking down a serial killer, but before she can accomplish that she must come to grips with an incident that occurred in her own life when she was about ten years old. That incident was the death of her father, a small-town policeman killed during an attempted robbery. But if you dig deeper into this extraordinary script (from the extraordinary novel by Thomas Harris), you'll find that this is really a story of Clarice's relationship with "three fathers." Jack Crawford (Scott Glenn) is the director of the Behavioral Science Division at the FBI Academy, and gives her the break to interview Hannibal Lecter that directly leads to her becoming involved in hunting and capturing the serial killer, Buffalo Bill. Hannibal Lecter (Anthony Hopkins) is her mentor, guiding and teaching her what to look for when pursuing a serial killer. It is through their relationship and his relentless psychological prodding and insight that she is forced to confront the death of her father, something she had buried deep in her unconscious.

It is a *Circle-of-Being* event. Because of her father's death she was sent away to live with an uncle in Montana. One night she was awakened by the screaming of lambs being slaughtered. So she tried to rescue one of the baby lambs, but was caught and sent away to live in an orphanage. It is Hannibal Lecter's forcing her to look at this emotional issue that ultimately frees her of it, and at the end of the film she can build a new life, both in a committed relationship as well as in her job as a top-notch FBI agent. But only when she can confront this incident of the past, the *Circle of Being*, can she be free. It's exactly the same with Louise in *Thelma & Louise*, except Louise never gave up holding on to the rape and it literally cost her her life. But Clarice, under the tutelage of Lecter, was strong enough to be able to surrender to it, deal with it, and let it go.

The Silence of the Lambs ends with Clarice receiving her diploma, and at the reception following her graduation she receives a phone call from Hannibal Lecter asking "if the lambs have stopped screaming. . . ." And then he shares his "admiration" for her by telling her that "I have no plans to call on you, Clarice, the world being more interesting with you in it. Be sure you extend me the same courtesy." He is the first to acknowledge Clarice's transformation from the trainee with an incomplete childhood into a trained professional, ready to fly.

So if you feel that your character is too thin and one-dimensional, too passive or too reactive, or speaks in dialogue that is too direct or explanatory, one way to solve the problem is to go back and explore his or her life in terms of the *Circle of Being*.

The Problem Sheet

DULL, THIN, AND BORING

- THE CHARACTERS ARE TOO TALKY AND EXPLAIN TOO MUCH

- DIALOGUE IS TOO DIRECT, TOO SPECIFIC

- CHARACTERS ARE FLAT, ONE-DIMENSIONAL

- THERE IS NO CIRCLE OF BEING

- ALL THE CHARACTERS SOUND THE SAME

- CHARACTERS' ACTIONS ARE PREDICTABLE

- THE MATERIAL IS FLAT AND BORING

- RELATIONSHIPS BETWEEN THE CHARACTERS ARE WEAK AND UNDEFINED

- I'M SAYING THE SAME THING OVER AND OVER AGAIN

- THERE IS NO SUBTEXT; THE STORY IS TOO THIN

14

Dull, Thin, and Boring

How often have you read something you've written and, much to your chagrin, found that the writing seems to be flat, the characters thin and one-dimensional, and as much as you want to deny it, or as much as you defend it, you cannot escape the cold, hard fact that everything you've written seems to be dull, thin, and boring? When you think about all the time and effort you've spent and all the sacrifice and denial you've had to endure, to end up with pages like *this*—oh, Lord!

Believe it or not, this is a pretty common refrain among screenwriters. And of course, as little as you want to admit it, it's true most of the time; the writing *is* dull, *is* thin, and *is* boring. Once you've recovered from the shock of your discovery, then you can rack your brains trying to figure out what you can do to make it work, or make it better; you might think about adding some action scenes, or adding a subplot, or creating a new character, like a love interest, perhaps, simply to liven up the action.

That's one solution, and it may work in some screenplays, at least for a little while. So you decide to add some new scenes and a new character to liven up the action, but when you sit down to reread the material, you suddenly notice something else isn't working and you get that sinking feeling in the gut that you really haven't fixed the material, you've just put a Band-Aid over it. Given it a paint job.

The real problem, *the source* of what makes the material dull, thin, and boring, persists. In despair, though hoping for the best, you have friends read it, but all they can tell you is that this or that needs to be strengthened, and when you try to fix this or that the material still doesn't seem to work. You're more confused than ever.

What usually happens when you're trapped in this scenario is that your confusion gives rise to frustration, which then funnels up into anger, then smothers you in a blanket of despair and depression, and the ultimate result is that you just give up. It's all part of the writer's journey.

The problem is still there. What can you do about it?

Let's take it step by step. The first thing you need to do is simply stop writing, sit back, and try to gain some kind of objective overview of your screenplay. And just because you're not writing does not mean *you're not writing;* it just means you're rethinking a creative problem. A script that's "dull, thin, and boring" is best approached from the perspective of *Character.*

In one of his literary essays Henry James suggested that the main character of a story occupies the center of a circle, and all the other characters surround him in an outer circle. James felt that each time the main character comes in contact with one of the other characters, some light or knowledge or insight should be revealed about the main character. And he used the image of someone entering a dark room and turning on the lamps in each corner, illuminating a specific part of the room.

James called this the *"Theory of Illumination."* It's a wonderful tool to use when you want to expand the dimensions of the character. In *Witness*, for example, a young Amish boy witnesses the murder of an undercover policeman. John Book (Harrison Ford) attempts to have the boy identify the killer in a series of mug shots and lineups, but they are unsuccessful. So, for lunch, Book takes the boy and his mother for a hot dog. The scene opens with Book picking up the food and setting it on the table. Without looking at the boy and his mother, he heaps some mustard on the dog and takes a big bite. As he's chewing, he notices that Rachel and her son are saying a short prayer over the food. Immediately, Book becomes embarrassed and self-conscious. With a silly little grin on his face he waits until they've finished their prayer before he finishes chewing.

As they eat, she launches into a conversation about what Book's sister (Patti LuPone) had told her about him; she told Rachel that "you [Book] should get married and have children of your own. Instead of trying to be a father to hers. Except she thinks you're afraid of the responsibility." "Oh," Book replies. "Anything else?" "Oh, yes," Rachel continues, getting into it. "She thinks you like policing because you think you're right about everything. And you're the only one who can do anything. And that when you drink a lot of beer you say things like none of the other police would know a crook from a . . . um . . . bag of elbows. Yes, I think that's what she said."

It's a wonderful little scene. In just a few lines (the scene is less than a page long), we literally know everything we need to know about John Book. Rachel sheds light on, and illuminates, what kind of person he really is. First, look at his name. It's no accident—he is a policeman who "lives by the book." He thinks he's "right" about everything—this is his *attitude*—and he constantly complains about the policemen he works with. He's unmarried, but he likes kids and "tries to be a father" to his sister's children.

This little scene reveals so much about Book's character. What makes it work so well is that within the body of the scene they're doing something, eating, putting mustard and ketchup on the dogs, not just sitting around talking. Even this little action of eating reveals the different points of view between these two characters. And two different points of view is the first step in generating a substantial source of conflict. In this case it represents a different way of life. As the boy and his mother bless their food, Book just wolfs it down, and so illuminates visually the difference between them.

James's *Theory of Illumination* is a good way to give your character a lot more richness and texture, which, in turn, makes him or her more interesting, full, not thin. In *Witness* the business of preparing the hot dogs for their meal gives the characters something do during their dialogue scene, which keeps the action moving. And it's all written into the screenplay.

There are many different ways to use the *Theory of Illumination* to reveal information about a character: you can have the main character reveal something about himself or herself to another character (do this only if you can't find another way to reveal the information); or another character might say something about the main character, as in the *Witness* scene. Or maybe a voice-over narration would be appropriate, as in *The Shawshank Redemption*, or *Dances With Wolves*, or *How to Make an American Quilt*, but just make sure this narrative device is appropriate to your story. Don't use a voice-over narration just once or twice during the screenplay, though, it's true, in *Apollo 13* it is used only once, at the very end of the script when Jim Lovell sums up the results of the mission. You can achieve the same purpose using some kind of subtitle, or crawl, or newspaper headlines. In *Stand By Me* (Raynold Gideon and Bruce Evans), the script ends with the Richard Dreyfuss character sitting at the computer writing the story we've just seen; you might also use some kind of magazine headline or partial story text on a computer screen. Occasionally something about the main character may be revealed in a dream sequence or in a flashback, like Andy's escape in *The Shawshank Redemption,* or maybe a flash forward (which is basically what *Apollo 13* accomplished with the voice-over at the end).

All of these various tools or devices are effective ways of illuminating some of the visual and emotional aspects of the main character. But you have to be consistent with whatever device you use, because *the integrity of the screenplay must be maintained.* That's what makes *Pulp Fiction* work so well; the humor, along with the nonlinear structure, are woven throughout the film. All the characters are introduced in the beginning and then the three separate stories are played out in their entirety.

Before you decide to use any of these various techniques, however, you must go back to the drawing board of your character. How do you do this? First, make an inventory about the relationships between your main character and the other characters in the story. Can you define these relationships clearly and succinctly? Are they deep enough, or interesting enough? In *Independence Day* (Dean Devlin and Roland Emmerich) the Jeff Goldblum character is very thin in his portrayal; all we know about him is that he still wears his wedding ring even though he's been divorced for three years. The only reason his wife left him, at least that we know of, is because she wanted to advance her career. What about their relationship? Was it working? Harmonious? What about children? What was their marriage like? Although this is back story, and not necessary to state in the body of the film, it's imperative that the writer know this in order to achieve the full dimension of character. It's pretty thin in the script; the only reason it works is because this is an "event" film, and, as in *Twister* and *Mission: Impossible,* the special effects are really the star; the main character only leads us to the effects. And while it works at the present time, you can't count on its always being the "current trend" in Hollywood. Most of the time these "event" films are really dull, thin, and boring.

Once you've examined the relationships of your main character, decide which ones need to be expanded, given more texture and dimension. One of the ways to do this is by writing a one- or two-page, free-association *(automatic-writing)* essay that redefines the relationship. In this exercise you want to recreate the relationship from the beginning. Where did these characters meet? How long ago? What kind of incidents or events can you create that will help define and clarify and strengthen their relationship?

Creative research means you enter the world of the character in order to define and redefine their lives and relationships. The more you know about your characters and the events of their lives, the more options you have to choose from in order to make them visually interesting and exciting.

Explore their first meeting. What were their thoughts and feelings about each other? What was it that made their friendship ripen or grow, or what was it that caused the relationship to turn sour? How long has this relationship endured? That could mean any relationship between man and woman, boyfriend, girlfriend, boss or associate; it could mean a rivalry on the tennis court or in the courtroom. In films like *Seven* we don't actually know why the Brad Pitt and Gwyneth Paltrow characters left the place they were living and moved to the big city. We really don't need to know, but you better bet that Andrew Kevin Walker, the screenwriter, knows. Their decision to leave the community they were living in and come to the city is what leads to the powerful conclusion of the film. So if you don't know things about your characters, about the important decisions and events that happened in their lives, who does?

If you feel the characters are talking too much, or the dialogue is too specific or too direct, or the characters are flat and one-dimensional, and the material is simply dull and boring, there are several ways to approach the problem.

Let's break it down into three distinct categories: What can you do if the screenplay seems *Dull*? Does the script plod along with excessive dialogue, or do the incidents and events take too long to develop, or are your descriptions too thick and dense, and do you have a hard time following the narrative line? All these are symptoms of dull writing. What can you do?

First, change the style of your writing. Don't try to write complete, literary sentences. Focus on short, descriptive passages, maybe one-word sentences, where the words are used to accentuate color and humor to the reader. Shane Black (*Lethal Weapon*, *The Long Kiss Goodnight*, among others) uses dynamic and imaginative writing in his work; for example, in a car-chase sequence with the cars squirreling through traffic and racing down sidewalks scattering pedestrians, the cars scrape each other; and the way he describes it is short, visual, and concise: "The cars trade paint." It's a great way to convey the thrill of the chase.

If you're writing more of a character piece, go back and redefine your characters by writing short two- or three-page essays dealing with the character relationships. Look for ways to strengthen your characters to make them more interesting. Go into their professional life, their personal life, and their private life, what they do when they're alone. That means hobbies, gardening, exercise classes, raising pets. In *Crimson Tide* the little dog the Gene Hackman character takes everywhere adds to and expands the characterization.

Then, of course, you have to look for conflict; to find ways of going deeper into the scenes in order to achieve maximum dramatic value (MDV) in your character relationships. That means possibly redefining your character's *point of view*, the way he or she looks at the world. Conflict is one sure way to avoid dull writing, but you have to go into your character's life in order to effectively portray this. Conflict, remember, can be internal, like an emotional problem, or external, a threatening force working on the characters, as that induced by the hunt for the aliens in *ID4* or the storms in *Twister*. It's up to you to design and integrate these conflicts into the story line.

You might possibly want to change your character's *point of view*. Look for the opposing points of view during your scenes; what are your characters thinking or feeling about the situation? When your character enters the scene, do you know where he or she has come from? What happened to him or her before the scene occurs? Do you know what the purpose or motivation of this character is in the scene? Does the scene reflect your character's dramatic need? Look within the context of the scene for ways to generate conflict; do the characters have a different point of view in terms of what's at stake in the scene? Is the problem external to them, like a physical or emotional threat? The film *Seven* is a good example of this. The tension between the serial killer, the Kevin Spacey character, and the Brad Pitt and Morgan Freeman characters, is taut and tense because we don't know what's going to happen, though we know something must happen for the story to resolve itself. Remember, in good writing we discover what's happening at the same time the character does. Reading a screenplay should always be an *act of discovery*. That's why the ending of *Seven* is so memorable.

What do you do if your material is too *Thin*?

Add something to fill it out; either create another character so you can add more scenes, and give more detail to the character, or think about adding an action sequence, and if that's not enough and you need to go deeper into the story line to give it more body and texture, you might think about adding a subplot (see Chapter 10).

Before you can make any decisions about what to do, go back into each scene and check out the action point of where you entered it. Many times a writer will enter a scene too late and leave it too early, and that results in cutting away from the action before it's fully realized. It dilutes the narrative line and is one of the causes of a script's being too thin. If you go back into the basic construction of each one of your scenes, you can always structure it into beginning, middle, and end. Set up scenes beginning in the preceding scene if possible, then determine what's going to happen in the middle of the scene, and finally the end of the scene, where you pay it off before you segue into your transition for the next scene. It might be a good exercise to list the components that make up the beginning of the scene, the elements that make up the middle of the scene, and what happens at the end; so, you have lists of actions for the beginning, middle, and end of the scene. Then you can take whatever elements you need and structure them into a new scene.

Take a scene like Andy Dufresne's entrance into Shawshank Prison. How many ways could you lay that out? Hundreds, and they'd all be good and visually effective. But if you look at the elements involved, you can go deeper, add things to fill out the material, and make it richer. In this case someone is arriving at the prison. So, you have the elements of the bus ride, the actual entrance into the facility, the checking in of the new inmates, and so on. But look what Frank Darabont did: first, he introduces Red, the Morgan Freeman character, with the parole board, then in voice-over narration he tells us about the first time he saw Andy Dufresne. Only then does he create this marvelous overview of the prison with the helicopter shot. (That shot, by the way, was created on location and is one of my favorite shots in the film.) Then he cuts to the bus to show the emotional fear and confusion of Andy sitting on the bus with the other cons. We see the tough prison guard Hadley, we see the screaming inmates howling, "Fish, fresh fish," and we see the new cons filing off the bus in their chains, and how they look to the hardened inmates.

All that material can be sorted out and structured into elements of the beginning, middle, and end. This doesn't mean you have to show all the ingredients you've laid out, just that you have to be selective as to whether to use them or not. Frank Darabont chose to use most of this introduction to Shawshank, but in isolated, fragmented bits and pieces of film. First, he cuts from the judge's gavel striking the block to the sound of a door opening in prison (a sound-to-sound transition), then we meet Red being evaluated by the parole board (it's really only half the scene, the beginning and middle), and then we see the stamp of rejection. We follow Red as he steps out into the prison yard and we get the magnitude of where we are:

> RED emerges into fading daylight, slouches low-key through the activity, worn cap on his head, exchanging hellos and doing minor business. He's an important man here.

> **RED (VO)**
> There's a con like me in every prison in America, I guess. I'm the guy who can get it for you. Cigarettes, a bag of reefer if you're partial, a bottle of brandy to celebrate your kid's high-school graduation. Damn near anything, within reason.

> He slips somebody a pack of smokes, smooth sleight-of-hand.

> **RED (VO)**
> Yes, sir, I'm a regular Sears and Roebuck.

> TWO SHORT SIREN BLASTS issue from the main tower, drawing everybody's attention to the loading dock. The outer gate swings open . . . revealing a gray prison bus outside.

> **CON**
> Fresh fish! Fresh fish *today*!

Red is joined by Heywood, Skeet, Floyd, Jigger, Ernie, Snooze. Most cons crowd to the fence to gawk and jeer, but Red and his group mount the bleachers and settle in comfortably.

INT.—PRISON BUS—DUSK

Andy sits in back, wearing steel collar and chains.

> **RED (VO)**
> Andy came to Shawshank Prison in early
> 1947 for murdering his wife and the fella
> she was bangin'.

The bus lurches forward, RUMBLES through the gates. Andy gazes around, swallowed by prison walls.

> **RED (VO)**
> On the outside he'd been vice-president
> of a large Portland bank. Good work for
> a man as young as he was, when you
> consider how conservative banks were
> back then.

This is a scene with texture, depth, and dimension, both in terms of visual presentation, as well as in utilizing the *Theory of Illumination*. The whole sequence (I've presented only the opening section) gives us the necessary information we need to know for the story to move forward. We've introduced the main characters, revealed information about them, and now watch as the story unfolds through the eyes of the main character. We see prison life from two points of view: from Red's and from Andy's.

Look at the elements inherent in the scene: first, the

prison and the cons; then Red and his group; then Andy arriving, then the welcome, hearing the rules of the prison, and seeing the way the cons create their own rules. These are the elements that become the foundation of the narrative line and are used to keep the story moving forward. It's definitely not dull, it's certainly not thin, and for sure not boring. It's great screenwriting, a very good illustration of how to employ the various elements inherent in the fabric of the scene. If you read the novella by Stephen King, you'll see how much Darabont had to add and adapt in order to mold and contour the story line into a dynamic cinematic presentation.

Which brings us to *Boring*. What if you're reading your script and your eyes hurt, your attention wanders, and it's hard to understand what's going on, it's hard to sit still, and you have to fight off the urge to get up to find something to eat, and reluctantly you have to admit to yourself that you're bored to tears? Your worst fears seem to have come true. How do you deal with that?

First, some practical pointers. Nothing turns a reader off more than having to read thick and dense single-line paragraphs that fill up half to three quarters of a page. To support the reader, make sure your descriptive paragraphs are not longer than four or five sentences. If you've laced your script with long descriptive paragraphs, break them up into shorter paragraphs. Make sure the descriptive prose is not too "thick," or "dense"; a good screenplay should have a lot of white space on the page. You don't have to cut the material, just break it up into new paragraphs every four or five sentences. So many times a screenwriter will write a thick descriptive paragraph that fills up most of the page and it just stops the reading process cold. Lean, clean, and tight. That's what you want in your screenplay.

What else can you do to remove the element of "boring"?

Check your writing style. You want to write in an active, present-tense style, so make your descriptive sentences shorter, tighter. Check the dialogue; is it too wordy, too long, and too explanatory? Cut it down. Be ruthless. Either dialogue moves the story forward or it reveals character. If it doesn't satisfy these two requirements, cut it.

After you've done this, see if there are places in the text where you can add some kind of action, either a car chase or a kiss; just know that whatever action you choose has to *fit within the fabric of your story line*. Obviously, you can't add something without reason, or something that doesn't fit, or something that's completely out of context. If you check your material carefully you might find a few places where an action sequence, or some humor, might help to relieve the heaviness or density of the reading experience.

After you've made that assessment, move into individual scenes. Are there places where your characters are just talking heads, sitting in a restaurant, driving a car, or walking through a park? What are they doing during the scene? What's happening around them? For example, if they're sitting in a restaurant having an intense conversation, give them something to do. Let them be eating shrimp, for example, or corn on the cob, or let a tooth chip or break; or let the character be coming down with a cold; try to add something to the detail of the scene that the characters have to deal with. If your characters are driving in a car, let another driver cut them off and maybe the driver overreacts, so you've now got two things going on at the same time; the conversation as well as the reaction to the other driver. This adds depth and tension to the action.

In *The Shawshank Redemption*, when Andy Dufresne has

locked himself in the warden's office and is playing the operatic aria, the guards and warden are banging on the door. Two different things are going on simultaneously. So look for ways to incorporate any kind of secondary action into your scenes.

When Andy makes contact with Red for the first time, Red is playing catch with a baseball and this action continues through the entire scene. Give your characters something to do during the scene. You don't have to explain anything, just show it.

There will be times when a dialogue scene isn't working. No matter what you do, or how many times you change the character's lines, the scene just doesn't seem to gel. If this is the case, there are a few things you can do: number one, go into the scene and clarify its elements. Define the purpose of the scene. What is the dramatic need of the main character? What does he or she want during the scene; what is he or she doing there? Where did the character come from before the scene began? Where is he or she going after the scene is over? You don't have to write this information into the scene, or explain it, but you, the writer, must know it. Don't assume anything; clarify and define the character's dramatic need until there's no question in your mind about what happened before the scene began and what's going to happen after it's over.

If the scene or sequence still isn't working, there's something else you can do: switch the lines of the characters. If Bill's the main character and he's in the scene with his ex-girlfriend, Sally, and he wants something from her, some information, or a package, whatever, simply switch the lines. Give Bill's lines to Sally and Sally's lines to Bill and see what happens. If that doesn't work, rewrite the scene and change the character's point of view. If Bill is the main character, and Sally is a major or minor character, write the scene from Sally's point of view and let Bill be the secondary character. That means you have to enter the scene from Sally's point of view and see the purpose of the scene through her eyes.

This is an amazing little exercise. It removes any resistance you might have to the scene, and somehow dissolves the blocks that keep it from working. Once you've written the scene this way, go back and rewrite it from Bill's point of view. See what happens.

These little things can literally change the tone and texture of the screenplay. They can add depth and dimension to the scenes so the reading experience does not end up being dull, thin, and boring.

The Problem Sheet

THE PASSIVE ACTIVE

- MAIN CHARACTER IS TOO PASSIVE, TOO REACTIVE

- THE MAIN CHARACTER IS TOO INTERNAL, DISAPPEARS OFF THE PAGE

- THE CHARACTERS ALL SOUND ALIKE

- CHARACTER CONFLICTS ARE TOO THIN

- THE CHARACTERS EXPLAIN TOO MUCH

- THE DIALOGUE IS DULL, UNINTERESTING

- MINOR CHARACTERS ARE MORE INTERESTING THAN THE MAIN CHARACTER

- CONFLICT IS EXPRESSED THROUGH DIALOGUE, NOT ACTION

- THERE IS NO SUBTEXT IN SCENE

- THE STORY IS PREDICTABLE AND CONTRIVED

15

The Passive Active

There are times during the screenwriting process when the main character seems to vanish, literally disappears off the page. No matter what the character does, either in terms of fulfilling the story's action or in revealing information about himself/herself, the personality, the behavior, or the dramatic need vanishes and the character is lost within the matrix of the action. And then, at other times, a minor character suddenly emerges, developing such a strong and vibrant personality that he or she totally overshadows the main character.

I call this phenomenon the *passive active*. It's where the main character seems to wander around looking for something to do, and, no matter what he or she does do, always reacts instead of acts, and is portrayed as passive instead of active.

It can be a real problem, especially if your story line is built around this particular character and he/she gets lost in the narrative story line or seems to disappear off the page. One of the best ways of becoming aware of this problem is to evaluate the material and determine whether the main character is *reacting* to the situation or is *actively creating* it.

You're writing for the visual medium. One of the strongest rules governing the craft is that your main character must be active, and be the catalyst of the action, the spark that *causes* things to happen. That doesn't mean you shouldn't let your character(s) react to a particular situation during the screenplay, just the opposite. Characters are always reacting to events or forces that affect them.

In *Three Days of the Condor* (Lorenzo Semple and David Rayfiel), the Robert Redford character is literally "out to lunch" when the entire cell of his CIA unit (they read books looking for information) is wiped out. When he discovers this, he understands it won't be too long before the assassin comes after him, and he enters the Second Act not knowing what to do or whom to trust. For the entire First Half of Act II the Redford character is only reacting. It is only at the Mid-Point, about sixty pages in, that he kidnaps the Faye Dunaway character and begins to be active again. And it works perfectly. If you haven't seen it in a while, check it out.

Action and *reaction* are two sides of the same coin. As a matter of fact, Newton's Third Law of Motion states that "for every action there is an equal and opposite reaction." It's just something to be aware of, and it can be a good rule to follow. If something happens to a character, if he or she is affected by an incident or event, the reaction is a normal part of character revelation. It only becomes a problem when the character is reacting constantly, not only to an incident or event, but also to other characters. Things always seem *to happen* to him/her; the character doesn't cause or trigger them. If you show your characters reacting too much of the time, they'll simply disappear off the page or, as sometimes happens, disappear off the movie screen.

A few nights ago I was watching television, and a Steven Seagal movie, *On Deadly Ground*, came on. I started watching. This was a film that Seagal starred in as well as directed. The film opens with some beautiful location shots of the Alaskan wilderness, and we cut to an oil well fire that's burning out of control. A helicopter wings its way over the rugged country, bringing the Seagal character to the fire. He lands, gets out, and approaches the team of firefighters. They can't handle it and they don't know what to do. So what does the Seagal character do? With only a few words he dons his fire suit and walks directly into the raging inferno. He stands there, surrounded by flames, casually plants some explosives, then just as casually walks out. The other characters scatter, looking for cover, but the Seagal character simply stands there as the oil well explodes, putting out the fire.

Pretty strong stuff, right? Strong action, a strong character, and some powerful visual images. What I saw during the thirty or forty minutes I watched the film was that it was a perfect example of the *passive active*. Why? Because the portrayal of characters was so thin, the film became laughable. Michael Caine, the fine English actor, played the mean and totally corrupt oil baron, but his performance (I'm sure it was written as it was played) was a one-dimensional, histrionic, over-the-top characterization of a man obsessed with carrying out his evil scheme.

Opposing him, of course, was the good guy, Seagal. The portrait of the Seagal character is the perfect expression of the passive active. As the main character he's the strong, silent type, a man who doesn't talk too much, a man who wants to avoid trouble, except when pushed too far, and only then will he react and take action—and as we see, he's a character who can literally do everything. Whether it's putting out the oil fire single-handed, or being a master of martial arts, or breaking into a computer and uncovering secret passwords, or protecting the rights of a drunken and downtrodden Eskimo. He is a man who is reacting to the situations caused by others, the bad guys. And all this is shown in the first fifteen minutes, by the way!

The unscrupulous oil baron, the bad guy, and the Seagal character, the good guy, quickly square off and it's pretty predictable who's going to come out on top.

It's easy to see what Seagal and the writer were striving for here; they wanted to portray the Seagal character as the strong, silent type, but because we're not privy to what he is thinking or feeling, he comes across as a character who only *reacts* to the events instigated by the Michael Caine character. That makes him a reactive character. Throughout the film the main character does not once instigate any actions, he only responds to actions initiated by someone else; so all we know about him is that he's reacting to what's happening to him and how it affects the tribal community of Eskimos.

His character, portrayed as the strong and silent type, is a man who seemingly knows everything, is right about everything, and lives according to a strict moral code that came out of the early westerns of Tom Mix. He was so busy being the "good guy," and reacting to the things the bad guys have done, that he becomes a boring character and literally disappears off the screen.

For example, here's a situation that is supposed to reveal an aspect of his character. It's a typical bar fight, and it could have been taken right out of a Tom Mix western. Seagal's sitting in the bar, drinking alone at a table. Three big tough guys, oil riggers, are hassling a drunken Eskimo who wants another drink. They taunt him, then begin pushing and shoving him around until he collapses into a corner. Seagal doesn't do anything, he simply stares at them. When they belligerently ask what he's looking at, Seagal at first does not reply. When they continue taunting him, he stands and the oil rig workers exchange words with him. Seagal walks toward them and, before they can continue talking, launches into them, throwing them all over the place, and in only a matter of minutes he reduces the oil workers, and there must be at least ten of them, into whimpering weaklings, begging and groveling for mercy.

Ho-hum. It's pretty standard fare. We've seen it hundreds of times, for it's a predictable bar fight: the hero sits alone minding his own business when some tough guys pick on someone who can't take care of himself, usually a drunk, and the hero steps in and rescues him. What makes this interesting for our purposes is that the Seagal character is so passive, portraying an attitude rather than any emotion. And that's the way he is during the entire film. We don't know anything about him, and all we see about this character is a strong, silent, passive attitude. He becomes the passive active. It's not very interesting.

The screenwriter's job is to keep the reader interested enough to keep turning pages, or in this case, keep my fingers off the remote. The real lesson to be learned in this case is that at no time do we know enough about Seagal to see or understand his thoughts, feelings, or emotions; all he reflects is his attitude. His humanity, or believability, is all contained inside his head.

That being the case, the only thing this kind of a character can do is react to the situation. By placing a character in these types of situations, reacting to something someone else has initiated, the screenwriter causes his main character literally to vanish, to disappear off the page.

In many of Robert Redford's films he portrays this type of active/reactive character. Take a look at *Sneakers* (Larry Lasker and Walter Parkes), *Indecent Proposal* (Amy Holden Jones), or *Out of Africa* (Kurt Luedtke). In *Sneakers* he plays a character who doesn't show any thoughts or feelings, he simply states that he has a plan and then we see him implementing the plan and then he seems to disappear into the background. He is a passive yet active character.

So if you're writing, or rewriting, a screenplay, and you sense that your character is washed out, or unseen on the page, or he or she is overshadowed by another character, or the story line seems contrived or predictable, or conflict seems to be missing, the chances are your character is too passive and is busy reacting to other characters or situations rather than creating or initiating the action.

One of the "rules" of screenwriting is that action is character. It must be remembered that film is behavior, and what a person does, his or her actions, reveals who he or she is. But there has to be a way for the reader to connect with the character; there must be a character-audience bond established for the script to be effective. If this bond is not formed, then there's a whole dimension missing in the illumination of character. And when that's the case, there is no "willing suspension of disbelief."

How do you go about solving the problem of the passive character? First, it has to be approached from the perspective of *Character*. A lot of writers try to solve the problem by approaching it through *Structure;* they seem to feel that if they can add enough action sequences, or tense dramatic mo-

ments, that will take care of the problem. All that does, however, is accentuate the passivity of the main character. Just
like *On Deadly Ground*. It's not enough to pile on a number of
action sequences, because it doesn't really solve the problem.

So, how do you recognize the problem of the *passive/ac-
tive*?

Take a look at the *Problem Sheet*, and see if you can recognize some of the symptoms. When you reread your material,
does your main character seem be lost in the background of
the action? Do you find that one of the minor characters
seems to leap off the page and draw attention away from the
main character? Do your characters all sound alike, as if there
is only one voice for all? What about conflict? Is there
enough? Is your character's point of view clearly established
and defined? Do you find your dialogue dull and boring? Or
maybe your main character is constantly explaining things,
and the story moves forward through dialogue rather than
action? Are your scenes focused, or flat and one-dimensional,
with no color and texture?

All of these symptoms could be indicative of the problem
of a character who's too passive.

So what do you do? There are many ways to solve this
kind of problem, but perhaps the easiest is to examine the
character from the perspective of *conflict*. Do you know the
character's *point of view*? Have you gone into the background
of the main character and established a strong *Circle of Being*?
What about the point of view within each scene? And what
about your character's *dramatic need*? Is it clearly defined in
your own mind? If not, go back and redefine your character's
dramatic need and *point of view* in relation to the conflict of the
story line. Go through and extract the elements of each scene
and make sure you've got enough conflict, either on an emo-

tional level in terms of the scene's *subtext,* i.e., what's not said during the scene; or on the level of direct confrontation or even physical conflict. Don't make things too easy for your character. If things happen too easily, the action becomes contrived and predictable.

Which brings up another point. Sometimes the screenwriter, wanting to avoid being too direct, or too "on target," in the dialogue, tries to be a little too subtle, a little too indirect. That creates a sense of confusion and a lack of understanding, so the needs of the character become lost in *what the character is not saying.* The dialogue seems vague and off center and the reader really doesn't know what's going on, and the story line seems to wander off in several directions. It's a symptom of the screenwriter's wanting to be too clever.

There are times in a screenplay when the dialogue has to be direct, for exposition purposes, in order to move the story forward, whether on a physical or an emotional level. And sometimes these scenes are the hardest to write just because they are so direct and on the mark. They're so easy, you think there's something wrong. This is where you don't need subtlety of action or dialogue, you need clarity and definition to keep your character active and interesting. The great American novelist F. Scott Fitzgerald always felt that the hardest thing a writer has to do is to "write down" to his readers; what he meant by that was that it's very hard to write material that is too specific and too direct, with no subtlety either in thought, action, or exposition.

This happens all the time if you "try" to make your character alive and interesting. If you think you're really being smart and clever writing "indirect" dialogue, there's a good chance the motivation and need of your character will simply wash out and disappear off the page, lost in the twilight zone between clarity and confusion.

That's when another character will start to take over and become more interesting than the main character. If you get the feeling a minor character is dominating or overshadowing the main character, and is more lively and more interesting, it's a pretty good indication the main character might be too passive, and you're going to have to strengthen the characterization. It should be noted that there will be moments when your main character will be reacting to another character, action, or situation, and that's not bad—it's when reaction becomes his or her only response that it proves a detriment, and that's why you have to be careful walking the line between action and reaction.

A case in point is *The Accidental Tourist*. Adapted from the novel by Ann Tyler by screenwriter/director Lawrence Kasdan and Frank Galati, the film, starring William Hurt and Geena Davis, is a quirky comedy about a man who has recently lost his son in a senseless shooting in a mall. William Hurt portrays a writer of travel books for people who detest traveling, and by nature he's a character who is withdrawn and reclusive. His only companion is his dog, who, it is understood, loves to travel. They're quite a pair together. And when the Hurt character accepts a new assignment, he takes his dog to be boarded in a kennel and there meets the delightful and wacky Geena Davis character. And she makes it her "mission" (her dramatic need) to bring him out of his shell because she's looking to find a father for her own son.

The novel is so unique that it poses major problems adapting it into a screenplay. In the first place you have a main character who's divorced, alone, and reclusive, and the fact that he's just lost his son in a senseless killing simply compounds the problem; his main action is moping around feeling sorry for himself. This is very delicate material that works wonderfully on the printed page under the gifted talent of Ann Tyler. But translating this kind of material to the screen is very difficult. If you want to visually portray a character reacting to the death of another person, you have to know from the beginning that the character's gaze will be mostly focused inward, that he will be self-absorbed in grief and somewhat reluctant to engage in any kind of action, physical or emotional. This depends on the story of course, but in the case of *The Accidental Tourist* it's a primary force that's working on the character.

The Hurt character is obsessed with the injustice of life, and withdraws into a comfortable routine of inaction and noninvolvement. This can work part of the time, but since we're trying to take a passive character and make him active, we have to find a way of incorporating some kind of emotional reaction and making it more visually active. Sometimes, in this situation, you can simply slide over the grief and get the character back on his feet by throwing him into a new situation. For example, one of my students was writing a script, a thriller, and the film opens up with a lovely anniversary dinner between a husband and wife. When the evening's over, they decide to exchange cars for the drive home. So the wife drives home in the husband's car, but as she's driving, the windows, doors, and sunroof suddenly seal shut, poison gas is released, and she's killed.

The man's dramatic need is to pursue and find the killer(s) of his wife and bring them to justice. But he never really accepts the mourning process, so he is constantly moving through the action devoid of any emotional reaction or grief. You could say that he's in shock and total denial, and that may be so, but he becomes so obsessed with justice and revenge that he literally becomes a passive character in the midst of nonstop visual action.

This is totally opposite the passive-active character portrayed by William Hurt in *The Accidental Tourist*. So it really doesn't matter what kind of story you're telling, whether an action, adventure, drama, or comedy. That the Hurt character is a writer makes him even more difficult to portray visually. And it just didn't work. What happened in the film is exactly what happened in the screenplay: the main character Hurt portrays literally disappears off the page. Oh, yes, he's there physically, but there's no connection with the audience, and no sympathy for him whatsoever. Which, of course, is part of his character.

The Geena Davis character, on the other hand, is striking in her "activity." She's always in motion, and livens up the page, and the screen, by her presence, delightfully active in her quest to bring the Hurt character back into life again.

But it isn't enough.

The passivity of the Hurt character drags the whole film down. It was an attempt to make a passive character work on the screen, and it didn't work; it was, as they say in Hollywood, an "interesting failure."

On the other hand you have a character like Dr. Richard Kimble in *The Fugitive* (Andrew Davis), who is constantly reacting to a particular situation; in this case he's wanted for the murder of his wife, and is on the run, trying to elude capture by the law in the form of the Tommy Lee Jones character. His dramatic need, to prove his innocence and find out who actually committed the crime, is what drives him through the screenplay. It's the engine that keeps the story moving forward. So even though he's continually reacting, he's an active character because he causes things to happen, he's always *doing something* to try and prove his innocence. And he's not adverse to helping a little child who's been misdiagnosed, by going back into the hospital and making a notation on the chart. The little side journey reveals his character through his behavior. Film, as I am so fond of saying, is behavior.

Even if you have a character confined in a physical location does not mean that he or she has to be passive. Hannibal Lecter in *The Silence of the Lambs* (Ted Tally) is a good case in point. Locked inside a prison cell, he is far from being passive. Through insight and perception he prods, probes, and finally provokes Clarice Starling to confront and deal with her past, for two reasons: One, of course, is that he is tutoring her to bring the serial killer Buffalo Bill to justice, and by doing that he can achieve his *dramatic need*, which is to be moved to another prison facility where he can be placed in a cell with a window. His motivation, and the way he manipulates Clarice, even though he's locked inside a small six-by-eight-foot cell, is honed to achieve his dramatic need; everything else is secondary. So, he manipulates her to serve his own purpose. That's makes him an active character even though he's locked in a passive location.

When I was working with the Brazilian filmmaker on the screenplay about the famous Brazilian composer Villa-Lobos, he was very nervous giving me the screenplay to read, he confided, because it was such an unconventional story line. It was a nonlinear screenplay told in a series of flashbacks that traced five different threads of the composer's life: his boyhood; his search for musical inspiration and direction; his relationships with the two significant women in his life; his life of celebrity and worldwide recognition; and lastly, his final concert and death.

He thought the problems in the screenplay were structural; but what I discovered was that structure wasn't really the problem; the main character, the composer, was the problem. Because of the nature of the script, the composer was always reacting to the forces that were shaping his life. That made him a passive character, not an active one. It made the screenplay a simple biography, not a visual experience of the man's life. That kind of story simply doesn't work well. No matter that the five different story threads were structured in a jigsaw-puzzle fashion; it didn't change anything. Throughout the screenplay the main character was constantly reacting to other people, and this created a kind of visual landscape that forced him into the background, and made the secondary characters stronger and more dynamic.

Once I identified the problem, we could approach it from the vantage point of *Character* and not *Structure,* even though it touched both. So we went back to the foundation of the screenplay in order to make the composer more active. The composer had *to create the action* that would cause other people to react. And this had to be set up from the very beginning, so we had to restructure the entire First Act, adding several new scenes in which the composer created the action, and the other characters reacted. Even though this was an unconventional script, it was not difficult to find a way to solve this particular problem once we identified it.

Another way to make the character more active is to go back into your scenes and redefine the dramatic need, both in terms of overall story and in the context of each individual scene. If you determine the point of view of each character in each scene, then it's possible to rewrite the scene adding conflict to achieve the maximum dramatic value. Part of the reason a character seems to be passive and reactive is because there's a lack of conflict. Nine times out of ten if you feel your character is too passive, or is reacting too much to an external situation or character, it's due to a lack of conflict. So go back and redefine the internal and external forces working on the character.

If it's an internal, emotional reaction to a situation or event, try to create a visual metaphor and *let us see* it. For example, in *Dances With Wolves* after the John Dunbar character arrives at the fort at Plot Point I, the first thing he does is give himself the task of cleaning up the area; his behavior tells us that he's cleaning up his life and putting things back in order.

If you find it too difficult, then write a new character biography that will create a new *Circle of Being,* and in this way you can establish a strong and perceptive point of view that will generate more conflict.

That's the essence of transforming a character from passive to active.

The Problem Sheet

THE FLASH POINT

- CHARACTERS ARE TOO TALKY AND EXPLAIN TOO MUCH

- MAIN CHARACTER IS NOT VERY SYMPATHETIC

- THE MAIN CHARACTER IS A LONER AND HAS NO ONE TO TALK TO

- THE MAIN CHARACTER HAS NO POINT OF VIEW

- THE ACTION IS TOO THIN

- THE EMOTIONAL STAKES ARE NOT HIGH ENOUGH

- SOMETHING SEEMS TO BE MISSING

- THE STORY LINE IS TOO EPISODIC, TOO JERKY, AND NEEDS TRANSITIONS

- THE STORY SEEMS CONFUSING

- THE STORY WANDERS AND GETS BOGGED DOWN IN TOO MANY DETAILS

16

The Flash Point

What's the best way to use a flashback? When does it work the best and when is it the most effective?

These are some of the most common questions I encounter regarding the flashback; it really doesn't matter what country I'm in, or whether the writers are students or professionals. For some reason, the use of flashbacks in a screenplay seems to elicit indecision and insecurity. So, when I'm asked what's the best way to use a flashback, I listen patiently, then ask why the screenwriter wants to use one in the first place. The person usually becomes very serious and states that the flashback gives information that's essential to the story.

That's cool, I respond, but if you use the flashback in this particular situation, does it move the story forward? Or, does it reveal something about the character? Remember, the flashback is simply a tool, a device, which the screenwriter uses to provide the reader with information that he or she cannot incorporate into the screenplay any other way. That's something most writers don't understand or take into consideration. That's why there seems to be so much confusion about whether to use a flashback or not.

The purpose of the flashback is simple: it is a device that *bridges time and place either to reveal information about the main character, or to move the story forward.*

When flashbacks are done well and integrated into the narrative line of the story, as in *How to Make an American Quilt, The Usual Suspects* (Chris McQuarrie), *Courage Under Fire* (Patrick Duncan), *The Long Kiss Goodnight* (Shane Black), *Lone Star* (John Sayles), *The English Patient* (Anthony Minghella), or are absorbed into the Third Act as in *The Shawshank Redemption,* the flashback works wonderfully. But when a flashback is thrown into the screenplay because the writer doesn't know how to move the story forward any other way, or decides to show something about the main character that could be better stated in dialogue, then the flashback only draws attention to itself and becomes intrusive. That's when it doesn't work.

The flashback is a tool; it should be used to give the viewer information about the character or story that he can't get any other way. It can reveal *emotional* as well as *physical* information (as with Andy Dufresne's breakout from Shawshank), though it often does both, and can show different points of view of the same event, as in *The Usual Suspects* or *Courage Under Fire.* Or it can reveal thoughts, memories, or dreams, as in *The English Patient* or *Shine* (Jan Sardi).

That's when the flashback is most effective. If it is incorrectly used, as the *Problem Sheet* reveals, it only highlights flaws: characters who are too thin and weak, action too subtle or episodic, and the story itself seeming to wander around searching for itself, like a dog chasing its tail.

I firmly believe that flashbacks are an aspect of *Character,* not story. As a matter of fact, I tell my students that a flashback is really a *"flashpresent,"* because what we're really seeing is what the character is thinking and feeling in present time, whether a memory, an event, or fantasy, or the illumination of the character's point of view. What we see in a flashback is shown through the eyes of the character, so we're seeing what he or she is seeing, thinking, or feeling in *present time;* in this time and in this place. No matter what it is. Take a look at *The English Patient* again, or *Shine,* or *Lone Star;* the action all takes place in present time with the character remembering moments in time past. The *"flashpresent"* is anything the character is thinking and feeling in the present moment, whether a thought, a dream, a memory, or a hope, a fear, or fantasy, for time has no restraints or limits. In the character's head the *"flashpresent"* could be past, present, or future.

In *Courage Under Fire,* for example, the same incident is seen through the eyes of different characters, and each one views it differently. The *subject* of the script is honor; it dramatizes how a person must learn to live with a mistake he made that resulted in the death of a friend. Not only that, but the Denzel Washington character is forced to lie to the dead man's family at the urging of the military. The *context* of the film, what holds it together, the circumstances or situation, is the Gulf War. Each particular flashback reveals what happened when a medic helicopter on a rescue mission was shot down by Iraqi soldiers.

What happened when the helicopter went down? That's the assignment of the officer in charge, Colonel Serling, played by Denzel Washington. The pilot who flew the mission is being considered for the Medal of Honor, America's highest and most prestigious military award. But it turns out there are some discrepancies in the survivors' stories, and to add further fuel to the fire, the captain of the medic helicopter is a woman, played by Meg Ryan. Colonel Serling is told by the White House that it is important politically for her to receive the medal, for it will be the first time a woman would have been so honored for courage under fire.

The script begins with an incident in the Gulf War that takes place at night, in the heat of battle. Colonel Serling makes a decision to fire at a tank that does not respond to his message. Only after the tank is destroyed, and all men lost, does he learn the tank was one of his own, captained by his friend. That's the *inciting incident* of the screenplay, the incident or event that catapults the story into motion. When he returns to the States, he's given the assignment of investigating the woman's actions, and is forced to look into the mirror of his own soul to examine his own actions under fire, which he cannot forgive or forget.

So we explore the subject of "courage under fire." As he's investigating the actions of the Meg Ryan character, he forces himself to seek out the truth, while under constant pressure from the White House and the military. He finds that for each step he takes, his actions are reflected back at him through his own experience.

But it's the perfect setup for using the flashback. This is the kind of story I call an "emotional detective story," for each member of the surviving crew sees the action differently. It's a *Rashomon*-type story, and it's up to the Denzel Washington character to sort things out and find "the truth." His search becomes a journey of transformation and self-forgiveness.

It's true there are two different stories in this screenplay, but both stories reflect the emotional scar that remains unhealed in Colonel Serling's heart, and his dramatic need is to resolve the conflict within himself.

Two other examples that use the flashback effectively are *The Long Kiss Goodnight* (Shane Black) and *The Usual Suspects*. *The Long Kiss Goodnight* is the story of an amnesia victim (Geena Davis) who has a memory of only "three thousand days," eight years by her count. Her name is Samantha, Sam for short, and she has no memory of her past life other than being washed up on the beach in a T-shirt and jeans. Since that time she has married a nice man, Hal, and has a wonderful eight-year-old daughter, and continuously wonders about her past. As she says in her voice-over in the opening scenes, when she woke up, her daughter was "two months grown in my belly. I don't know who put her there. I may never. I just know she's mine, and she's about to turn eight."

When the script opens, it is near Christmas Eve and as she's driving her father-in-law home, she inadvertently hits a deer that kills her father-in-law, and she lands in the hospital. But something's wrong, something she can't explain, and she feels the need for a cigarette, even though she doesn't smoke. As she lights up, she sees herself in the hospital mirror and suddenly her reflection becomes alive, drenched in blood, and the reflection says her real name is Charly and she smokes Marlboro Reds. This starts a series of quick-cut flashbacks where she learns more about her identity.

Things start heating up on Christmas Eve when a group of carolers are singing carols in front of the house. Only something's wrong; the carolers are singing horribly off key. And when Sam throws open the door to welcome them and offer some Christmas cheer to them, no one is there except a trained killer pointing a shotgun at her. And he calls her Charly. And she reacts, yanking the gun out of his hand, leading to a wild and woolly fight sequence where we learn (as she learns) that she definitely has the ability to take care of herself. She ends up killing him, brutally, shocking herself as much as her family. Plot Point I. She's really incredible at what she does and she's astonished that somewhere within her memory banks is this amazing killing machine. It frightens her and she begins her journey of self-discovery to recover her lost life.

It's easy to see how the script is an ideal vehicle for the flashback. Every time Sam finds herself in a certain situation, the screenwriter draws upon a wonderful tool to show us some of the incidents and events of her past life. And it's not until the Mid-Point that she fully steps into her identity as Charly, and learns (at the same time we learn) that she was an assassin for the CIA. And they want her dead because she "knows too much."

She is truly a lethal weapon—so lethal, in fact, that she wonders, as we do, how she could have lived so contentedly as a wife and mother with this killing machine inside her. And this is what she's trying to resolve.

We're not talking about the quality of writing here, or how good or bad the film is, we're simply talking about creating the cinematic *context* of taking a particular situation and effectively incorporating flashbacks into the material. All the flashbacks used are points of present time, the *"flashpresent."*

Which is illustrated very clearly in *The Usual Suspects*. What makes the screenplay so unique is that we're examining one particular event, an explosion on board a ship in the San Pedro harbor that kills some twenty-seven men over a reported $91 million in cocaine. This event is seen through a series of voice-over flashbacks narrated by "Verbal" Kint (Kevin Spacey), a palsied con artist with a twisted foot and a penchant for talking. Verbal is one of two survivors of the blast (the other is an aged Hungarian gangster), and under the relentless questioning of the customs agent played by Chazz Palminteri, Verbal tells the story of "what happened." The context of the script is tailored to become the perfect vehicle to show the events leading up to the shipboard blast, the inciting incident that opens the film.

There is no linear story-line progression here, meaning we don't go through the story from beginning to end, chronologically, but the flashbacks reveal what happened in visual bits and pieces.

As Verbal is being questioned, he tells us, in voice-over, how the five suspects were picked up, placed in the same holding cell, and questioned about the hijacking of a truckload of gun parts. And as Verbal answers the policeman's questions, we start fitting the individual pieces of the visual jigsaw puzzle together. These questions work as *lead-ins* to the individual flashback sequences and, again, should be thought of as a *"flashpresent"* because Verbal is literally making the story up as he goes along. It's a bold cinematic demonstration of taking a singular incident, as in *Courage Under Fire,* and presenting it in a nonlinear fashion.

Which brings us back to the question of when to use a flashback, and when not to, and how to solve a problem with it, either by incorporating it into the story line or by removing it.

There are no "rules," of course, about this; it really depends upon whether you've designed the flashback to be an integral part of the story, as in *Courage Under Fire, The Usual Suspects, The Long Kiss Goodnight, How to Make an American Quilt,* or *The English Patient.*

If your screenplay was not conceived to incorporate flashbacks and still doesn't seem to be working, see whether "the problem" exhibits some of the symptoms listed on the

Problem Sheet. If the answer is yes, and you think a flashback may solve the problem, whatever it is, then the simple rule If you can say it, don't show it, may apply.

Now, I'm sure this sounds like a contradiction, because the object of a screenplay is to tell the story in pictures, not words. The dialogue only becomes an adjunct to the visual information that moves the story forward; either that, or it reveals information about the character. Suppose, for example, you want to show an event that has affected your character, and you decide to incorporate it into the script. So you go through the scene and find a place to lead into the flashback, which naturally results in your cutting away from the middle of the scene to insert the flashback. What happens? In the case of *The English Patient* it works wonderfully, because the patient is a mystery, and slowly we begin to learn who he is, and his affair with Katherine, but each time we cut away there is a natural and solid transition point. Plus, the entire love affair, though told in flashback, is really the structural foundation of the entire film. We learn what happened to the English patient at the same time Hana (Juliet Binoche) does. It works wonderfully.

By the same token there's also a good chance that you might destroy the integrity of the scene. And that, of course, is not the point of the flashback. If you cut away in the middle of a scene, it could also create another problem instead. Why?

Take a look at *The Silence of the Lambs*. When Clarice Starling visits Hannibal Lecter in his makeshift prison cell after he's been transferred to Memphis, she wants to obtain the name of the serial killer Buffalo Bill. And she knows that Lecter knows the identity of the killer. She wants that name, but they don't have much time before she'll be forced to leave. His reply is that "we don't measure time in the same way, do we, Clarice?" and then he insists that she tell him more about her childhood after the death of her father. Knowing the guards will return any moment (which creates a tremendous tension in the scene), she proceeds to tell him that she was sent to live with her uncle in Montana. One night, she tells Lecter, she woke up hearing "screams," and when she sneaks out of bed to investigate, she finds men slaughtering the spring lambs in the barn. Horrified, she tries to save one of the lambs, but can only carry it about a mile before she's caught and returned to the ranch. Her uncle is furious, and, in retaliation he sends her away to an orphanage, and that's where she spends the rest of her childhood growing up. It's a powerful scene, and especially significant since the title of the book and screenplay was taken from it.

The scene was originally conceived as a flashback with the dialogue in present time playing over the images of Clarice as a little girl. But when Jonathan Demme filmed it, he saw the emotional dynamic of the scene between Anthony Hopkins and Jodie Foster was so intense that if he cut away to show the child discovering the slaughtering of the spring lambs, he would absolutely destroy the integrity of the scene. As mentioned, this is one of the most important scenes in the film because it is the final flashback that shows her confronting the events of her past. Without completing this incident in her childhood, Clarice would have been incomplete in her growth, both as a person and FBI agent. Which is a major part of her character. On film the scene was so strong that the director couldn't cut away and incorporate the flashback. The price would have been too high had he chosen to use it. He would have lost the emotional integrity of the scene. So he decided to keep the action in present time to maintain that. And, if you remember, the entire scene is played in close shot and it's so powerful that it remains firmly fixed in the memory. The information revealed about the character was more revealing and more dramatic stated in dialogue than it would have been in flashback.

This is not a hard-and-fast "rule," but it is something to remember. So *if you can say it, don't show it.*

You can use flashbacks for any number of reasons but their primary purpose is to bridge time and place; to reveal a past emotional event or physical conflict that still affects the character, as in *The English Patient;* or to move the story forward, as in *Courage Under Fire;* and to give insight into, and understanding of, a character's behavior, as in *How to Make an American Quilt.* Or to solve a mystery of the past, as in *Lone Star.*

Using a *"flashpresent"* is also effective at showing memories, or visually giving expression to a thought or expectation or to wishful thinking; remember that scene in *True Lies* (James Cameron) where Arnold is driving in the Corvette with the salesman he thinks is having an affair with his wife and he busts him in the nose? Only wishful thinking. You can show that, no problem. You can also use the flashback to show how, or why, an event happened, or maybe flashforward to an event that may or may not happen in the near future. These all are ways to incorporate the *"flash point"* into your screenplay and *make it work.*

In *The Shawshank Redemption* the flashback of how Andy Dufresne escaped from the prison at the end of Act II is a very good example of how and when to use the flashback. It's important to remember that there are one or two things that are unresolved when you reach the Plot Point at the end of Act II. These must be resolved during Act III. In *The Shaw-*

shank Redemption two things remain unresolved: one, how did Andy escape, and two, what happens to him and Red?

The flashback that opens the Third Act is beautifully structured, and incorporates the flashback at this point as an integral part of the story. It's what every flashback should do and be. "Get busy living or get busy dying," Andy tells Red in the scene after Tommy is killed by the warden. The sequence opens with Andy waiting in his cell as the lights go out, and Red, in voice-over, tells us that "I've had some long nights in stir. Alone in the dark with nothing but your thoughts, time can draw out like a blade. . . ." No one knows what Andy's going to do. We watch as Andy gathers his belongings, pulls on the rope, and then we cut away to Red, waiting, wondering.

The next morning Andy is missing from cell count. No one knows where or how he disappeared, and it drives the warden crazy. As the warden questions Red and the guards, he throws one of the rocks Andy left behind at the large poster of Raquel Welch hanging on the wall. But a strange thing happens; the rock goes right through the paper. Everybody stops. The warden moves toward the poster, pokes his finger through the hole, then shoves his entire arm through. He yanks the poster off the wall and we discover (as the characters discover) that a tunnel has been hollowed out of the wall. We cut to a montage of several police cars racing down the highway, and guards combing the countryside, and all they find is part of Andy's torn shirt and his loyal rock hammer, which has been worn down to the nub. That's the flashpoint by which we lead into the flashback and Red tells us, in voice-over, how Andy got out of Shawshank Prison.

We see a couple of scenes of Andy picking at the wall with his rock hammer to carve his name when a chunk of rock falls out; then we see him in the movie requesting the Rita Hayworth poster; then shots of Andy digging into the tunnel at night, and emptying the gravel from the tunnel into the prison yard. Then we flashback again and see Andy's last night as he polishes the warden's shoes, only this time we see it from Andy's point of view; we see him substituting the false ledger for the warden's, and he puts the false one into the safe. Then we see him walking back into the cell block, only this time we see the shoes he is wearing; bright and shiny. In Andy's cell we see him taking off his prison garb, revealing the warden's shirt and tie underneath, then he places his goods into the plastic bag and starts his escape to freedom. Red tells us in voice-over that "Andy crawled to freedom through five hundred yards of shit-smelling foulness I can't even imagine. Or maybe I just don't want to. Five hundred yards. The length of five football fields. Just shy of half a mile."

This is just a wonderful flashback. Structured in a non-linear way, it moves the story forward and reveals a part of his character that we never knew existed. Not once during the entire Second Act did he ever mention that he was considering escape. But if you think about it, that is his character's dramatic need; to get out of prison must be the dramatic need of every convict doing time. We don't need to state it, but the screenwriter must know it.

Andy's escape is a *physical* use of the flashback. It shows us how he escaped. But there's also an *emotional* use of the flashback. In *How to Make an American Quilt* there are six different stories that deal with various aspects of love. The subject of the quilt, "Where Love Resides" is what the story is about. The screenplay itself is structured very much like a quilt; piece by piece, story by story, certain situations in life and love are shown that allow Finn to ferret out what she needs to learn so as to let go of her fear of commitment.

What works so well is the lead-in point where the flashback dovetails into present time, and it's this weaving of narrative story line between past and present that illuminates Finn's dilemma so well. Each piece of the quilt the women are making gives us some insight and understanding into the nature of love.

Using flashbacks in this manner offers a unique perspective on the action. Before she can deal with the commitment of marriage, Finn must learn to confront her own emotional fear. This is shown in two ways: one, through the dissertation she's now working on (her third, she explains); we see her past history is constant as we learn, that when her thesis is almost complete, she decides that's not the subject she really wants, and so begins another thesis on another subject. I think we're all like Finn in a way, because most of us have struggled with the fears and insecurities of an emotional commitment at some point in our lives.

The first thing we learn about Finn is that her fear of commitment has been passed down to her from her mother. "Maybe she was just afraid that their relationship had become just like everyone else's," she confides, and that's why her parents separated. So, when Sam proposes to Finn, she, caught in this emotional turmoil, runs away to the safety of her grandmother's house.

As mentioned, each of the quilters' particular stories reflects a certain emotional aspect in relationship to love and commitment. There is something Finn must learn from all the stories so she can resolve the conflict of "where love resides" within herself. This is a very good example of the way flashback reveals the emotional conflict that resides at the core of Finn's character.

Which brings us back to the basic question of this chapter: When can you use a flashback to solve a particular problem?

The examples given illustrate the basic context of the flashback; either physical or emotional, it is the point at which you slide into the *"flashpresent."* If you feel you have a problem the flashback creates or can solve, what do you perceive the problem to be? First, ask yourself what you want to use the flashback for. Is it to reveal character? Or is it to show *how* an event reveals the character, in terms of their actions and reactions? What incident are you going to show, and what does it reveal about the character, and how is it going to move the story forward?

If, for example, you have a situation where you think your story is wandering around in circles, or your character is too talky and explains too many things, you might consider using a flashback to reveal a certain aspect of your character. If your character is too passive and reactive, or feels too thin or one-dimensional, you could use a flashback to provide more depth and dimension to your story line.

But—and it's a very big *but*—you just can't insert a flashback because you think it will work to expand character. You need to go back into the character and define those forces that are working on him or her during the screenplay; if need be, write essays about the relationships between the characters just to clarify them in your own mind.

"What is character but the determination of incident? And what is incident but the illumination of character?"

These are questions you must ask yourself as you start contemplating the use of flashback to solve a particular problem. If you decide to use it, think of it in terms of a *"flash-present"*; what is your character thinking or feeling in the present moment? If you can get into your character's head, and find some thought, memory, or event that reflects, or acts, upon the present moment, and, through it, show how it affects your character, you gain an optimal advantage. Go into your character's *Circle of Being* (Chapter 13) and see what you can find.

The best use of the flashback is to provide some kind of emotional insight and understanding for your character. The transformation between Sam and Charly in *The Long Kiss Goodnight* is all about regaining a side of her character that's been buried for the last eight years. That's why I always think of a flashback as a *"flashpresent."* It's what's inside your character's head at the present moment; it either moves the story forward or reveals information about the main character.

Could you have used a flashback in *Thelma & Louise* to show her *Circle of Being*? Possibly. There might have been an opportunity to show what happened to Louise when she was raped in Texas. It might have helped clarify why she killed Harlan in the parking lot. But would it have been as effective? Not really. There's no sense spoon-feeding the reader or audience. We've become too sophisticated in terms of movie culture to do that. As far as I'm concerned, a flashback revealing this event in Louise's life would have been redundant and surely not be as effective as the way Callie Khouri originally conceived it.

So be careful when you use a flashback.

Some films incorporate the flashback as a major part of the story; they use it to *"bookend"* their main story line, meaning they open the script with an incident or event, and then flashback to the actual story, then end it in present time again.

A few films that do this well are: *The Bridges of Madison County*, *Sunset Boulevard*, *Annie Hall*, and *Citizen Kane*. And, of course, *Pulp Fiction*.

Should you decide to use a flashback, make sure it doesn't intrude upon the flow of the action, or get in the way of the story, or draw too much attention to itself.

If you can say it, maybe you don't have to show it after all.

Part IV

PROBLEMS OF STRUCTURE

The Problem Sheet

SCENEUS INTERRUPTUS

- THE SCENE HAS NO DRAMATIC PAY-OFF

- THE ACTION IS INCOMPLETE; SOMETHING SEEMS TO BE MISSING

- THE STORY LINE GETS LOST

- THE DRAMATIC NEED OF THE MAIN CHARACTER IS UNCLEAR

- THE SCENE IS LOADED WITH TOO MUCH EXPLANATION

- DIALOGUE IS TOO DIRECT, TOO MELODRAMATIC

- THERE ARE TOO MANY CHARACTERS

- THE CHARACTERS ARE NOT TRUE TO THE EMOTIONAL REALITY OF THE SCENE

- THE TEMPO OF SCENE IS TOO SLOW OR TOO FAST

17

Sceneus Interruptus

  Structure is the foundation of screenwriting. The word itself means "to build, or put together," so when you start structuring your script, you're building and putting scenes, sequences, and acts together into a unified whole with a definite beginning, middle, and end, though not necessarily in that order. Structure can be either linear or nonlinear, depending on the needs of your story.

  The second definition of *structure*, as it relates to screenwriting, is "the relationship between the parts and the whole." Since you have to build, or put together, various parts of the screenplay, whether a scene, or the individual shots that comprise the scene, or the separate scenes that make up a sequence, or the necessary character elements you need to integrate into the narrative line, the insertion of a flashback or flashforward structure becomes the glue that holds everything together. It's like gravity, the force that sustains the entire physical universe.

  When you read and analyze a good screenplay it's like seeing bits and pieces of film joined together to create a series of moving images, the story told in pictures. A clock ticking, a car moving slowly down a crowded city street, a woman peering out a window, the sound of a baby crying or a dog barking, the car pulling into a parking space, all these bits and pieces of little pictures can be joined together to create a tense and suspense-filled sequence that has the reader, or audience, on the edge of their collective seats. That's what film is all about, building, or putting together, these little bits and pieces of images that are joined together to create an organic story line. Remember the definition of a screenplay: "a story told with pictures, in dialogue and description, and placed within the context of dramatic structure."

When we approach the dynamics of *Problem Solving* in screenwriting, all the solutions, to whatever the problem, will utilize *Structure*. That's because when you fix, or correct, a particular problem, you have to reconstruct, or rebuild, the elements, or content, that make up the narrative line. A story is a *whole* made up of specific *parts:* the action, the characters, the locations, sets, scenes, sequences, Acts, Plot Points, music, effects, and so on, all these *parts* go into the craft of building and putting together a story. It's the understanding of this relationship between the *parts* that make up the story, the *whole,* which allows you to approach Problem Solving from the confidence and security that you know what you're doing.

Yes, structure *is* the foundation of screenwriting, and it's also an essential part of the problem-solving process. If you have a scene that doesn't play well, for whatever reason, and you define it as a problem of *Plot, Character,* or *Structure,* you're going to have to go back and create new incidents, episodes, or events to blend into the material, and that's going to create a new mix. Anything you add is going to have to be restructured and rebuilt; as Newton's Third Law of Motion states, "For every action there's an equal and opposite reaction." For every cause there is an effect, and if you've not fleshed out a particular scene to the necessary degree, you're going to have to go back into that material and change a few things. And whatever you change, you're going to have to restructure. It's as simple as that.

So what kind of problems are you dealing with within the context of *Structure*?

First, you have the context of story. Is your story focused, clear, and precise, or does it seem to wander around trying to find its line of action? Even the most complicated script, like *The Usual Suspects,* is clear and concise, at least from the writer's point of view. Does your story seem to skirt on the edge of things and not go deeply enough in terms of action and character? Does it appear that your scenes have no dramatic payoff? Do your characters seem to be wandering around searching for their dramatic need?

All these are symptoms of something that's not quite right with your structure. It could be the scenes are too short, or not paid off, or the story line seems to wander around with no sense of development, which, remember, is defined as "a line of direction." In short, with a problem of *Structure*, something seems to be missing.

I believe that good structure in a screenplay should not be seen. Good structure should simply disappear into the content of the story line. When I first started developing my concepts of structure, I would go to a movie, watch and notebook in hand, and dutifully time the individual Plot Points, because I wanted to clarify and define screenplay form. Form, not formula. Looking back on it now, I see I was trying to locate and define the building blocks of the screenplay, and what I discovered was that structure was like the DNA of screenwriting.

When I read a screenplay now, or see a film, I really don't pay too much attention to structure; I just let the material wash over me. If the script or film doesn't feel right, if there seems to be some kind of problem, then I'll go into the material and analyze it structurally. I can recognize structure by the particular beats in the story line. I've always maintained that the screenwriter's job is to keep the reader turning pages, so if I find myself becoming bogged down in the reading experience, that's a signal there may be something wrong structurally. If I can't follow the story line, if it wanders around, or something seems to be missing, or if too much is happening, or there are too many characters, or nothing seems to be paid off, that's a symptom that something's wrong; that's when I'll start breaking it down into its component parts.

Good structure alone does not make a good screenplay. That's simply a fact of life that everyone has to remember. So many times people will tell me they've written a screenplay "just the way you say it should be done," and immediately I get suspicious. By the same token the opposite is also true: you can't have a good screenplay without good structure. Structure is only the foundation, the start point, not the be-all and end-all. Characters, action, dynamic visuals, and strong situations are only some of the things that make up a good screenplay. So many times people ask me for examples of movies that don't have a good structure and I really can't give too many examples. That's because a film without good structure doesn't hold up. It wanders, is slow to develop, and the only thing that can save it is the dimension of its characters. The audience perceives this, so the film only has a run of a few weeks and then disappears deep into the bowels of the film graveyard.

The definition of structure, remember, is *to build*, or *to put something together*, and as so often happens, when you correct one problem in a screenplay it always affects something else, so you have to add elements, or remove elements, to make it work. That means building, or putting together, a new scene or sequence.

So what we'll try to do in this section is uncover various problems that exist as a result of structure, and which can be solved by restructuring the material. And, at the risk of repeating myself again, no matter what the problem, you're going to have to restructure the material, whether it's a problem of *Plot*, *Character*, or *Structure*. In the arena of Problem Solving, *Structure* is an integral part of every solution.

One of the problems I've become aware of in my teaching experience is that writers will sometimes write key scenes, either action or dialogue, which are not paid off; the scenes usually end too early. In a dramatic scene, for example, the screenwriter will cut to the next scene before the purpose of that particular scene is realized. And then, when I'm reading the material, I get the feeling something's missing; the action feels incomplete. It's so important—essential—to determine the purpose of the scene in order to dramatically realize the intention of that scene.

A few years ago I was commissioned to read and analyze a screenplay for a producer/writer. It was an action-thriller set in the Cayman Islands, a marvelous location for this kind of film. The story, about a photographer who accidentally stumbles into a situation where he becomes a target for murder, was interesting and well written. There were good action sequences and the script was well structured.

But as I was reading the screenplay, I kept getting lost in the story line. I was confused and so many characters were pulled into the narrative line, I didn't know who the main character was and what the whole thing was about.

Even though the premise was good, with solid visuals and locations, good action sequences, and interesting characters, somehow I got the feeling that something was missing, something just wasn't right. I couldn't pinpoint the problem, so I started examining it more closely. As I read through the screenplay again, I saw that many of the key scenes were not complete, that the action had stopped before the dramatic requirements of the scenes had been satisfied. In the middle of a confrontation scene, for example, the writer would cut away to another scene, or to another character, and this altered the focus of the story line. I had the impression that something was definitely missing.

With that in mind, I went back and looked at the material again, and saw that this particular trait had become a tendency on the part of the writer. In scene after scene, a scene or situation would be set up, and then before the purpose of the scene was realized, he left the scene; the scene was not really paid off. So while the idea of the scene had been planted, it had never come to fruition, and therefore the action and story line seemed hazy and uncertain.

Now, I had been aware of this phenomenon before, but I never had a name for it. But this was such a clear example of the problem that I labeled it *Sceneus Interruptus.* Leaving the scene too early simply means the *purpose of the scene is unsatisfied, unfulfilled.* It does not accomplish its dramatic function and therefore leaves a gaping hole in the action. And when that happens, something is definitely missing.

This particular problem could be approached from either *Character* or *Plot*, of course, but I chose to put it under the heading of *Structure* because if you leave the scene too early, you've got to add components back into the material in order to reconstruct the unit of dramatic action. That's how you build tension and pacing, by going into the elements of the material and finding ways of expanding it visually. That's why when you see a shot of a key being placed in a lock, or thread being stitched into a piece of fabric, or a bullet placed into the chamber of a gun, it expands the visual tension of the scene. That's why film is such an art form where time can be stretched or condensed and becomes larger than life. Pacing is always related to *Structure*. If there aren't enough elements in the scene to hold it together, the chances are it will bog down and not go anywhere. The tension will be dissipated. Conversely, if you have too many elements in the scene, the pacing will also be off, and the material will have a slow, wandering feel to it. Again, no tension.

In the particular screenplay I had been asked to read, there is a series of short scenes that I'm going to use as an example to illustrate what I'm talking about in terms of *Sceneus Interruptus*. Now I know the material I'm using is totally out of context, and therefore may not be as illustrative as I would like it to be. But I'm going to take a shot at it anyway.

The main character, DeFoe, a professional photographer, had been commissioned by the local museum to photograph some ancient artifacts, and a few days later these treasures are stolen and several people are killed. He becomes involved when his studio is ransacked and his assistant killed. In this particular section of the screenplay (it occurs in the Second Half of Act II), one of the major characters, the policeman Gary, is on the hunt, tracking down the first major lead. Gary has uncovered a clue, a utility vehicle a witness claims he had seen leaving the museum around the time the cime was committed.

The owner of the vehicle has been tracked through the Motor Vehicles Department to a man named Helo, and we know that he is definitely involved in the crime. Gary is snooping around, trying to find out if Helo is really the owner of the vehicle, so he inquires at a neighbor's apartment hoping to establish that fact. That's where we'll start:

INT. HELO'S APARTMENT BUILDING—AFTER-NOON

Gary makes his way down the long, dark, and dingy corridor, stops in front of Apartment 207. Carefully, he scans the area, ready for anything. He knocks on the door.

We HEAR a muffled voice inside, then the door swings open and a YOUNG WOMAN, obviously expecting someone else, stands in the doorway of her apartment, her smile fading when she sees Gary.

> **GARY**
> Excuse me, but I have a terrible
> confession to make. I scraped the white
> truck that's parked in the garage, and
> I'm trying to find the owner. Is that your
> truck? It's only a scratch, but I'd like to
> settle things without going through the
> insurance company.

The woman looks at him for a moment, weighing his words.

WOMAN

You a cop?

Then she slams the door in his face. Gary stands for a moment, breathing deeply, then moves to the next door, Helo's apartment. He adjusts his gun, then rings the bell.

CUT TO:

EXT. LINSEY'S HOUSE—DAWN

Linsey (the man responsible for the crime) stares out the window, his back to a woman, Marta, who smokes casually and idly leafs through a fashion magazine.

CUT TO:

INT. STAIRWELL, BED AND BREAKFAST—DAY

A WAITER carries a breakfast tray up the curved, polished wood stairwell and limps down the long corridor bathed in early morning sunshine. He stops at a door and knocks loudly.

CUT TO:

INT. BED AND BREAKFAST—DAY

CARRIE, lying in bed, opens her eyes and looks around for DeFoe (the main character), but the bed is empty. There are photographs spread haphazardly all over the floor.

CUT TO:

INT. HELO'S FLAT—DAY

Helo stands in the doorway, defiant, belligerent, refusing to look directly at Gary.

GARY

Are you telling me you don't know
anything about that truck. . . . It is
yours, isn't it?''

And then the writer cuts to yet another scene which is
totally unrelated to anything that has been seen or alluded to
so far.

Now, at first glance it may appear that nothing is really
"wrong" here, that whatever problem there is might be fixed
by simply adding some dialogue or opening up the scenes
visually. But if you take the context of the story line into
account, you'll see there's really no narrative thread. The
writer cuts away from the scene before the purpose of the
scene is established. And that's what made me so uncomfortable reading it. This little scene where Gary confronts Helo is
way too thin, and really doesn't say anything that will move
the story forward or reveal information about the character.
Granted, the whole section is taken out of context, but it's
pretty clear that more has to be added, not only from the story
line's point of view, but also from the character's perspective.
Helo is Gary's first link to the crime, so we must see these two
men warily circling each other before they confront each
other. As you can see, the writer cuts away from every scene
before anything significant happens. Because the purpose of
the scene has not been satisfied (establishing a link between
Helo and the crime), cutting away too soon simply dissipates
the action. Whatever tension there might have been has simply vanished.

The result of *Sceneus Interruptus* can lead to serious problems in the screenplay. Once the tendency of cutting away
before the purpose is established, chances are it's going to be

reflected in a variety of scenes, and that means it's going to influence the entire story line.

That's what happens here in this short section. The action seems disjointed and listless, the natural transitions are forced and contrived, and the action moves along like a car with a flat tire. For the reader, concentration is lost, the interest in the story line wanes, and the script is usually shelved before it's been completely read.

I think the most difficult thing about this problem is simply recognizing it. So many times we read and reread the material looking for ways to improve it, and we have a hard time seeing that a scene ends too early.

Once you become aware that the problem exists, you can fix it. And the way to do that is to break every scene down and restructure it into a beginning, middle, and end. First, what's the purpose of the scene? What's it doing there? What does the character want to win, gain, get, or achieve during the course of the scene? In what way does this scene relate to the character's dramatic need in the screenplay? Where has the character come from, and where is he/she going after the scene is finished? These questions must be addressed and resolved before the scene begins.

If you don't know what's going on during the scene, who does? That means knowing what the thoughts, feelings, and emotions of your character are, and keeping them clearly in mind as the scene plays out.

How do you know when you've satisfied the requirements of the scene? There's no real way of knowing that, of course, except that each scene becomes a link in the chain of dramatic action. Each scene, as mentioned, is like a living cell; it should contain everything within it, either to move the story forward or to reveal information about the character.

Just like the DNA molecule in living cells. Every scene serves a particular function, and it's up to you, the screenwriter, to know or determine what that function is. What is its purpose? If you don't know what it is, or what it does, or why it's there, you'll probably have to drop it. Just cut it. The chances are it doesn't belong in the screenplay. You have to be ruthless when you're writing a screenplay, especially when you're trying to solve a problem. Screenwriters all over the world have the same complaint; they always have to cut what they think are their best scenes, their best writing, out of the scripts.

To solve the problems of *Sceneus Interruptus*, start by rethinking the parameters of the scene. What are the character's thoughts, feelings, or emotions when the scene begins? Where is he or she coming from, and what is the emotional reality working on the character? Does your character have a sore throat and does he seem to be cold? Has he/she just managed to escape from a would-be attacker? Is he/she preparing for a big showdown, or confrontation scene? So, define the emotional forces working on your character when the scene begins.

The next step is to find out what elements you have to work with within the scene. Where does it take place? What time of the day or night? Is there anything within the setting of the scene that you can use to your advantage, dramatically? The weather, a crowded art gallery, a crowded restaurant, a market, or on the street? Or is it late at night, where the silence and emptiness of the location seem to create their own ambience? Once you establish the environmental elements, you can break the scene down into beginning, middle, and end.

On a separate piece of paper, break down the scene. To start, where does your character come from before the scene begins? Write it down. If the scene takes place in a library, for example, your character may have come from the office, or maybe an exercise class; if the latter, then it means that he will have to dress, leave the area, walk to the subway or car, ride or drive to the destination, park, get out, walk up the steps, and enter the lobby. That's the beginning. And remember conflict. Maybe something happens on the way to the scene that affects the character, so you might want to create a little back story to the scene.

Then, find a way to dramatize the purpose of the scene. Why is the character at the library? To find a certain book, do some research on the Internet, or have a clandestine meeting?

Isolate the flow of events that make up the middle of the scene. The character arrives, walks into the lobby, searches for someone or something, then finds the person or book he or she is looking for, finds a corner table to sit down at, and then the purpose of the scene begins to unfold. What's the nature of the dialogue? Is it direct, for exposition, so the story can move forward? Or is there a subtext to the dialogue, a hidden meaning, or an indirect threat? Is this a scene that reveals something about the character, that gives us some insight into the emotional or physical landscape of the character? It doesn't have to be much. In *Courage Under Fire* we can tell what Colonel Serling is thinking or feeling when he pulls out a bottle of Scotch and takes a long pull. We don't need any more explanation than that.

Then, the end. The character(s) get up, leave the library, and then where do they go or what do they do? Do you follow the main character, or the other person? In *Pulp Fiction* the interesting thing about the bar scene in the beginning where Vinnie (Travolta) meets Butch (Willis) is that we could have followed the Butch character just as easily we do Vinnie on his "date" with Mia Wallace (Uma Thurman). This is all creative choice. Does anything happen on the way to the next scene? How much time elapses between the scene in the library and the next scene?

Look it over. Have you satisfied the purpose of the scene? That is, does it contain the correct information, either visually, or emotionally, or physically, or through the dialogue, to be complete within itself, or to act as a link to another scene? As we'll see in Chapter 19, it's always better to enter the scene late and get out early, but the only way you can really do that is if you are totally clear on what each beat or movement is, within the body of the scene.

Is there enough conflict within the scene? Are the characters' points of view clear, concentrated, and focused? That's something you have to be clear about yourself. That's your homework, and nobody can do it but you.

If you're not clear about the relationship between the main character and the person he or she is meeting in the library, then write a short, free-association essay of two or three pages about their relationship. When did they first meet, and where? What happened? What you're really trying to do is to get enough information so you can make sure your scene works and is totally effective for the purpose it serves in the screenplay.

When you complete the necessary preparation, then do your breakdown of beginning, middle, and end, and then select bits and pieces from each category to set up and then pay off the scene. For example, we could start with a shot of the office clock, followed by a shot of the character looking and thinking, then cut to him or her riding in the subway, or driving, then entering the lobby of the library, searching for the other character, their meeting, and then pay it off with a shot of the character leaving, and walking down the steps, or simply go into a transition. Clean, lean, and tight.

In this way you know that the purpose of the scene is satisfied, complete unto itself, providing as well a necessary link in the chain of dramatic action, so the story can move forward with concise skill and visual continuity.

The Problem Sheet

SET-UPS AND PAY-OFFS

- INCIDENTS AND CHARACTERS ARE NOT PAID OFF

- SCENES LACK DIRECTION (A LINE OF DEVELOPMENT)

- NO TRANSITIONS BETWEEN SCENES

- SCENES ARE TOO LONG AND TOO EXPOSITORY

- TEMPO IS TOO SLOW

- TOO MUCH OR NOT ENOUGH INFORMATION IS BEING REVEALED

- TOO MANY PLOT TWISTS, TURNS, AND CONTRIVANCES

- STORY LINE SEEMS UNSTRUCTURED, WITH TOO MUCH, OR NOT ENOUGH, ACTION

- THE CHARACTER'S CONFLICT IS TOO INTERNAL

18

Set-Ups and Pay-offs

In the first few pages of *Thelma & Louise*, Thelma is "packing," literally throwing stuff into a suitcase for their weekend excursion to the mountains, and the last thing she does is open the nightstand drawer next to the bed, and "we see a gun, one Darryl bought her for protection. It is unloaded, but there is a box of bullets. She picks up the gun like it's a rat by the tail and puts it in her purse . . ."

This little scene, more like a mention, doesn't seem like much at the time, just part of her ditzy character, like eating a frozen candy bar for breakfast one bite at a time. Later, when Thelma and Louise are driving toward their anticipated weekend, Thelma hands the gun to Louise, saying, "You take care of this." Louise is shocked: "What in the hell did you bring that for?" "Oh, you know . . ." Thelma replies. "In case there's any crazy psycho killers on the loose," and they both laugh at her outrageous behavior. Louise tells her to "put it in my purse."

In reality, this little bit seems like a "throwaway," something to shed light on the character, nothing that's really too important. It's only later, when Harlan is in the parking lot, forcing himself on Thelma, that the gun comes into play. Louise takes it out of her purse, orders him to stop, which he does reluctantly, and when he exchanges words with her, she loses it and blows him away.

This gun is integral to the plot of the screenplay. If Thelma had not taken the gun with her, had not given it to Louise, Harlan would not have been killed, they would not become fugitives from the law, and the whole story wouldn't have happened; in short, if there were no gun there wouldn't have been any *Thelma & Louise.*

Setting up some of the various story elements of the screenplays is essential to the art of Problem Solving. Whether a particular element, an object or an event, deals with setting up the story, setting up a character, or character trait, understanding when and when not to establish a story point is the difference between a script that works and one that does not.

The setting up of these story elements often becomes the "glue" that holds everything together, which is why it's a problem of *Structure,* not *Plot* or *Character.* If it ain't on the page, it ain't on the stage is the old Hollywood expression, and knowing when to set something up and then pay it off is fundamental to the craft of screenwriting.

Different things must be set up, then incorporated into the story line—that's one of the principal rules of all writing. One of the most important elements is setting up the *dramatic premise* of the screenplay; that is, *what the story is about.* The Set-Up also refers to setting up the first ten pages of the screenplay, establishing the inciting incident, as well as providing enough exposition to move the story forward. Setting up these elements gives texture and direction, the natural line of development, to the narrative.

Characters also have to be set up, along with their characteristics and manners of behavior. Character aspects serve a variety of dramatic functions, like Louise knowing how to handle a gun. What happened to her in Texas when she was growing up, the *Circle of Being*, is a character element that is essential to know. As mentioned earlier, it was Louise, the young girl raped in Texas, who really pulled the trigger, not the Louise of the present.

If certain elements of character are set up, then they have to be paid off. In *The Shawshank Redemption*, Andy Dufresne had been a respectable banker in a Portland, Maine, bank, before being convicted of his wife's murder, so he knows enough about the *system* to create a fictitious identity, to establish a phony driver's license, birth certificate, and passport as well as duplicate a set of account books. So we believe he could take the warden's money—which he has laundered and deposited in banks all over the Portland, Maine, area—to Mexico. "On the outside," he says to Red, "I was an honest man. I had to come to prison to learn how to be a crook." And that information, which had been set up early in the screenplay, was not finally paid off until the end of the Second Act. So it really doesn't matter where the story point is paid off, as long as it's set up properly, whether it's related to the character or the plot.

There are other elements that need to be set up in a screenplay, specific objects, for example, like the gun in *Thelma & Louise*, or the rock hammer in *The Shawshank Redemption*. These particular objects are essential to the story line, so they need to be planted in the screenplay at different points within the landscape of the story. In *The Shawshank Redemption* we have seen the warden giving Andy clothes to take to the prison laundry, and shoes to shine, so when he gives Andy his clothes and shoes on the night he makes his escape, it's totally believable, meaning it's paid off. The "willing suspension of disbelief" has been set up and we buy it. It's good writing.

So understanding how to set up characters, situations, and objects in a screenplay and then paying them off is necessary to the Problem-Solving process.

This was something I had to learn in my own screenwriting experience. When I first started writing screenplays, I didn't know anything. I didn't know what a screenplay was, I didn't know what it meant to tell a story with pictures, I had no idea about structure or building a story, and didn't know anything about setting up a story or situation, or paying it off, for that matter. Though I had been an English major at UC Berkeley, as well as a published film and book reviewer, I still didn't have the foggiest notion about the nature and craft of screenwriting.

When I began experimenting with the screenplay form, I understood I had to learn it, literally, from the ground up. Which meant I had to teach myself how to write a screenplay. There were no books or anything about it, and the only thing I had at my disposal was Lajos Egri's great book *The Art of Dramatic Writing*, written in the forties about the craft of playwriting. So I did the only thing I could do: I got hold of some screenplays from the two filmmakers I admired the most and started reading and rereading the material.

These were really my mentors in the art and craft of screenwriting. I have mentioned Jean Renoir's contribution to my understanding of film education in both *Screenplay* and *The Screenwriter's Workbook*. But I consider two writer-directors to have been my teachers, and both were masters of the cinema. One of them was the great Sam Peckinpah (*The Wild Bunch*, *Pat Garrett and Billy the Kid*, and *The Ballad of Cable*

Hogue, to name just a few). I was so impressed with Peckinpah's *Ride the High Country* that I wrote a piece for the magazine *Film Quarterly* on it. A few years later I had the great good fortune of being with Sam when he was actually writing *The Wild Bunch*, and we spent many an afternoon in Malibu talking about the West from Peckinpah's point of view. It was quite an extraordinary time in my life. Peckinpah's style, his mastery of storytelling, was an incredible education in the art of screenwriting. Especially the way he introduced and set up certain story points.

The other filmmaker I studied was the magnificent, revolutionary, and influential Michelangelo Antonioni. The Italian director is a master of setting up and weaving emotional attitudes and characterizations throughout his films. I was so impressed and inspired when I saw *La Notte (The Night)*, that I literally began my writing career with it, and thus entered the world of contemporary film. *La Notte* is masterful study about the relationship and values of a well-to-do Italian couple. The way Antonioni sets up his characters, his mastery of the situation, the visual expressions of behavior, were revolutionary in terms of film, and when you see any of his films today, they stand firmly on the timeless pedestal of great film art. During the last few years I've had the privilege of getting to know Antonioni (he's the only director I address as Maestro), and I'm as much in awe of him today as I ever was. The way he sets up an emotional situation in just a few visual strokes is phenomenal.

These filmmakers taught me everything. And, as mentioned, I was so struck with Peckinpah's *Ride the High Country* that I decided that this was what great screenwriting was all about. So when I managed to get hold of the script of *Major Dundee* (written by Peckinpah with Oscar Saul), I think I must have read it at least a hundred times, analyzing it, taking it apart, memorizing it scene by scene, action by action, character by character, trying to understand what made it tick and what made it work so successfully. It was a wonderful education.

The script, like so many of Peckinpah's films, was a Western (he loved the theme of *"unchanged men in a changing time,"* which he incorporated in almost every film he did), and takes place right after the Civil War. The story concerns an obsessed renegade Union officer, Charlton Heston, who refuses to accept the peace between the North and South even though the war is over. A major in the Confederate army, he fled to Mexico rather than accept the peace treaty. He's determined to fight his own war. In this case he breaks a group of misfits out of prison and together they hunt the band of Apaches responsible for the slaughter that opens the screenplay.

The script opens at a ranch on the frontier on Halloween. The men, women, and children are preparing for the large celebration and it's a joyous and festive time, with the children playing "cowboys and Indians" in makeshift holiday masks and warpaint, as the grown-ups dance and enjoy themselves getting ready for the evening's feast.

But as the children play their games, we suddenly start cross-cutting between the costumed children and a band of renegade Apaches creeping toward the ranch house in what will eventually turn into a bloody massacre. The fierceness of their faces, emblazoned in war paint, contrasted with the children's decorated faces, and surrounded with the festive music of the fiddles playing and the people dancing, is as visually striking as it is terrifying. When the massacre begins, the laughs and squeals of the children are interwoven with the war cries of the attacking Apaches, resulting in a truly memorable sequence.

The opening is a remarkable example of the power and magic of film. (Unfortunately, because of budgetary problems, the studio brutally recut the film. Peckinpah wanted to take his name off it, but the studio prevailed.) It is this particular incident, the inciting incident, that sets up the entire film, and the story line is a reaction to this event, tracing the obsession of the renegade Union officer, Major Dundee (Heston), who relentlessly tracks down the Apaches, hoping to avenge the massacre of the homesteaders.

The script of *Major Dundee* is a wonderful illustration of how to set up the dramatic premise of the story line. Sometimes, going back over the material you've written, you may find a scene or a sequence that seems unclear, or maybe you think the dialogue needs to be sharpened, or another scene added to clarify the narrative or define the character, and many times the problem can be solved by making sure that certain story elements have been set up appropriately. Setting up necessary story elements, then paying them off, allows you to keep the story moving forward. No moments are too small or too subtle to be set up. If these points are not set up appropriately, the reader will sometimes shift his or her focus away from the story. And this, of course, results in a "problem."

There are a several good examples of how you set things up in order to pay them off later. If you do want to set something up, think of it as a *"noun"*; you're going to be setting up a *"person, place, or thing,"* either a character, or a situation, or an object. As mentioned, *Thelma & Louise* is a great example: the gun Thelma puts into her purse at the beginning of the film is paid off at Plot Point I when Harlan is shot in the parking lot. In that case it was setting up an object, or "thing." Setting up her character, in order to expand the situation, is revealed later when Louise was raped in Texas. As a matter of fact, when you read the screenplay of this film, everything is carefully set up from the very beginning; Louise's relationship with her boyfriend, Jimmy, actually the back story that results in the two women going to the mountains for the weekend; and tracing the emotional arc of Thelma's growth from being locked in her marriage with Darryl in the opening allows her to grow into a free-thinking, independent woman.

When and where to set up things in a scene, sequence, or act, and when, where, and how to pay them off, means knowing your story and characters well. If you don't know the basic and essential elements of your story line, or if you're vague and unclear about the progression of events, or the character's arc, this lack of information, this lack of preparation, will often create problems in the screenplay. This is really what writing's all about, asking yourself the right questions so you can reach levels that keep the story moving forward with depth and dimension. It creates a framework of universality around your work. This is your responsibility as writer; if you don't know what's going on in your story, then who does?

There are times in the screenplay when a particular piece of information, or a physical item, is set up in one scene, and then paid off in the very next. Or the information or object can be paid off several scenes later, or even later than that, as is the case in *The Shawshank Redemption* and *Crimson Tide*.

In *Shawshank*, at Plot Point I, Andy Dufresne approaches Red for the first time and asks if he can get him a rock hammer. Red asks some questions about it, and through Andy's answers we begin to see and understand a little bit about his character; on the outside, before he was sent to prison, he was a "rock hound." That, of course, sets up an important piece of information we need to know, that will be paid off at the end of Act II. Later, we see the hammer being "delivered," and then, as Act II unfolds, the rock hammer, and rock cloths, are only referred to, and shown in a few shots. After we've seen the hammer a few times, it's something we simply take for granted. Only at Plot Point II is the rock hammer really paid off and we "see," through the flashback, how Andy escaped from prison. Suddenly, all those little scenes and references make a lot of sense.

What happens when you don't set up these story points properly, or pay them off appropriately? You'll notice that the story line appears to lose momentum and seems to wander around in search of itself. When I'm reading a script and I feel my focus shifting and my interest waning, I start looking for what's going on, the "through line" of the story. If I don't find it, if I have to keep looking for what the story's about, that's an indication that something's missing; either a particular story point or a character or an object needs to be set up, or accentuated more.

The symptoms of a failure to set things up properly are pretty obvious, and different for every screenplay, of course, but they all share some similar traits; take a look at the *Problem Sheet*, and you'll see that problems of this nature seem to make the material *soft,* so it might seem that there's a lack of conflict, or the story line has no focus and wanders around looking for direction, insight, and clarity. Sometimes various story points will be introduced and then left hanging and unresolved. As you're rereading the material, you'll probably find yourself asking, "What happened to this or that point?"

or "What's this story really about?" so the action appears to be washed out and the story unfolds on a single narrative line without any dimension, tension, or suspense.

It doesn't work. Things that are set up have to be paid off. Structure, as we've seen, is the relationship between the parts and the whole, and each part is directly related to the whole, so if you set something up, whether it's a story point, or situation, or a particular object, it has to be paid off. Otherwise, whatever you've set up doesn't make any sense. Can you imagine a film like *The English Patient* (Anthony Minghella) working as well as it did without the principal issues of the story line in relationship to the characters having been set up?

If you feel there's a problem because something has not been set up properly, or paid off, go back into the material and determine where you set it up, and then how it's paid off. Whether it helped to set up the story's premise, or a particular plot element, find out the specific location where you first introduced it, then how you did it, and whether through a visual image or in an exchange of dialogue.

We can learn so much from *The Shawshank Redemption* in terms of setting up the dramatic premise and the inciting incident. As mentioned earlier, the opening sequence incorporates three threads of dramatic action; one, Andy Dufresne is sitting outside in his car drinking, when he takes the gun out of his glove compartment as we witness his wife and her lover in the house wrapped in an erotic embrace; two, we see him on trial being cross-examined by the prosecutor for the murder of his wife and her lover; and, and three, the judge sentences him to two life terms back to back, and then we cut to the prison, where we're introduced to Red.

That's the first ten pages of the screenplay. In the second

ten pages he enters prison and we see things through his eyes; this audience-character bond allows us to identify with him and what he's going through. Audience and character should always be united by the dramatic action; the audience learns as the character learns what's going on.

At this point in the story I really didn't know whether Andy Dufresne was guilty or innocent. But as the story line unfolded, it really didn't matter. At Plot Point I, the first moment he approaches Red to request the rock hammer, he learns the "truth"; in prison, everybody's innocent, so as I was watching the film, it never really occurred to me to wonder whether he was innocent or guilty. That wasn't the story; the story was about his relationship with Red and how he adapts to life inside prison. It's only later, at Pinch II, when Tommy tells him that a former cell mate had confessed to committing the murder of his wife and lover, that we understand Andy is really innocent. And while this is set up within the first ten pages of the screenplay, Andy's actual guilt or innocence is not paid off until almost the end of Act II.

So what's your story about? Have you set it up properly in the first ten pages? If you feel there's a problem in setting up something, go back into the material and see what it is that you've failed to establish. What needs to be set up? Is it essential to the story? Is it a story point within the script, or a "thing," like the gun in *Thelma & Louise*, or the rock hammer in *Shawshank*? Or maybe it's an integral part of the character that needs to be set up. Or maybe it's answering the question of what happened and why the plane is shot down and crashes at the beginning of *The English Patient*. It's up to you as the writer to clarify and define what it is that needs to be set up, and then go back into the script and determine the best way to solve that particular problem.

In *Crimson Tide* the story is set up from the opening scene of the screenplay. A news reporter is shown at sea on an aircraft carrier and he explains, with the help of actual newsreel footage, that a band of Russian rebels have taken over the government and are threatening to launch a nuclear attack against the U.S. In response, the nuclear sub *Alabama* is ordered to sea, and Act I is devoted to setting up the Russian threat, introducing and setting up the Denzel Washington character—Hunter, the XO—and the Gene Hackman character—Ramsey, the captain of the vessel—and preparing the sub for its mission. At Plot Point I the sub casts off and begins its underwater mission.

That basically sets up the story. But there's another dimension here, and that's the setting up of the characters. I've already mentioned Captain Ramsey's dog, and how the little Jack Russell terrier goes everywhere with him. It's a wonderful touch. But the Hunter character is somewhat different. First of all, we learn that he spent a year at Harvard, which makes him "suspicious" in the eyes of Ramsey; he's an "intellectual," and that sets up a situation that might create problems with Ramsey's journeyman ethics as the captain of the nuclear sub. More important, however, is when Ramsey asks Hunter about his likes or hobbies, and Hunter replies that he rides horses. "What's the best horse you've ever ridden?" Ramsey asks. "Arabian," Hunter replies. That impresses Ramsey. Just a little exchange, and, at first glance it could easily be a throwaway line, something to just illuminate the difference in character.

But that line about the horses is introduced where it is so it can help set up the clash between the two characters that explodes at Mid-Point; because the radio has been damaged when the emergency action message has been cut off before it is complete.

The First Half of Act II deals with expanding the characters and clarifying their points of view. Drama is conflict, remember, so one of the first scenes in this unit of dramatic action shows the officers sitting at their first meal, in a scene said to have been written by Robert Towne. Hunter is the new member of the crew, so the captain, Ramsey, is trying to find out what his philosophy of war is, and what kind of "man" his new XO is, what he believes in. The difference between "you and me," Ramsey explains, is that when "I was taught, things were simpler in a war situation; I was taught how to push a button and told when to do it." It's not a question of strategy, he states, but simply a matter of military and political procedure. And he quotes von Clausewitz. He pauses for a moment, then continues his observation: it's different now, he says; the brass, meaning the Pentagon, want you (referring to Hunter) to know "why you're doing it." The Denzel Washington character nods in agreement, then responds "that in a nuclear world the true enemy can't be destroyed, because the real enemy is war itself."

This little dialogue exchange succinctly summarizes the differences in their philosophies of war. It also shows us the differences in their points of view, because it is this conflict that fuels the entire film. If the differences in their points of view had not been set up and established, the entire story would fail to work; there would be no conflict, no mutiny attempt, no story, and the *Alabama* would just cruise the waters until the situation in Russia resolved itself. Basically, their differing points of view would be like two parallel lines moving toward infinity without ever connecting. That's not how you build and structure a screenplay.

Some screenwriters might argue that the scene is too direct, too obvious, and they would either omit it or write it in a more subtle way. But some scenes in a screenplay have to be written directly, no matter how obvious, or expository, they are, and this happens to be one of them. It is set up to be paid off later so it can follow the natural law of cause and effect, action and reaction. If the essential seed of the screenplay is planted appropriately, in the right place and at the right time, it can blossom into a full-grown narrative, replete with the structural and character dimension.

It's all in how you set it up. Establishing Hunter's interest in riding horses in the very beginning, the third scene of the screenplay to be exact, sets us up for what follows. When the conflict between their characters explodes at Mid-Point, Ramsey insists they follow the orders received to launch ten nuclear missiles against Russia rather than wait for the confirmation of the incomplete second emergency action message received. This results in Hunter's taking over the sub and placing Ramsey under arrest.

Later, when a small group of men regain control of the *Alabama* for Ramsey the radio is almost repaired. Ramsey gives Hunter three minutes for the radio to be fixed so the message can be completed; if, at the end of three minutes, the message is not received, he's going to launch the missiles as ordered.

So begins a long three-minute wait. It's an ideal moment for tension and suspense. In the scene, which it is said that Quentin Tarantino wrote, Ramsey asks Hunter if he knows about the Lipizzaner stallions. They're all white, he adds, almost as an afterthought. Hunter nods, yes, he knows about them. Again, this kind of dialogue emphasizes their character differences; it illuminates that one of them is "right," and one of them is "wrong." When the EAM message is finally received, it orders the *Alabama* to cancel the previous orders of the nuclear missile strike. Hunter has been proven "right."

This "right" and "wrong" scenario is then resolved, or paid off, in the last scene of the film, the little tag. The military tribunal assembled to weigh evidence in the case of the two men, clearly determines that both men "were right" in their actions. What they did only points up the ambiguity of the military law that was then on the books. As they stand outside the courthouse, Hunter pays off the horse scene that was set up early in the film. He tells the captain that the Lipizzaner stallions are from Spain, not Portugal, and at birth, they are black, not white. (See explanation page 332.) Another case of "being right," as it reflects the basic conflict in the film. It is a powerful statement, made more powerful in the way it is set up at the very beginning.

Crimson Tide is a very good film and it reflects the nature of the classic "tragic situation." Hegel, the nineteenth-century German philosopher, always proclaimed that the true nature of tragedy is not a conflict between "good and evil," or "right and wrong," but resides in the conflict between "good versus good," or "right versus right." Both sides of the conflict are right in the actions they pursue. And *Crimson Tide* personifies this in an exciting and entertaining presentation. It's a very good film.

The setting up and paying off of story points is integral to the art and craft of screenwriting. Every scene, every sequence, every Plot Point and story point, must be set up, established, and then, at the right moment, paid off. Nothing can be set up without later being paid off.

For every action, remember, there is an equal and opposite reaction.

The Problem Sheet

ENTER LATE AND GET OUT EARLY

- DIALOGUE IS TOO WORDY, TOO EXPLANATORY

- THE SCENES ARE TOO LONG, WITH NOT ENOUGH ACTION

- STORY LINE IS THIN AND EPISODIC

- PLOT ELEMENTS AND STORY POINTS HAVE TO BE EXPLAINED OVER AND OVER AGAIN

- THE SCRIPT IS TOO LONG

- THE STORY IS NOT VISUAL ENOUGH

- CONFLICT IS EXPRESSED THROUGH DIALOGUE, NOT ACTION

- CHARACTERS ARE REACTIVE, RATHER THAN ACTIVE

- THE SECOND ACT IS WEAK AND WAY TOO LONG

- THE WRITING IS TOO EASY, IT CAN'T BE GOOD

19

Enter Late and Get Out Early

In William Goldman's book *Adventures in the Screen Trade,* he talks about the best place to enter the scene, and to hypothetically illustrate his point he gives an example. Suppose, he says, you're writing a scene in which a reporter is interviewing a subject, and it's laid out like this: The reporter arrives at the place of the interview, the two introduce themselves to each other, get comfortable, chat for a while, and after a few moments the reporter suggests they start the interview. So he turns on the cassette recorder, pulls out his notepad, and starts asking his questions. They discuss the topic, going back and forth for a while until the reporter is satisfied and terminates the discussion. He turns off the recorder, thanks the subject, picks up his belongings and prepares to leave, says his good-bye, and walks to the door. But when he reaches the door, he suddenly stops as if struck with an afterthought, turns back to the subject, and says, "Oh, by the way. One last question . . ."

Where is the best place for the screenwriter to enter the scene? When the reporter arrives? When he turns on his recorder? At some point during the interview? At the end?

None of the above, Goldman says. Instead, he feels the best place for the screenwriter to enter the scene is when the reporter is standing at the door, on his way out, and remembers "one last question."

Every screenwriter deliberates this question, mulls it over and over, and finally, at some point, decides where to enter the scene. What's the best point to enter the scene? When I first read this in Goldman's book it always struck me as being a good rule of thumb, so when I was writing my book *Selling a Screenplay*, I thought I might give it a try just to see what happened.

I had an interview with Peter Guber scheduled, just before he took over control of Sony Pictures, so I decided to see whether Goldman's advice worked in real life as well as in the screenplay. We met in his office on a beautiful cloudy day in L.A., and I had a list of questions laid out in my notepad, and we spent an informative session together discussing what a buyer looks for when a company is considering purchasing material.

When I completed the interview and it came time to leave, I turned off the cassette recorder, got up, and put on my jacket. I walked to the door, then I paused, turned to him, and said, "Oh, by the way, one last question: Why do some movies get made and others don't?" Which had been my key question right from the beginning. He laughed, and asked why I'm wearing the jacket I'm wearing, and why is he wearing the jacket he's wearing? Still standing at the door, we started talking about the market and personal taste, but as he started getting into it and answering my question, I took off my jacket, sat back down, and turned the cassette recorder back on. Peter Guber is a pretty amazing, as well as astute, producer and we sat there for another forty-five minutes talking about why some movies get made and others don't. It was really a fascinating discussion and provided the most intriguing and insightful part of the interview with Peter Guber. And most of the chapter on producers draws upon this part of the interview and gives great insight into the moviemaking process.

I use this interview in many of my screenwriting courses as an example to help clarify and define the best point at which to enter the scene. So many times a screenwriter starts a scene and fills it with unnecessary dialogue that basically says nothing, and by the time the purpose of the scene is revealed, the scene is way too long and whatever dramatic tension should have been, or might have been there, is lost in a plethora of empty dialogue.

So, what's the best point to enter the scene? A good rule of thumb is to *"enter late and get out early."* Which means that in many scenes (depending on their purpose) it's best to enter the action at the last possible moment. I usually tell my students that you enter the scene about two lines before the purpose of the scene is revealed. In this way you only need a minimum of dialogue to state the dramatic purpose.

Now this, of course, is only a *general rule;* it doesn't apply to every scene in the screenplay, because the dramatic function of each scene is singular and unique. Some scenes have to be constructed, or built, in terms of their beginning, middle, and end, and it always depends on what information you need to communicate, either to move the story forward, or to satisfy the dramatic purpose of the particular scene. Where you enter the scene is absolutely an *individual decision,* and hopefully the scene itself will dictate the best point to enter. If you're able to see it.

The same principle applies to ending the scene. At what

point do you leave one scene so you can move into the next? The main things to remember about getting out of one scene and into the next are: First get out with a sense of tension so the reader will want to see what happens next. Second, make the transition from one scene into the next interesting, visually arresting, smooth. Remember that it's the writer's responsibility to keep the reader turning pages.

If you write a scene that is complete unto itself, it will have a definite beginning, middle, and end, and if you do that consistently, you'll end up with an episodic, or sequential, screenplay. Every scene has a definite end, a definite place to get out; you just have to find it, and it doesn't matter whether it's transitional, or deliberate (like a fade-out). Every scene should lead into the next one, like a force of nature, spring turning into summer. The connection between these units of dramatic action, whether effected by picture-to-picture, sound-to-sound, dialogue-to-dialogue, or special-effect-to-special-effect transitions, should always be pulling and guiding you from one scene into the next. The story must always move forward, from beginning to end, beginning to end.

Just look at *The English Patient*; the relationship between the two lovers is the focal point of the story, and how the love affair grows and blossoms between the Ralph Fiennes (Almásy) and Kristin Scott Thomas (Katherine) characters is always unfolding. As Fiennes is languishing on his deathbed, vividly recalling his memories, we learn what happened between them. The script itself is a distinct mosaic being pieced together by the context of their emotional relationship. So the end of the film is seen at the beginning of the film, a "bookend" device that works wonderfully.

In order to keep the tension going, and keep the reader

turning pages, enter late and get out early. That's what screenwriting is all about.

If you don't pay attention to the point at which you enter the scene, there is a possibility that your screenplay will drag and sag, or be too long, so that the sense of tension and suspense is lost, and if that happens, the chances are you'll be overwhelmed with problems of a script that is not working. This is really not too unusual. Many times I've received screenplays that are very long, well over a hundred and fifty pages, and as I go through the material, the first thing I notice is that the screenwriters have usually started their scenes too early and have had to fill them with unnecessary dialogue. You know: "How are you? Nice to see you again. Won't you sit down? What's going on?"

When and where you enter the scene is the central question as you set about structuring each particular moment of the screenplay. To do that you need to ask yourself certain questions: What is the purpose of the scene? Why is it there? Does it move the story forward? Does it reveal information about the character? Is it driven by the need for exposition, or transition? If you don't know the answers to these questions, who does?

There are many times when the scenes are too long and episodic and the writer has to rethink and create a new approach to them. What is the problem? If it's *Plot*, you have to approach it from one perspective; if *Character*, from another; and if it's a *Structural* problem, still another. The writer can approach the problem by first breaking the scene down into its component parts, *beginning, middle,* and *end,* and then spend time rethinking the elements of the scene; describing the location, what it looks like, the various aspects or dynamics of character that need to be revealed. By refocusing on these components, it's easy to judge whether you are entering too early or too late. If too early you'll probably find the scene is approximately two or three pages long and top heavy with trite and unimportant dialogue, redundant and verbose. Yet there are other times, when you enter too late, where the true dramatic purpose is unrealized, and then the scene comes out short and the story line seems vague and unfulfilled.

Every scene, as we know, has a definite beginning, middle, and end. If you have a problem that answers to some of the symptoms listed on the *Problem Sheet*, restructure and redefine the scene into its basic parts of beginning, middle, and end. This way you can reevaluate some of those long scenes that seem to achieve no dramatic purpose except to slow the narrative down. The same exercise can be used if the scenes are too short and don't give enough information to move the story forward.

How do you determine the best place to enter the scene? That's the real question. I think the only way to gauge this is to ask yourself what happens before the scene begins, what happens during the scene, and what happens after the scene is over. Whether your scene takes place in an office, or at a concert, or in a car, where does the scene begin, what is its middle, and how does it end?

Let's say you have an important scene that's too long, too wordy, and drags the action down. And let's say, just as an example, that your scene takes place in an office. The first question to ask yourself is where is your character coming from before the scene begins? From his or her office? From a meeting outside the office? From home or the airport? What is the purpose of the scene, and what function does it serve? In other words, why is it there? And from the other characters' point of view, what are they doing when your character enters the office? Are they in the middle of a phone call or conversation? What's the back story to the scene? Are there any pleasantries exchanged? Or are the characters irritated and pissed off? When the characters enter the office, maybe your main character might be asked to wait before entering in turn. Conflict, remember? Getting your character into the office would be the beginning of the scene. So you could enter the scene anywhere along the flow of physical action of getting the character to the office.

The middle would be the actual conversation taking place. What's the conversation about? How does it fit within the context of the story? What function does it serve? Does it move the story forward or does it reveal information about the character? Is it a dramatically charged scene, or is it mainly subtext, meaning that what's not said is more important than what is said?

As far as I'm concerned, subtext should, if possible, become a major part of each scene. For example, in *The English Patient*, a formal dinner party is being given and Katherine (Kristin Scott Thomas) and her husband, Colin, are getting ready to leave. The war is becoming a reality and getting too close and their archeological expedition has been shut down. Now, we know that Almásy and Katherine are deeply in love. The scene opens with the group seated around the long table, when Almásy walks through the door drunk and, with only a few lines of dialogue, makes a total fool of himself. The dramatic purpose of the scene is not found in the dialogue, it is seen in what is not said: the looks, the uncomfortable glances from Katherine; her husband, tense and uptight; and the other people there trying to endure the embarrassing behavior of Almásy. It is during this scene that Colin, Katherine's husband, suspects, maybe knows, that his wife and Almásy are having an affair. From Almásy's point of view, he knows he has fallen hopelessly in love with her, does not want her to leave, and cannot stand to see her with her husband. It's a beautiful scene that on an obvious level shows us the drunken words and gestures of a person who is hurting deep inside, but more importantly conveys the character's thoughts, feelings, and emotions by the words that are not said. The dialogue itself during this encounter is really irrelevant. That's subtext.

Getting back to our office scene, what happens at the end? Does the character say his or her good-byes and simply leave? Does the character go back to his or her own office, leave the building, or get into a car or cab and then we move into the next scene? In other words, what's the ending of the scene?

When my students find themselves in this dilemma, and have to deal with this kind of problem, I have them break down the scene and lay out the parameters of beginning, middle, and end. Again, what is the purpose of the scene? Where does it take place? How does the character get into the scene? When those answers are known, then I have them list these events on a separate piece of paper so they can determine which elements lead up to the character's entering the scene, what events take place during the scene, and what happens when the scene is over. When they have completed this little exercise on a separate piece of paper, they have three complete columns of *beginning, middle,* and *end,* for these events lead up to, are part of, and conclude the scene.

Then I ask them to examine the characters' emotional state. What are the characters thinking and feeling before they enter the scene? Is there an emotional subtext? What is their dramatic need in this particular scene? What do they really want to say (basically stating the purpose of the scene), and what is said to them? If there's any doubt or question in the students' minds, I have them write the scene out in an obvious and direct way. What is this scene really about? Just write it and don't worry about whether it says what you want it to say. There's still time for that. Sometimes I'll have them do this in a free-association essay, of a couple of paragraphs or a page. This is only background to the scene.

Then, move on. What is the character's point of view during the scene? Does it alter or affect the scene? How so? What about the other person(s) in the scene? What are their thoughts, feelings, and emotions before the scene begins? And what is their point of view during the scene? What is their dramatic need in the scene? Do they achieve it? Every character in the scene has a different agenda, a different dramatic need, and it's important, absolutely essential, for writers to know what that need is so they can express it either visually or through dialogue.

If you're unclear about what the relationship is between the characters interacting in the scene, write a short two- or three-page essay about them. Free-associate. What is their relationship? Where or how did they meet? What is their purpose in being together? Do they like or dislike each other? What is their point of view? What is it that keeps them together? Where did they come from before the scene begins, and again, what thoughts, feelings, or emotions do they carry into the scene? Why are they there and what do they want to get or achieve in the scene? All these points should be determined so you can enter the scene at the best moment dramatically. Once you know the answers to these questions, then enter the scene a few lines before the purpose of the scene is stated.

Enter late and get out early. It makes for a good reading experience, as well as moving the story forward. Here's a example from *The Shawshank Redemption*. It's a scene that takes place in the First Half of Act II, and occurs right after the tarring-of-the-roof sequence when Andy tells the prison guard Hadley how to keep the $35,000 he inherited from his brother and, in exchange, manages to obtain some beer for his fellow inmates, which he does not drink. Be aware of the scene in terms of beginning, middle, and end.

EXT—PRISON YARD—THE BLEACHERS—DAY

Andy and Red play checkers. Red makes his move.

                         RED
            King me.

                         ANDY
            Chess. Now, *there's* a game of kings.
            Civilized . . . strategic . . .

                         RED
            . . . and totally fuckin' inexplicable.
            Hate that game.

                         ANDY
            Maybe you'll let me teach you someday.
            I've been thinking of getting a board
            together.

                         RED
            You come to the right place. I'm the man
            who can get things.

ANDY

We might do business on a board. But
the *pieces,* I'd like to carve those myself.
One side done in quartz . . . the
opposing side in limestone.

RED

That'd take you years.

ANDY

Years I've got. What I don't have are the
rocks. Pickings here in the exercise yard
are pretty slim.

RED

How's that rock hammer workin' out,
anyway? Scratch your name on your
wall yet?

ANDY

Not yet. I suppose I should.

RED

Andy? I guess we're gettin' to be friends,
ain't we?

ANDY

I suppose we are.

RED

I ask a question? Why'd you do it?

ANDY

I'm innocent, remember? Just like
everybody else here.

Red takes this as a gentle rebuff, keeps playing.

> **ANDY**
> What are you in for, Red?

> **RED**
> Murder. Same as you.

> **ANDY**
> Innocent?

> **RED**
> The only guilty man in Shawshank.

And we cut to the next scene.

This little scene is a masterpiece of understatement, and though short, it reveals many different facets of their character. Even though the scene is taken out of context, it is an insightful illustration of entering late and getting out early.

First, what's the purpose of the scene? You could say there are a couple of things here; first and foremost the scene reveals information about the characters. As mentioned, this particular scene takes place near the beginning of the Second Act, so it's really a scene about them solidifying their relationship. As Red says, "I guess we're gettin' to be friends, ain't we?"

We can also see the difference between Andy and Red, in terms of background and interests; they're playing checkers, a game that most everyone knows, but Andy would rather be playing chess and as far as Red is concerned, chess is "totally fuckin' inexplicable. Hate that game," he says. So much for that. What it does reveal is a vast difference in terms of their backgrounds and interests. The two men met because Andy wanted to obtain a rock hammer and to further pursue his interests as a rock hound, he wants to carve the chess pieces himself, "one side done in quartz . . . the opposing side in limestone." This says something about him. He was probably raised in a solid middle-class or upper-middle-class family, he's intelligent, logical, a good craftsman, he pays close attention to detail, likes to make things, and is always looking to see how things work by taking them apart. He's a hands-on kind of person, and of course Red's line about "scratching his name on the wall" is setting us up for the way he escapes from Shawshank Prison.

But there's another element in this scene as well: when Red asks why he killed his wife, Andy replies humorously, "I'm innocent, remember? Just like everybody else in here." And the stage directions say that "Red takes this as a gentle rebuff, keeps playing." Andy senses this and asks, "What are you in for, Red?" "Murder. Same as you." "Innocent?" Andy inquires, smiling slightly. But Red is serious: "The only guilty man in Shawshank." We hold for a moment, then cut to the next scene.

The scene ends on a statement that really raises more questions than it answers. Whom did Red murder? Why? How old was he when he committed the crime? What were the circumstances surrounding his act? We leave the scene before we have any answers. We get out at a moment of thoughtfulness, a natural end to this particular scene, but it spurs us on to know more about Red. Only later do we learn about the crime that brought Red to Shawshank. But entering late and getting out early keeps the tension going and the reader turning pages.

It's a good "rule" to remember.

If we wanted to break this scene into the elements of

beginning, middle, and end, it would begin with Andy and Red in the yard, walking up the bleacher steps, laying out the checkerboard and pieces, and they would start playing the game. The middle would deal with the game itself, and the dialogue would play, as it does, over the action of checker moves of the two men. The end would be when the game is over. They'd pack up their goods, either with dialogue or in silence, and they would walk back to the cell block. They're getting closer as friends, but there's still a distance between them, otherwise Andy would have answered Red's question on a more serious note. It's the manner in which he says it that implies that he actually committed the crime, and of course, that's what we're being set up to believe.

The scene is structured so we begin toward the end of the middle section. "King me," Red says in the opening line. Which means they've been playing awhile, because you don't king someone in checkers until you've made several moves to get into the right position. So the scene opens toward the end of the middle section and that's exactly what this little dialogue exchange is; a little "window" allowing us to learn what we're supposed to learn about their characters, and then moving on.

That's where we enter. And we get out early, after the last thought, Red's admission of guilt, is stated but before it's completed. If the author had wanted to continue the scene, Andy would have asked Red why and how he committed the murder. But he doesn't. We don't learn that until much later. We entered the scene late and then we got out early, before the explanation of how and why Red did what he did.

Where you enter depends upon the dramatic purpose of the scene, and where you end it depends on what you're leading into for the next scene. Structuring the scene so you enter late and get out early is what keeps the action moving forward smoothly, seamlessly. When I read a good screenplay, the reading experience is smooth and easy, and the pages have an almost liquid texture, with each scene continually moving the story forward. The only way I can describe it is by saying a good read is like "honey on the page."

And a good read is what we're all looking for.

The Problem Sheet

OKAY, FASTEN YOUR SEAT BELTS

- THE ACTION GOES NONSTOP

- ACTION SCENES ARE TOO DETAILED, WITH TOO MUCH DESCRIPTION

- NO TRANSITIONS BETWEEN SCENES

- STORY LINE IS THIN AND EPISODIC

- THE STAKES ARE NOT HIGH ENOUGH

- THE ACTION IS DULL AND BORING, AND GOES FROM INTERIOR TO INTERIOR TO INTERIOR

- THE SCENES ARE TOO EXPOSITORY, AND THE CHARACTERS EXPLAIN TOO MUCH

- THE CHARACTERS ARE TOO THIN, AND DO NOT REVEAL ANYTHING ABOUT THEMSELVES

- I'M NOT PAYING ATTENTION TO THE BUDGET

20

Okay, Fasten Your Seat Belts

OKAY, BUCKLE YOUR SEAT BELTS, HERE IT COMES. . . .

That's the line that begins the Third Act of *Terminator 2: Judgment Day*, one of the most significant action films of the last decade. Not only is the action singular and the characters sound, but it is the uniqueness of James Cameron's vision that drives the film into our consciousness. The same holds true with any great film, whether it be an action-adventure, science-fiction, or mystery thriller, or simply a great action sequence nailed into the scenario of a good drama or detective story. The Star Wars trilogy has been rereleased with astonishing results, once again proving that the action film, accompanied by the mythic vision of the filmmaker, is what truly drives the film into our collective celluloid immortality.

The action film is actually a significant staple of our movie fare, and at least half of a major studio's production schedule is devoted to developing and nurturing this particular brand of entertainment. And now, with the advent of the computer-graphic revolution, it's only going to become more popular. Writing the action film, or even an action sequence, is really an art unto itself. So many times I read screenplays whose pages are filled with nonstop action—in fact, there is so much action that it becomes dull and repetitive, with little or no characterization. The reader, and the viewer, are overwhelmed and numb. Sometimes, it's a good action script with strong individual action sequences, but the premise is weak and derivative of earlier films. In other words, we've seen it all before. It needs a "new look," or a more interesting concept. And when that happens, you're in trouble.

Why? Because there are problems. Lots of problems. Either with the plot, or the characters, or the action itself. Some writers have a natural ability to write action films, and there are others who are more comfortable writing character, but it's important to note that before you can write any kind of an action film, or sequence, it's essential to understand what an action film is, what its nature is. I had a student who wrote a screenplay about a navy pilot sent on a mission to a foreign country to rescue a kidnapped scientist being held hostage. It's a good premise, and there were several opportunities to create some notable action sequences and keep the story moving forward at a fast pace. So that's what he did, and his entire screenplay was one action sequence after another; the story moved like lightning, but it didn't work at all. What he didn't do was create an interesting main character. Because he didn't know his main character, most of the dialogue consisted of expository elements designed to keep the story moving forward. It didn't work. We didn't know anything about this person sent to rescue the scientist, had no idea about his thoughts or feelings, or about the forces working on his life.

This is not all that uncommon. When you're writing an action screenplay, the focus must be on the action *and* character; the two must reside in and interact with each other. Otherwise there are going to be problems. What usually happens is that the action overpowers the story and diminishes the characters, resulting in a screenplay that, no matter how well written, is flat and uninteresting. There has to be an appropriate balance of peaks and valleys, places in the material where the reader and audience can pause and catch their collective breath.

So, what do we have to know in order to avoid creating these problems in an action screenplay? Let's start from the top. *Action* is defined in the dictionary as "a movement or a series of movements," or "the state of being in motion," so film, a medium that moves at twenty-four frames per second, is a natural medium for "showing" action. Writing an action script, or sequence, is a definite skill, and good action scripts are written with color, pacing, suspense, tension, and, in most cases, humor. Remember the Bruce Willis character mumbling to himself in *Die Hard* (Steven de Souza) or the bus making the leap across the enormous freeway chasm in *Speed* (Graham Yost)? We remember good action films like *Jurassic Park* or *The Fugitive* (David Twohy) or *The Hunt for Red October* (Larry Ferguson and Donald Stewart) by the uniqueness of the action, but we usually forget all the cool car chases and explosions that occupy the majority of action films that fill our theaters. They all look alike.

The key to writing any action film lies in writing the action sequence. (Plot and character come later.) In an action film like *Terminator 2: Judgment Day*, for example, the entire film is structured and anchored by six major action sequences. After the introduction of Terminator, the T-1000, and John and Sarah, the *first* major sequence is where young John Connor is rescued by Terminator; *two*, Terminator and John break his mother out of prison; *three*, the "rest period" at Enrique's gas station where they load up with weapons; *four*, Sarah's attempt to kill Miles Dyson, creator of the microchip that makes possible the future Age of Machines; *five*, the siege at Cyberdyne Systems; and sequence *six*, their breakout and chase, winding up in the steel factory. The entire Third Act is literally one long nonstop action sequence. These key sequences *hold* (the function of structure) the entire story together, but within this structural framework Cameron and Wisher have created a dynamic and intriguing premise, as well as some interesting characters. That along with the special effects, is what makes this a truly memorable action film. And let's not forget that at the Mid-Point, there is the "rest period" at the abandoned gas station so we can "breathe" and learn more about the characters. Then we're off and running again.

What is it that makes a good action film great? The electricity of the action sequences. Remember the chase scene from *Bullitt*? Or "the walk" at the end of *The Wild Bunch*? Or Butch and Sundance jumping into the river's gorge after being relentlessly chased by the Super Posse in *Butch Cassidy and the Sundance Kid*? The list goes on and on.

The key word in writing a great action sequence is the way it's *designed*. A sequence, remember, *is a series of scenes, connected by one single idea, with a beginning, middle, and end*. A sequence is usually a complete entity, held together by *one single idea:* a chase sequence, wedding sequence, party sequence, fight sequence, love sequence, storm sequence. As mentioned earlier, *Twister* is a film that is really four major sequences, held together by the characters' racing from one to the next. And, of course, each new sequence is more intense than the last.

So let's take a look at an action sequence. This little tidbit is from *Terminator 2: Judgment Day* and takes place at the beginning of Act III, right after the Terminator, Sarah, and John, with the help of Miles Dyson, have broken into Cyberdyne Systems to destroy the microchip left behind in *The Terminator*, seven years earlier. The police are summoned, there's a huge gunfight action sequence, and, at Plot Point II, they break out of the building and flee with a SWAT team van. They race away, followed by the T-1000, who's chasing them in a police helicopter. This is the beginning of Act III.

OKAY, BUCKLE YOUR SEAT BELTS, HERE IT COMES. . . .

INT./EXT. SWAT VAN/HIGHWAY—NIGHT

Terminator looks back at his two passengers as he turns the boxy van onto a divided highway. Sarah and John are catching their breath, still coughing from the CS gas. Terminator looks to the rearview mirror. He sees the xenon searchlight of the chopper behind them, gaining.

Sarah looks around the inside of the SWAT van. It is a rolling armory. There are rifles, ballistic vests, all manner of equipment. . . . Then she grabs two M16's from the wall rack and loads them. She starts on a shotgun as—

The SWAT van weaves through sparse traffic at high speed. Terminator slews the unstable van around cars and trucks, which seem to be crawling. The van hits its top speed of eighty. They swerve to miss the back end of a WHITE EIGHTEEN-WHEEL TANKER.
The chopper [*flown by the T-1000*] swings in behind them, closing fast.
T-1000 reaches through the shattered canopy with the

MPK machine pistol and FIRES. The back of the van CLANGS WITH HITS. The door windows are BLOWN IN.

Terminator weaves the van, trying to throw off the T-1000's aim.
The unstable vehicle screeches and wobbles on the edge of control.
One of the doors is kicked open. Sarah, wearing a ballistic vest, crouches in the doorway, whipping up the M16. SHE OPENS FIRE.

Bullets riddle what's left of the chopper's canopy as the T-1000 returns fire. The van is stitched with hits.
INSIDE THE VAN holes are punched through the thin sheet-metal walls, ripping up the interior. The vests covering John are hit repeatedly. We see that Sarah has hung two Kevlar vests on the inside of the back door and she ducks behind these as bullets hit around her. She pops back out and fires in controlled bursts. The M16 empties and she grabs another.

Terminator swerves around a car which is changing lanes, hitting it and knocking it skidding.

Sarah reloads and keeps firing. The van swerves around a Toyota. A moment later the helicopter passes it, the rotor just clearing the top of the car.

T-1000 FIRES the machine pistol.
Sarah has popped out to fire. She takes a HIT in the thigh, and several rounds hammer into her Kevlar vest. She is blown back onto the floor of the van. She lies there, an exposed target—

Terminator sees the T-1000 preparing to fire again.

He locks up the van's brakes. Tires scream as the vehicle shimmies. Sarah is thrown forward, sliding up to the bulkhead next to John.

And the helicopter SLAMS RIGHT INTO THE BACK OF THE VAN.

The rotor disintegrates. The back doors of the van are crushed in as the canopy, the whole front of the fuselage is HAMMERED INTO JUNK, trapping the T-1000 inside twisted metal. The chopper hits the pavement, flips sideways, and cartwheels . . . smashing itself into a shapeless mass of twisted metal.

It falls away behind the van, tumbling end over end.

Whew! And, that's just the beginning of the Third Act. The chase sequence continues on from there, the action building upon itself, the pace quickening, the tension heightening. Just reading this little section, even though it's taken completely out of context, brings thrills and chills and has me clinging to the edge of my seat.

If you're writing an action film, and you feel there's a problem, determine what it is. Go through the *Problem Sheet* and see if there's anything that applies to your specific script. Is the action too dull, or too slow? Does your story move from INTERIOR to INTERIOR to INTERIOR without moving the action to an EXTERIOR location? Are scenes too expository? Are the stakes high enough? Does your character talk about an action that may have happened in the dialogue, and is it possible for you *to show the action they're talking about*? This is what happens when you adapt a play into a screenplay. *You show what the character is talking about,* and that means creating action sequences to keep the story moving forward and reveal information about the main character.

And you most definitely have to pay attention to the film's budget. Films like *Terminator 2: Judgment Day*, *Speed II*, *Waterworld*, *Jurassic Park*, *The Lost World*, or *Titanic* are budgeted at millions and millions of dollars. But they're also written and directed by people whose previous movies have grossed millions and millions of dollars. Pay attention to the budget. It costs so much to produce a film today, almost $12,000 to $15,000 a minute, that you have to make an effort to keep the production cost under some kind of control, if possible. If you're fortunate to have a major studio or production company buy your screenplay, great, then let them drive the budget up and add things that will visually enhance your story.

If your script doesn't seem to be working as well as it should, or you have some problem areas in terms of pacing, or it seems dull and boring, you might think about adding some kind of action sequence to keep the story moving and the tension taut. Examine the material and see whether the proposed action will blend in with your original concept. Your script is only a start point; sometimes you have to make some drastic creative choices to allow you to fix your film. But always remember that *you can't just throw in an action sequence because your story line drags and sags, or is dull and boring*. To approach any action film or sequence, the material has to be designed for and incorporated into your story line and be executed to the best of your ability.

In today's market I think it's essential that every screenwriter should know how to write a good action sequence, no matter what kind of film he or she is working on; whether a character study like *Shine* (Jan Sardi), or *The English Patient*, or *Lone Star* (John Sayles), even a comedy like *Michael* (Nora Ephron). You'll find that most of the screenplays funneled through the studio pipeline will have some kind of action sequence woven into the story line. The trick is to make sure it fits into the overall concept and design. I can't stress this enough.

There are many problems in screenwriting that can be solved by a knowledge of good action writing, but there is always the tendency to sacrifice character for action. The trick is to weave the two together in such a way that the characters support the action, and the action supports the characters. *Crimson Tide, Die Hard, Lethal Weapon,* and *Terminator 2: Judgment Day* are good examples in which the action and characters complement each other.

In my many travels and workshops I meet a lot of writers who confide in me that they have difficulty crafting an action sequence; when I ask why, their answers, generally, are the same: because film is really "a director's medium," they say, anything they do will be ignored anyway. If I probe a little deeper, it turns out that, depending on what their strengths or weaknesses are, it's because they don't want to write everything out. As a result they will be the first to admit that their efforts lack focus. Either that or they write such detailed action that it becomes bogged down in a lot of words. The result is usually what I term *"thick pages,"* pages that are so dense, they're difficult to read. In the nineties and beyond, it is the screenwriter's responsibility to design the action scene or sequence in the screenplay. You can't give that responsibility to the director; it's your job to write the best action you can.

It wasn't always that way. In the sixties and seventies a screenwriter could simply write the words *There is a chase,* and the director would do the rest. One of the most memorable action scenes in the action genre was written that way—the dynamic chase sequence in *The French Connection* (Ernest

Tidyman) stunningly directed by William Friedkin. No longer. Today, action sequences have to be designed and choreographed with the utmost care, skill, and patience.

So, how do you write a good action sequence?

William Wisher (*Terminator 2, Judge Dredd*) says that "ideally, the action is on the page. It's a very smart thing to do because the script serves different purposes at different times in the [filmmaking] process. The first people who read it are going to be the producers. Your job is to get them to actually see the movie on the page and get them excited enough to write you a big check so that you can make the movie. The second group of people who read your script are directors and actors. Your job with them is to not just get them excited, but to give them a sense of character and structure. There should be enough information to let the actors know how to play their roles and give the director an understanding of how the movie should be made."

There's a fine line to be drawn here, because it's important not to write too much. David Twohy (*The Fugitive, Waterworld, Terminal Velocity*) says that "if it gets too detailed, then you're doing the director's job and you're taking things away from him. And he won't appreciate that. It's best to give the maximum effect with the minimum amount of words."

That means finding the right visual components to describe the sequence. David Koepp, who wrote *Mission: Impossible, Jurassic Park,* and *The Lost World,* to name a few, says that the key to writing a good action sequence "is finding more ways to say that someone runs. You tend to use a lot of adjectives. For example: He runs to hide behind the rock. He races over to the rock. He scrambles over to the rock. He crawls frantically on his belly over to the rock. . . . Those are the things that drive me crazy. Hurries, trots, sprints, dives, leaps, jumps, barrels, slams. The word *slams*, that'll appear a lot in your action script.

"In an action scene," Koepp continues, "the reader is sometimes forcing their eyes along because what's tremendously entertaining to watch on film is not necessarily so thrilling to read. I think the challenge is to make that stuff fly by at the pace you would like it to fly by in the movie. So you've constantly got to find ways to make the action sequences readable and easy for the reader to picture in his mind."

What's the best way to write an action sequence?

Design it, choreograph the action from the beginning, through the middle, and to the end. Choose your words carefully when you're writing. Action is not written on the page with a lot of long and beautifully styled sentences, the way Tom Clancy does in his novels. Though Clancy builds his cross-cutting scenes with rapid style movements, his intention is to hook his readers so they will move from scene to scene quickly. It's a very cinematic style. Writing an action sequence has got to be more intense, more visual. As Bill Wisher says, the reader must see the action as if he or she were seeing it on the screen. We're dealing with moving images that hopefully keep you glued to the edge of your seat, filled with excitement, or fear, or great expectation, locked in that great "community of emotion" that unites everybody in the darkened movie theater. Just look at the great action sequences: *Bullitt*, *The French Connection*, *Psycho*, *Terminator 2*, the long walk and final shootout from *The Wild Bunch*. These are all action sequences that have been designed and choreographed with immense care and strict attention to detail.

Sometimes people tend to write too little, and then the

action line becomes thin and doesn't carry the gripping intensity that you must have in a good action sequence.

Suppose, for example, your screenplay is slow, it drags and sags, and seems dull and boring. If you reexamine the material, it may be possible to insert some kind of action into the narrative that pumps up the story line. But you must be careful that the action you want to insert belongs in the tone and style of the script. Often the easy way out, a car chase, or a kiss, or a shootout, or a murder attempt, draws attention to itself and therefore will not work.

And there will be times when the problem will not be in the action, but in how the action is conceived and written. We've become so sophisticated, in terms of reading screenplays, that the reader wants some kind of "involvement," so you want to include the reader in such a way that he or she will be drawn into the action.

Shane Black (*Lethal Weapon*) is a master at this. And even then, as in *The Long Kiss Goodnight*, for example, he overdoes it and somehow the action loses its effectiveness. Cute and clever does not always work. A few pages into the screenplay, Sam, the main character, and her father-in-law, are driving at night. Snow is everywhere. And "that, gentle reader, is when the DEER walks into the road—Fucks up their night altogether."

DEER FACT #25: It's been said, confronted with roadway deer, that the best course of action is to *punch the gas*. The idea, presumably, is to pop the animal over the roof, rather than risk dragging him under the car.

It may work once or twice, but that's about it. Screenwriters sometimes have the tendency to overwrite their action sequences; that is, they get bogged down in detail, thinking that every piece of "business" needs to be written and explained with absolute minuteness. In that case the pages become "too thick," and it makes for a very difficult read.

If the reader ever sees a single-spaced full page or three-quarter page of dramatic action, it becomes a burdensome reading experience. I tell my writers that a good action sequence should be lean, clean, and tight, as well as being totally visual. Each action paragraph should be no longer than four or five sentences. Any more than that and it appears to be a "thick" page. And make sure there's a lot of white space on the page.

Here's an example of an excellent action scene; it's lean, clean, and tight, totally effective, extremely visual, and not bogged down with details. This is a little piece out of *Jurassic Park*, by David Koepp. The scene takes place on the island off Costa Rica just as it has been hit by a violent tropical storm, and the security systems have been shut down by an employee trying to smuggle out dinosaur embryos. The two remote-controlled electric cars, one with the two children and the attorney Gennaro, the other with the Sam Neill and Jeff Goldblum characters, are stalled next to the massive electric fence that keeps the dinosaurs enclosed in their restricted area. The power is out all over the island, and the kids are scared, nervous.

Tim pulls off the goggles and looks at two clear plastic cups of water that sit in recessed holes on the dashboard. As he watches, the water in the glasses vibrates, making concentric circles—

then it stops—

—and then it vibrates again. Rhythmically.

Like from footsteps.

BOOM. BOOM. BOOM.

Gennaro's eyes snap open as he feels it too. He looks up at the rearview mirror.

There is a security pass hanging from it that is bouncing slightly, swaying from side to side.

As Gennaro watches, his image bounces too, vibrating in the rearview mirror.

BOOM. BOOM. BOOM.

> **GENNARO**
> (not entirely convinced)
> M-Maybe it's the power trying to come
> back on.

Tim jumps into the backseat and puts the night goggles on again. He turns and looks out the side window. He can see the area where the goat is tethered. Or *was* tethered. The chain is still there, but the goat is gone.

BANG!

They all jump, and Lex SCREAMS as something hits the Plexiglas sunroof of the Explorer, hard. They look up.

It's a disembodied goat leg.

GENNARO

Oh, Jesus. Jesus.

Tim whips around to look out the side window again. His mouth pops open, but no sound comes out. Through the goggles he sees an animal claw, a huge one, gripping the cables of the "electrified" fence.

Tim whips the goggles off and presses forward, against the window. He looks up, up, then cranes his head back farther, to look out the sunroof. Past the goat's leg, he can see—

Tyrannosaurus rex. It stands maybe twenty-five feet high, forty feet long from nose to tail, with an enormous, boxlike head that must be five feet long by itself. The remains of the goat are hanging out of the rex's mouth. It tilts its head back and swallows the animal in one big gulp.

Well, there it is. . . . Quite impressive. The sequence is the beginning of the action that will carry us through the end of the film. We literally see the action as it unfolds, step by step, bit by bit. Notice how visual it is, and how short the sentences are, almost staccato in their presentation, and how much "white space" is on the page. This is the way a good action sequence should read.

What do the sequences from *Terminator 2* and *Jurassic Park* have in common? First, the reader and the characters experience the same thing at the same time. We are literally bonded together, "one on one," so we can experience what the characters are experiencing.

Take a look at the sequence dynamics: there is a definite

beginning, middle, and end to the action. Each visual moment builds the action line, incident to incident.

We open at the beginning, with the cups on the dashboard vibrating. We know something's going on here, we just don't know what.

Notice how visual it is, then look how the writing of the sequence builds upon the fear and terror of the characters. "BOOM. BOOM. BOOM." Relentlessly, each sound expands and heightens the moment, stimulating the antennae of our imaginations. The writing style, besides being visual, uses short, clipped words or phrases. No long, beautifully formed sentences here. And of course, Spielberg is a master at putting this kind of sequence on film. Go back and take a look at the opening sequence of *Close Encounters of the Third Kind*.

So far everything still remains unseen, which heightens the fear and causes us to expect the worst. The goat is another visual aid that amplifies the tension and pacing. Generally, a good action sequence builds slowly, setting things up, drawing us into the excitement so the action gets faster and faster. Good pacing allows the tension to build upon itself, no matter whether it's a chase sequence like *Speed*, a thriller sequence like *Seven*, the killing of Harlan in *Thelma & Louise*, or the tense waiting period for the emergency action message to arrive in *Crimson Tide*.

A good action sequence builds image by image, word by word. Notice after the goat has vanished and the chain is swinging freely, suddenly there's a BANG! and we literally jump in our collective seats. Then, we see the "disembodied goat leg." That's when the fear starts rising among the characters, and that's when our palms begin sweating and our mouths become dry, waiting for and dreading what we know is coming . . . Tyrannosaurus rex.

It's just good writing. Sometimes writers will try to cover a weakness in character writing by inserting action sequences, thus avoiding any attempt at characterization. Sometimes the action sequences are written up in such detail that it looks like there's a blanket of words on the page, and any attempt to create a good reading experience is simply lost in the excess verbiage.

Writing a good action film, or a good action sequence, can often create as many problems as it solves. But if you find that your script drags and sags, and needs an extra shot of something, consider some kind of action sequence that can be incorporated into the story line to visually expand the attributes of your character.

Action and character, joined together, can often sharpen the focus of your screenplay and make it a better reading experience. And that's what it's all about.

The Problem Sheet

ENDINGS

- STORY'S RESOLUTION IS NOT PAID OFF

- THE ENDING DOES NOT WORK

- THE ENDING IS TOO SOFT, TOO WEAK, CONFUSING

- THE ENDING SEEMS CONTRIVED, TOO PREDICTABLE, UNSATISFYING

- MAIN CHARACTER DIES (THE EASY SOLUTION)

- THE MAIN CHARACTER DISAPPEARS AT THE END

- A SURPRISE TWIST COMES OUT OF NOWHERE

- EVERYTHING HAPPENS TOO FAST

- ENDING IS NOT BIG OR COMMERCIAL ENOUGH

- ENDING IS TOO BIG, AND THERE MIGHT BE A BUDGET PROBLEM

21

Endings

Endings.

If there's one problem that screenwriters have to deal with more than any other, it's the problem of *endings*. How to end the screenplay so it works effectively, so it's satisfying and fulfilling, so it makes an emotional impact on the reader, so it's not contrived or predictable, so it's real, believable, not forced or fabricated; an ending that resolves all the main story points; an ending, in short, that works.

Endings have always fueled the industry dream factory; is there anyone who hasn't heard about the problems of ending *Casablanca* (Jules and Philip Stein) or *Fatal Attraction* (James Deardon)? And what about the endings of *White Palace* (Alvin Sargent) or *The Silence of the Lambs* (Ted Tally) or any of the myriad of other films released each year? Stories abound about endings that did not work, or the trials and tribulations of screenwriters and filmmakers trying to achieve the "right" ending.

What's so interesting about endings is that, most of the time, the ending is not really the problem, it's the fact that it *doesn't work effectively*. It's either too soft, or too slow, too wordy or too vague, too expensive or not expensive enough, too down, too up, too contrived, too predictable, or too unbelievable. Sometimes it's simply not dramatic enough to resolve the story line, or maybe a surprise twist in the story line comes out of nowhere, with no relationship to the story or characters; it just creates a solution to the script, is an easy way to end the story line. This happens a lot with young film students; the easiest way to end the screenplay is by having the main character die, or having everybody die.

So many times we hear stories about film endings having been changed after audience previews. In many cases the ending of a screenplay is agreed upon, then changed, or sometimes two or three endings will be shot during production, and then a decision will be made in the cutting room, or after audience previews, about which one to use. It happens all the time, and because of the high financial risk factors that go along with making movies, the filmmakers and studios have learned to take their cues from the preview audience, so changing the ending has become part of the moviemaking process.

Strong endings are an essential part of the screenplay. Whether it's a drama, comedy, or action thriller, or whatever, doesn't really matter; what's important is that the ending be a dynamic conclusion to the story line.

By itself the *ending* means the last part, or finish, or the conclusion. The best way to achieve the ending of the screenplay is to let it evolve, or be born, from the resolution of the story. Like a star evolving from the interstellar dust, a good and appropriate ending will always be born from the resolution. That's the start point, the beginning of a good ending.

Understanding the basic dynamics of a story's resolution is essential. By itself *resolution* means "a solution or explanation; to make clear." And that process begins at the very start of the screenwriting process. When building or constructing a story line, you must first determine the resolution. What is the resolution of your story? At the initial conception of your screenplay, when you were still working out the idea and shaping it into a dramatic story line, you made a creative choice, a decision, and determined what the resolution was going to be: does your character live or die? Succeed or fail? Successfully escape from Shawshank Prison and make it safely to Mexico? Reenter the earth's atmosphere and survive the ordeal of the damaged spacecraft as in *Apollo 13*? Confront her fear of commitment and access her own inner courage and commit to marriage as in *How to Make an American Quilt*? Does Larry Flynt win the court decision in the legal battle over the First Amendment or not, as in *The People vs. Larry Flynt* (Scott Alexander and Larry Karaszewski)? Does the Emergency Action Message arrive in time to prevent the launching of nuclear missiles in *Crimson Tide*?

The resolutions of all these films contain the seeds of each particular ending. It's important to note that *resolution* and *ending* are not the same thing. They are connected, in the same way that an ice cube and water are connected, or fire and heat, or the green in a leaf, in terms of their relationship between the parts and the whole. The resolution is a whole, whereas the ending is made up of parts. It is the resolution that contains the seed of the ending, and, if planted and nurtured correctly, it can bloom into a full-fledged dramatic experience. And that's what we all strive for. Endings are manifested in the resolution, and the resolution is conceived from the beginning. It's a natural law that endings and beginnings are related; the ending of one thing is always the beginning of something else. Be it a wedding, or a funeral, or a life change like a new job or career, the ending of a relationship or the beginning of a new one, or a move to a new city or country, or whether it's winning or losing in the lottery, it's all the same; the end of one thing is always the beginning of something else.

The surest way for your ending to work is to know the resolution, then find the best way to show the specific scene or sequence so you can make it visually and dramatically effective.

What happens at the end of your story? If you don't know (and this ambivalence usually occurs when you're first evolving your story line), then ask yourself *what you would like the ending to be,* regardless of whether it's too simple, too trite, too happy, or too sad. And please don't get caught up in the game of "What kind of an ending would *they* like?" Whoever *they* are. What ending do *you* want?

The ending of the screenplay is that point where the entire story line is paid off, so you have to design it carefully from Plot Point II. *Seven* has a great ending, and that's what makes the film so disturbing, so you literally carry it with you when you leave the theater. If necessary, retrace your steps from Plot Point II.

When you reach the Plot Point at the end of the Second Act, what elements are left unresolved? There will be one or two things that need to be resolved in Act III. What are they? Can you define them? In *The English Patient* the two things left unresolved at the beginning of Act III are whether Almásy comes back in time to save Katherine, seriously injured from the plane crash and waiting for his return in the Cave of the Swimmers; and two, does Caravaggio carry out his mission to kill the English patient as he had planned? The other points to be resolved are what happens to the English patient and to the nurse, Hana.

These elements must be resolved before you can even think, or construct, the ending. So we follow Almásy as he trudges through the desert looking for help to save Katherine, but drama is conflict, and he's captured by the English and believed to be a German spy. We see how he escapes, then learn he traded the maps of the desert to the Germans for an airplane. But when he arrives at the Cave of the Swimmers, he's too late; Katherine has died, but she shares her love and her death with him in the notebook she left behind. He picks her up and carries her in his arms to the airplane and they take off, which, of course, is the opening shot of the movie.

At that point we cut to present time, where Caravaggio (Willem Dafoe) tells the English patient he had intended to kill him, but the dying man replies that he can't, because he's "already dead." At this point his life is over, and Hana (Juliette Binoche) fulfills his wish and gives him an overdose of morphine, so he's able to leave his body and join his true love. Day breaks, and we follow Hana as she climbs aboard a truck, to begin a new life as a new person, the ghosts of her past buried, and as the truck pulls away, she begins her journey into the light of a new day.

That ending had to be designed, mapped out. It had to be conceived as emotional, yet symbolic. The same with *The Shawshank Redemption*. As mentioned, Act III begins with two basic things unresolved: how does Andy escape, and what happens to Red? Act III resolves those two story points; it shows how Andy escapes, and in the process the warden and Hadley are brought to justice. Red is finally paroled, knows he can't make it on the outside, for he has become institutionalized, and decides to break his parole and join Andy in Mexico. That's the resolution. The end shows Red walking toward Andy on the sands of the Pacific and their embrace as they are reunited.

The ending cannot be a separate and isolated incident or event. Everything is connected in a screenplay, everything exists in relationship between the parts and the whole. So, if you feel your ending does not work, if it's too soft or subtle, or comes out of nowhere, or the main character seems to be lost, or you really don't know what to do to write an ending that works, then it's time to sit down at the drawing board and begin the ending from a specific point: Plot Point II.

First, set up what you have to pay off. Determine what elements of the story must be resolved at the end of the screenplay. If need be, write an essay about what happens in Act III so the story line can be resolved. Then you might want to go through the action and, in free association, in a page-or-two essay, begin to list the ways this film can end. Don't be attached to any one single shot, scene, or sequence. Just list the various ways the ending can be achieved. If that doesn't clarify the action, and you're still unclear about how the material should end, simply write down how you would like it to end, regardless of budget, believability, or anything else that gets in the way. Just throw down any thoughts, words, or ideas, without any regard as to how to do it. That's really the first step in the completion process. It's important to tie together all the loose ends of the narrative line so the screenplay becomes a complete reading experience that rings true and is integral to the action and the characters.

There are other ways to end your screenplay as well. There may be an instance where Act III becomes an entire sequence, a full and complete unit of action; *Apollo 13* is such a case; so is *Witness,* so is *Crimson Tide.* And if you look at *Pulp*

Fiction, the end is really the "bookend" ending with the Tim Roth and Amanda Plummer robbery attempt in the restaurant, which, coincidentally, opens the movie. Endings and beginnings are connected, right? In each of these scripts the ending completes the action of Act III.

In *Apollo 13* the entire Third Act focuses on their reentry back to earth, and we follow the action from the moment the LEM separates from the spacecraft, cutting back and forth to the command center, to the anxious three minutes that turns out to be four, waiting for them to plunge through the atmosphere, not knowing whether the heat shield will protect them or not. When they finally do break through the cloud cover and safely land in the ocean and are rescued, that is the resolution; the ending is simply the voice-over of Jim Lovell telling us what happened to the three astronauts after their ordeal in space. It's played over shots of them on the aircraft carrier.

The Plot Point at the end of Act II in *Witness* has John Book (Harrison Ford) and Rachel (Kelly McGillis) completing their relationship as they embrace underneath the birdhouse that Book had broken when he first arrived, and has now restored. Act III opens when the three crooked cops pull over the ridge, park their car, pull out their weapons, and make their way down to the farmhouse. Once there, they break into the farmhouse and hold Rachel and the grandfather hostage while they hunt Book and young Samuel, trying to kill them. So the entire Third Act is really a shootout, and the end comes out of that action; John Book says good-bye to Rachel and young Samuel, and over the end credits, as he drives the car up the long dirt road leading back to Philadelphia, Daniel, played by Alexander Godunov, Rachel's suitor, walks toward the farmhouse. *Witness* is a great little film that works on all levels. The ending of one thing is always the beginning of something else.

It's different with *Crimson Tide*. At Plot Point II the emergency action message is interrupted and the Denzel Washington character takes over the command of the sub as the countdown to launch the nuclear missiles continues. Act III is the entire sequence, and ends when they finally receive the complete message telling them to cancel the nuclear strike. That's the resolution.

The ending is something else. There is a little tag added on after the action is complete; a naval inquiry is held, and it is decided that both men were right in their actions, because the naval regulations happen to be unclear in this particular situation and must be changed. The Gene Hackman character retires from active duty, the Denzel Washington character will be promoted to captain and receive command of his own ship. When the two men walk outside, the Denzel Washington character tells Gene Hackman that the Lipizzaner horses are really from Spain, not from Portugal, as the Hackman character had claimed, and they're born black at birth and as they grow into adulthood, they turn white. And, that's the final comment on the film; the conflict between them was not really a question of right versus wrong, but a question of right versus right. Which is what the entire screenplay is all about. The Lipizzaner is of mixed Arabian, Italian, and Spanish ancestry. The breed was founded in Trieste. Lipizzaner show horses are trained at the Spanish Riding School in Vienna.

Two different points of view, resolved, effective, complete. It's what a good ending is meant to do.

A good ending is only as strong as Act I; in other words, a good ending is set up from the very beginning of the screenplay. It will always come out of the integrity of the story. In many scripts the ending seems predictable; that is, we know what's going to happen, we just don't know *how*. *Jerry Maguire* (Cameron Crowe) is a script like that. We know from the very beginning what's going to happen, and the two people are going to get together, but the fun comes in watching how it happens.

Of course, there are other ways to approach an ending in relationship stories. One of my favorite examples is Michelangelo Antonioni's classic *L'Eclisse (The Eclipse)*, with Alain Delon and Monica Vitti. In the opening shot two people are sitting silently in a room. The only sound we hear is the whirring of a small fan as it swings back and forth. For almost four minutes nothing is said. That's because there is nothing left to say, it's all been said. The curtains are drawn. The silence is loud except for the fan. And we know, by the words not spoken, that the relationship, whatever it might have been, is over. The woman suddenly turns and draws back the curtains, letting in the light of a new day. "Well," she says, "I've got to go." The man, obviously exhausted, jumps up and says, "Let me drive you." "No, no . . ." she replies. He insists. She walks out and he follows her; "Please," he begs, "let's have dinner tonight . . . let's talk it over." She doesn't reply but strides forward with purpose and determination.

That's the opening. It's wonderful, because even though nothing has been said, we understand immediately what has happened; the relationship is over. Film is behavior.

The Monica Vitti character goes back into her life, and meets Alain Delon, a very attractive and successful stockbroker. They like each other, and begin seeing each other, and as they get closer and spend more time with each other, we like them; they're attractive, they have many things in common, and we "hope" they can stay together. But as the film progresses, we begin to see things that separate them; he lies to his clients, which she can't stand, and sometimes he'll do something dishonest, and then try to justify it to her. She believes in being totally honest, living with integrity, and while we notice her reaction to this part of his personality, nothing is really said. We only see it.

The end of the film is incredible. There are two scenes very close together. First, they are in his apartment, and he asks if she thinks "we can get along together." She considers this, hesitating. "I don't know," she replies. "There you go again," he says, "I don't know, I don't know, I don't know. . . . Why do you see me, then? . . . And don't tell me you don't know." She pauses for a long moment and says, "I wish I didn't love you. . . . Or that I loved you much more." He looks at her, not understanding.

Then, in a continuation of the first scene, we cut to his office, late afternoon. The phones are off the hook. They embrace after they've made passionate love, and talk of this and that, when suddenly, the doorbell rings. He freezes, telling her to be silent. He puts on his jacket, as she prepares to leave. He puts the phones back on the hook, and one by one they start ringing. It's time to go back to work. "See you tomorrow?" he asks. She nods yes. "And the day after, and the day after that . . ." he says playfully. "And, tonight . . ." she replies, smiling. "Eight o'clock. Same place," he says. And they continue to look at each other, the phones ringing incessantly; they embrace passionately, then she turns and walks down the stairs and we follow her outside.

There follow seven minutes of the most incredibly striking sequence. The two characters we've followed for almost the entire film are nowhere to be seen during it, only the places they've been together. Shot after shot after shot fill the screen. We see someone who looks like her from behind, but it is not her. We see someone walk out of his building, but it's not him. Places and faces and objects are focused on, and at the end a bright streetlight fills the frame. The film ends, wrapped in discordant music.

It's breathtaking, perhaps the greatest ending I've ever seen. We continually expect to see the couple again, and only at the very end do we realize that their relationship was not strong enough for them to stay together. It's a visually haunting and demanding sequence and derives its power from the opening scene. Both relationships, at the beginning and at the end, have failed to bear fruit for her, and we're left wondering what it was that she wanted in a relationship and whether it was realistic or idealistic. We'll never know, for the landscape of love and relationship is always challenging.

In one way this is an ambiguous ending, and yet it has been totally paid off. We know that she's a person searching for love, and we understand that she never found it, but because we don't see the actual ending of the relationship, it lets us make our own decisions as to what really happened. As an ending it works effectively, even though our expectations, however unrealistic, would like to have a more romantic resolution. But the power of that ending is like an eclipse: extraordinary.

So what makes a good ending? It has to work, first of all, by satisfying the story; so when we reach the final fadeout, or walk out of the movie experience, we want to feel full and satisfied, much as if we were leaving the table after a good meal. It's this feeling of satisfaction that must be fulfilled in order for the ending to work effectively. And of course, it's got to be believable. An unsatisfying ending occurred in the thriller *Jagged Edge* (Joe Eszterhas). The story, about a woman

attorney called out of retirement to represent a wealthy pub-
lisher accused of murdering his wife (the script opens with
the murder), totally believes he is innocent and despite herself
falls in love with him. She convinces the jury that he's innocent and gets him an acquittal. Only then does she begin to
suspect that he really is guilty. When she investigates her
suspicions, she searches a closet and there finds the critical
piece of incriminating evidence. Uh-oh. Too pat, too contrived, too forced, too simple, totally unsatisfying. Doesn't
work.

The same is true of *Presumed Innocent.* Taken from Scott
Turow's best seller, and adapted by Frank Pierson and Alan
Pakula (who also directed), a well-known prosecutor is assigned to investigate the murder of an attractive assistant
prosecutor with whom he'd had an affair. As the evidence
piles up, he is charged with the murder, manages to get ac-
quitted, and guess what? Trite and unconvincing.

If you contrast this with *Deceiver* (the Pate brothers), Tim
Roth portrays a wealthy liar suspected of killing a hooker.
Two detectives believe he is guilty, but when he takes the lie
detector test, he literally defeats the machine; the two cops
know he's guilty but can't prove it. After he suddenly, and
mysteriously, "dies," the case is closed; and then, in the last
shot, we see Tim Roth approaching another woman, and we
know, with chilling certainty, that he has staged his own
death in order to beat the rap. This particular ending is more
satisfying than the endings of the other two films. It's a new
twist on an old theme.

In order for an ending to truly work, it has to satisfy the
requirement of believability. *Absolute Power* (William Goldman) is slick and well done, and Clint Eastwood's direction is
marvelous. The story moves along with tense sophistication

and ease. Now, this is a case, at least for me, where I admired the film even though it did not engage the "willing suspension of disbelief." Not for one instant did I believe that the President of the United States, with only three people in the Secret Service, could bring this all about: The opening sequence, the inciting incident, shows a man and woman, drunk, staggering into the bedroom of a large mansion, just as a burglar is cleaning out the vault. The thief can only watch as the sexual encounter turns violent and the woman, defending herself from the man, picks up the letter opener and prepares to stab him. The door bursts open and two Secret Service agents appear and kill the woman.

When the chief of staff and the two agents discover that the Clint Eastwood character, the burglar, has seen the whole thing, they go after him. Naturally, they find out who he is, but, of course, they must break all laws to kill him. In this case I don't buy it at all, but what's so interesting to me is the relationship between the father (Eastwood) and his estranged daughter. This relationship is a significant part of the film, and when the President orders the Secret Service agents to kill Eastwood's daughter, Plot Point II, the master thief gets really pissed and decides to take on the President. And, in the end, justice is served, and father and daughter are reconciled.

So, even though I did not "willingly suspend my disbelief," I bought the ending. It was a fulfilling and satisfying experience.

What you want to accomplish is the "best" possible ending that works. You want to be true to your story line, and not have to resort to any tricks, gimmicks, or contrived elements, in order to make it work. What's the best way to do this? First, and I think this goes without saying, you have to be clear on what kind of film you're writing; then you can begin to devise and execute an appropriate ending.

So, how would you like it to end? What is the resolution? Then, what do you have to do to achieve it? If the ending doesn't work the way it is, or how you think it should, feel free to go back and play with it a little. Think about the ending in terms of the reader or viewer's satisfaction, because the key to a successful ending is the feeling of satisfaction or fulfillment. Whether it's happy or sad makes no difference. Is the story line resolved? In *The English Patient*, the ending and the beginning are the same.

If I could sum up the concept of endings, and declare what is the one most important thing to remember, I would say that *the ending comes out of the beginning.* Someone, or something, initiates an action, and how that action is resolved becomes the story line of the film.

So, whatever problem you might have, whether it's one of *Plot*, *Character*, or *Structure*, know that if you created the problem, then you can solve it. Don't be afraid to rethink the material, don't be afraid to rewrite. Anthony Minghella *(The English Patient)* told me he did twenty-one rewrites on the material, and he was still rewriting in the editing room while they were cutting the film. It's not how many times you need to rewrite the material, *it's what you need to do in order to make the material the best it can be.* That means being able to recognize, define, and then solve whatever problem you might have.

If there's one quality I feel is the most essential within the cauldron of *Problem Solving*, it's patience. If you become impatient with the material, impatient with yourself, impatient with a lack of progress, impatient with how many times you have to rewrite the same material, impatient with the results, just put your impatience aside and keep to the task at hand. Your job, your responsibility, is to make the material the best it can be, regardless of how long it takes. I know people who write their first draft, dabble a little on some scenes, then send it out into the world. It's not ready, and it comes back with the results that you would expect. Nobody's interested, everyone has an idea on how to make it better, and you hit the wall of rejection that is so debilitating it's possible you'll put the script on the shelf somewhere and never go back to it.

There's another side to this coin. The more people you give your script to read, the more diverse and contradictory the opinions will be about what you have to add, change, or delete in a rewrite. So many times writers give their material to people to read and the opinions and criticisms they receive are so diverse, so contradictory, and alter the story line so much, they don't even recognize the material anymore. That's because it's not their story anymore.

That happens all the time in the studio system of making movies. The cost of making studio movies has become so exorbitant, costing almost $12,000 to $15,000 per minute, and that, coupled with the cost of prints and advertising and distribution rising at an almost fifteen-percent increase every year, makes the studios hedge their bets. So they appeal to the lowest common denominator; the higher the budget, the more people become involved in adding things to the screenplay. It doesn't matter whether it's "right" or not, or whether it "works" or not, studio executives and producers give their input all the time, and their opinions and suggestions are not always right for the material. But because of the money at stake, the ideas are accepted and written into the shooting script. Most of the time the results are a disaster. Look at *Waterworld*, or *Judge Dredd*, as two such examples.

The same happens in writing classes. Everyone in the class is invited to give their opinion about what the writer should do to make the script better, and since everyone has their own opinion, you have a tendency to think that "maybe they're right," and you're "wrong," because you're so close to the material you can't see it anymore. If you think that, if you really buy into that, you'll very soon succumb to the haze of confusion and uncertainty.

If you follow everybody's suggestions, just to follow the suggestions, you'll find it's no longer your screenplay. At that point it doesn't belong to anybody; the changes will be so far removed from what your original intention was that it's neither your screenplay nor theirs. If their suggestions feel right and you think they're accurate, use them. But if you know they're wrong, and what they suggest won't work for your story, don't use them. Whatever works, works, and whatever doesn't, doesn't, it's really that simple. At least in theory.

If you make changes that you don't feel are right for your screenplay, that's when it can become a real problem, indeed a nightmare. It never works. The only thing that works, in terms of your material, is whether you feel satisfied with it when you put it out into the world. Deep down inside, when you're "one on one," you have to know that you've done the best job you can do, at least at this time. Only you can know that with certainty. Only you can trust your own instincts, your own creative Self.

As I've said many times over, everybody's a writer; everybody has an opinion about how to make your script better, how to sharpen the characters, how to make it more "commercial," how to be more acceptable to the current temper or trend of the times.

There will be occasions when someone will make a particular comment or observation that strikes a chord, or a feeling, within you. That's what you're looking for, that's what you have to follow as you walk along the path of *Problem Solving;* that's the only map you can follow, that's the spark of truth and light that illuminates your own creative vision.

Are you willing to do what has to be done to make your screenplay the best it can be? Are you willing to be true to your own vision? Are you willing to sit down and honor your own inner voice, and mine whatever problems the material might have and turn them into a workable solution? A solution that becomes an opportunity for your own growth and expansion, a solution, whether you know it or not, that will only sharpen your skills as a screenwriter?

Problem solving is really two sides of the same coin, a process that contains both sacrifice and commitment, for it's either a challenge or an obligation.

Writing is a personal responsibility; either you do it or you don't. *"The World is as you see it,"* reads the ancient scripture. Either you see it as an opportunity, or a burden. Either you honor your own creative vision, or you don't.

It's your choice.

22

The Troubleshooter's Guide

The *Troubleshooter's Guide* is exactly what it says it is; a checklist, or guide, that helps identify and define the *"problem,"* whatever it may be. Once you've gone through the material, and begun to isolate and define the problem as it applies to your screenplay, locate it on the *Troubleshooter's Guide*. If you feel there are many problems, go through the guide and checklist the chapters where the solutions might be found. Define them one at a time, whether the problem is one of *Plot*, *Character*, or *Structure*.

Check what applies:

1. *Are you:*

   ☐ Preparing to write your screenplay?
   ☐ Writing the first words on paper draft?
   ☐ Rewriting?

2. *Is it a problem of:*

   ☐ PLOT?
   ☐ CHARACTER?
   ☐ STRUCTURE?

3. *Where are you encountering the problem?*

☐ Throughout the screenplay?
☐ In Act I?
☐ In the First Half of Act II?
☐ In the Second Half of Act II?
☐ In Act III?

4. *Where does the problem occur?*

IF THE PROBLEM IS IN ACT I, IS IT:

☐ In the first 10 pages?
☐ Second 10 pages?
☐ Plot Point I?

IF THE PROBLEM IS IN ACT II, WHERE IS IT?

☐ The First Half of Act II
☐ Between the end of Plot Point I and Pinch I
☐ Between Pinch I and the Mid-Point
☐ The Mid-Point
☐ Between the Mid-Point and Pinch II
☐ Between Pinch II and Plot Point II
☐ As Plot Point II

IF THE PROBLEM IS IN ACT III, WHERE IS IT?

☐ What are the one or two points left unresolved
   at Plot Point II?
   Define them . . . just write them out.
☐ What is the resolution?
☐ Does the ending work effectively?
☐ How is it connected to the beginning?

THE TROUBLESHOOTER'S GUIDE

PLOT	Chapter 8	Chapter 9	Chapter 10	Chapter 11
SYMPTOM:				
The Story Is Told in Words, Not Pictures	✓			
The Action Does Not Move the Story Forward	✓			
The Dramatic Premise Is Not Clear	✓			
Who Is the Main Character?	✓			
Characters Are Too Expository	✓			
Main Character Is Too Passive and Reactive	✓			
There Are Too Many Characters	✓			
Everything Has to Be Explained	✓	✓		✓
The First Act Is Too Long	✓			
The Story Line Is Choppy and Disjointed	✓			
Too Much Happens Too Fast	✓			
Visual Arena Is Too Static		✓		
Story Seems Confusing, Too Complex		✓		
Events Are Contrived, Predictable		✓		
The Stakes Are Not High Enough		✓	✓	
Not Enough Visual Action		✓		

PLOT	Chapter 8	Chapter 9	Chapter 10	Chapter 11
SYMPTOM:				
The Story Builds Too Slowly, and Wanders Off in Too Many Directions		✓		
Characters Are Not Defined		✓		
Characters Are Too Internal		✓		
The Minor Characters Seem to Take Over the Action		✓		
Story Lacks Tension and Suspense			✓	
The Story Line Is Too Plotty, Too Complex, Things Happen Too Fast			✓	✓
Story Is Too Vague, Too Thin, Too Contrived			✓	
Too Many Plot Twists and Turns			✓	
Dialogue Is Too Talky, Too Direct			✓	
Characters Are Flat, One-Dimensional			✓	
Main Character Is Not Very Sympathetic			✓	
Character Always Reacts to the Situation, and Has No Real Point of View			✓	
Minor Characters Stand Out More Than the Main Character			✓	
The Script Is Too Long				✓
Story Is Episodic, Too Expository				✓
Too Many Things Happen, with No Focus in the Story Line				✓

PLOT	Chapter 8	Chapter 9	Chapter 10	Chapter 11
SYMPTOM:				
Too Many Characters				✓
The Main Character Is Too Weak, Overpowered by Other Characters				✓
Scenes Are Too Long, Too Complicated				✓
Too Many Subplots				✓
There Seem to Be Two Stories in One				✓

THE TROUBLESHOOTER'S GUIDE

CHARACTER	Chapter 12	Chapter 13	Chapter 14	Chapter 15	Chapter 16
SYMPTOM:					
The Main Character Explains Too Much about Himself/Herself	✓	✓		✓	
Main Character Is Not Very Sympathetic	✓				✓
The Main Character Is Too Reactive, Too Internal, Seems to Disappear Off the Page	✓			✓	
I Am the Main Character	✓				
All the Characters Sound the Same	✓	✓	✓	✓	
Minor Characters Are More Interesting, Stronger Than the Main Character	✓			✓	
Relationships Are Too Vague, Not Clearly Defined	✓				
Dialogue Is Too Literary, Too Flowery, Too Obvious	✓				
The Main Character Is Dull, Boring		✓			
The Characters Lack Depth, Dimension		✓			
The Character's Emotional Arc Is Too Thin and Undefined		✓			
There's Not Enough Conflict		✓			
The Emotional Stakes Are Not High Enough		✓			✓
The Dialogue Is Stilted, Awkward		✓			
The Dramatic Need of Main Character Is Vague, Undefined		✓			

CHARACTER	Chapter 12	Chapter 13	Chapter 14	Chapter 15	Chapter 16
SYMPTOM:					
There Seems to Be a Lack of Tension		✓			
Story Goes Off in Too Many Directions		✓			
The Characters Are Too Talky and Explain Too Much			✓		
Dialogue Is Too Direct, Too Specific			✓		
The Characters Are Flat, One-Dimensional			✓		
There Is No *Circle of Being*			✓		
Character's Actions Are Predictable			✓		
The Material Is Flat and Boring			✓		
Relationships Between the Characters Are Weak and Undefined			✓		
I'm Saying the Same Thing Over and Over Again			✓		
There Is No Subtext: The Story Is Too Thin			✓	✓	
Main Character Is Too Passive, Too Reactive				✓	
Character Conflicts Are Too Thin				✓	
The Dialogue Is Dull, Uninteresting				✓	
Conflict Is Expressed Through Dialogue, Not Action				✓	
The Story Is Predictable and Contrived				✓	

CHARACTER	Chapter 12	Chapter 13	Chapter 14	Chapter 15	Chapter 16
SYMPTOM:					
The Main Character Is a Loner and Has No One to Talk To					✓
The Main Character Has No Point of View					✓
The Action Is Too Thin					✓
The Story Line Too Episodic, Too Jerky, and Needs Transitions					✓
The Story Seems Confusing					✓
Something Seems to Be Missing					✓
The Story Wanders Around and Gets Bogged Down in Too Many Details					✓

THE TROUBLESHOOTER'S GUIDE

STRUCTURE	Chapter 17	Chapter 18	Chapter 19	Chapter 20	Chapter 21
SYMPTOM:					
The Scene Has No Dramatic Pay-off	✓				
The Action Is Incomplete: Something Seems to Be Missing	✓				
The Story Line Gets Lost	✓				
The Dramatic Need of the Main Character Is Unclear	✓				
The Scene Is Loaded With Too Much Explanation	✓				
Dialogue Is Too Direct, Too Melodramatic	✓				
There Are Too Many Characters	✓				
Characters Are Not True to the Emotional Reality of the Scene	✓				
The Tempo of Scene Is Too Slow or Too Fast	✓				
Incidents and Characters Are Not Paid Off		✓			
Scenes Lack Direction (A Line of Development)		✓			
No Transitions Between Scenes		✓		✓	
Scenes Are Too Long and Too Expository		✓			
Tempo Is Too Slow		✓			
Too Much Or Not Enough Information Is Being Revealed		✓			
Too Many Plot Twists, Turns, and Contrivances		✓			

STRUCTURE	Chapter 17	Chapter 18	Chapter 19	Chapter 20	Chapter 21
SYMPTOM:					
Story Line Seems Unstructured		✓			
The Character's Conflict Is Too Internal		✓			
Dialogue Is Too Wordy, Too Explanatory			✓		
Scenes Are Too Long, with Not Enough Action			✓		
Story Line Is Thin and Episodic			✓	✓	
Story Points Have to Be Explained Over and Over Again			✓		
The Script Is Too Long			✓		
The Story Is Not Visual Enough			✓		
Conflict Is Expressed Through Dialogue, Not Action			✓		
Characters Are Reactive, Rather than Active			✓		
The Second Act Is Weak, and Too Long			✓		
The Writing Is Too Easy, It Can't Be Good			✓		
The Action Goes Nonstop				✓	
Action Scenes Are Too Detailed, with Too Much Description				✓	
The Stakes Are Not High Enough				✓	
The Action Is Dull and Boring, and Goes from Interior to Interior				✓	

STRUCTURE	Chapter 17	Chapter 18	Chapter 19	Chapter 20	Chapter 21
SYMPTOM:					
Scenes Are Too Expository, and the Characters Explain Too Much				✓	
The Characters Are Too Thin, and Do Not Reveal Anything about Themselves				✓	
I'm Not Paying Attention to the Budget				✓	
Story's Resolution Is Not Paid Off					✓
The Ending Does Not Work					✓
The Ending Is Too Soft, Too Weak, Confusing					✓
The Ending Seems Contrived, Too Predictable, Unsatisfying					✓
The Main Character Dies (The Easy Solution)					✓
The Main Character Disappears at the End					✓
A Surprise Twist Comes Out of Nowhere					✓
Everything Happens Too Fast					✓
Ending Is Not Big or Commercial Enough					✓
Ending Is Too Big and There Might Be a Budget Problem					✓

Index